HELPING CHILDREN AND FAMILIES

HELPING CHILDREN AND FAMILIES

A New Treatment Model Integrating Psychodynamic, Behavioral, and Contextual Approaches

Peter Goldenthal

WILEY

JOHN WILEY & SONS, INC.

This book is printed on acid-free paper. ∞

Copyright © 2005 by Peter Goldenthal. All rights reserved.

Published by John Wiley & Sons, Inc., Hoboken, New Jersey.
Published simultaneously in Canada.

No part of this publication may be reproduced, stored in a retrieval system, or transmitted in any form or by any means, electronic, mechanical, photocopying, recording, scanning, or otherwise, except as permitted under Section 107 or 108 of the 1976 United States Copyright Act, without either the prior written permission of the Publisher, or authorization through payment of the appropriate per-copy fee to the Copyright Clearance Center, Inc., 222 Rosewood Drive, Danvers, MA 01923, (978) 750-8400, fax (978) 646-8600, or on the web at www.copyright.com. Requests to the Publisher for permission should be addressed to the Permissions Department, John Wiley & Sons, Inc., 111 River Street, Hoboken, NJ 07030, (201) 748-6011, fax (201) 748-6008.

Limit of Liability/Disclaimer of Warranty: While the publisher and author have used their best efforts in preparing this book, they make no representations or warranties with respect to the accuracy or completeness of the contents of this book and specifically disclaim any implied warranties of merchantability or fitness for a particular purpose. No warranty may be created or extended by sales representatives or written sales materials. The advice and strategies contained herein may not be suitable for your situation. You should consult with a professional where appropriate. Neither the publisher nor author shall be liable for any loss of profit or any other commercial damages, including but not limited to special, incidental, consequential, or other damages.

This publication is designed to provide accurate and authoritative information in regard to the subject matter covered. It is sold with the understanding that the publisher is not engaged in rendering professional services. If legal, accounting, medical, psychological or any other expert assistance is required, the services of a competent professional person should be sought.

Designations used by companies to distinguish their products are often claimed as trademarks. In all instances where John Wiley & Sons, Inc. is aware of a claim, the product names appear in initial capital or all capital letters. Readers, however, should contact the appropriate companies for more complete information regarding trademarks and registration.

For general information on our other products and services please contact our Customer Care Department within the United States at (800) 762-2974, outside the United States at (317) 572-3993 or fax (317) 572-4002.

Wiley also publishes its books in a variety of electronic formats. Some content that appears in print may not be available in electronic books. For more information about Wiley products, visit our web site at www.wiley.com.

Library of Congress Cataloging-in-Publication Data:

Goldenthal, Peter, 1948–
    Helping children and families : a new treatment model integrating psychodynamic, behavioral, and contextual approaches / Peter Goldenthal.
      p. cm.
    ISBN 0-471-43130-3 (cloth)
    1. Child psychotherapy.   2. Family psychotherapy.   3. Contextual therapy.   I. Title.

    RJ504.G645   2005
    618.92'8914—dc22

                                                    2004065762

Printed in the United States of America.
10 9 8 7 6 5 4 3 2 1

To my patients

Every day you may make progress. Every step may be fruitful. Yet there will stretch out before you an ever-lengthening, ever-ascending, ever-improving path. You know you will never get to the end of the journey. But this, so far from discouraging, only adds to the joy and glory of the climb.

—Sir Winston Churchill (1874–1965)

CONTENTS

Contents

SECTION THREE
Synthesis

PREFACE

Clinicians who work with children face a number of challenges not shared by those who work only with adults. Child therapists must be specialists and generalists at the same time. They need to have specialized knowledge and training in problems of childhood that either do not occur in adulthood or occur only in very different forms. They must be trained in child development and have strong consultation skills. Because the range of problems they will see is so great, they must also be generalists. Therapists who work with adults can define their practices by a specific problem or set of problems, as do medical specialists in fields such as cardiology or endocrinology. An adult therapist may choose to specialize in depressive disorders, in sexual dysfunction, in eating disorders, or in the treatment of substance abuse. Child therapists, with very few exceptions, can't do this. Rather, they have to evaluate and treat the whole child, applying their expertise to the full constellation of problems and issues presented by the child and his or her family.

The second major challenge that faces clinicians who work with children is that they will inevitably be working with the child's family, too, and so need to develop some special skills in this area as well. Most training tends to emphasize either family systems issues, concepts, and techniques or concepts and methods for working individually with children. Among those training programs that emphasize individual approaches, most choose either a psychodynamic or a behavioral approach. It takes all of these to engage and help our youngest patients and their families. Neither individual child therapy (psychodynamically or behaviorally oriented) by itself nor "pure" family systems therapy will do. Neither will the disembodied application of technique, no matter how skillfully done, help very many people.

Although training in individual psychotherapy (behavioral and psychodynamic) and family therapy tend not to overlap, neither does such training need to be exclusionary. The best clinicians from all camps quickly realize that flexibility is paramount for those who work with children; they learn to overcome their biases and adjust to what children and families need. Those trained in child psychoanalysis recognize the importance of engaging and developing rapport with the child's family. Some practitioners conduct family therapy sessions on occasion, even while regarding the real work as being done individually with the child. Similarly, behaviorally trained child psychologists learn to engage and work with their patients' families. Pediatric psychologists, by the nature of the populations they serve and the medical settings in which they work, are almost universally trained in behavioral approaches and techniques ranging from applied behavior analysis to cognitive-behavior therapy. Family therapy training is only occasionally part of their background. And yet, somewhere in the middle of that range are the techniques associated with helping parents develop more appropriate and useful techniques for managing children's challenging behaviors, all of which require working intimately with families. Nowhere in that range, however, are there specific techniques for managing difficult, confused, and anxious parents.

Some clinicians receive intensive training in working with children individually and far less in working with their families; others receive intensive training in marital and family therapy and far less in working with children, especially very young children. Individually trained clinicians sometimes feel handicapped in dealing with issues that come up daily in clinical practice, namely, how to engage parents and keep them engaged, how to manage severe parent-child conflict, how to respond when it becomes clear that a parent has significant psychological issues of his or her own, what to do when one parent is undermining the other parent's authority, how to respond to marital dysfunction, sibling conflicts, and issues of separation and divorce.

Those trained in marital and family therapy may feel equally lost with some of the problems that are specific to working with children: engaging very young children and setting them at ease, what stance to take with reluctant adolescents, specific behavioral interventions for oppositional children, relaxation techniques for anxious children, being a child's advocate with a school system, and being directive and willing to give advice about parenting. They also need more knowledge about specific childhood disorders—not the diagnostic characteristics, or research on their etiology since they've studied those in childhood psychopathology courses—but what to do about it.

Both individual and family therapy approaches have much to offer. A clinician who works within only one framework with children is likely to experience some inefficiencies: 6 months or longer treatment for a 4-year-old who refuses to use the potty; long supportive therapy for a 10-year-old boy who swears at and occasionally hits his single mother—therapy that scapegoats parents and blames them for a child's difficult temperament. An experienced child psychiatrist who attended one of my workshops summarized one side of this challenge: "We know we need to work with the families of our [child] patients but have no idea how to do it." I've met marriage and family therapists with excellent clinical skills who are at a loss when it comes to treating a child with selective mutism or a pervasive developmental disorder. I've also met psychologists specializing in couples and family therapy who have only the fuzziest of ideas what those two disorders are. Both sets of clinicians may find themselves conceptually at sea, wishing for a GPS device, or at the very least for a compass and a set of charts.

I wrote this book to meet the needs of both neophyte and experienced practitioners including clinical child and pediatric psychologists, child and adolescent psychiatrists, developmental and behavioral pediatricians, social workers, school counselors, and all others engaged in clinical work with children. It addresses the need that advanced graduate students, interns, and residents have for a practical guide to doing the work of a child and family clinician. It will also prove useful to those already providing therapy to families, children, or both, as well as non-therapists who work with children and families: elementary and middle school principals, guidance counselors, clergy, pediatricians, and nurse practitioners.

In this book, I provide specific and practical guidance tied to a new conceptual model that incorporates concepts and techniques I've found most helpful, integrating them in a way that retains flexibility.

As you read this book, the extent that I borrow from these approaches will become clear, as will my divergence from them. This book presents not only a conceptual model but real and practical guidance for clinicians facing oppositional 3-year-olds; single mothers with bossy and aggressive 10-year-olds; selectively mute 8-year-olds; short-tempered and impatient fathers of children with mild PDD; anxious children with anxious parents; teachers who believe that every child has an attention-deficit disorder until proven otherwise, depressed pot-smoking teenagers, and the myriad of other clinical problems busy clinicians see every day.

The book is divided into three sections: Preparation, Treatment Techniques for Resolving Specific Problems, and Synthesis. The first two chapters lay the theoretical groundwork for the integrated model. In them you will find explanations, illustrations, and applications of some of the most useful and elusive concepts associated with Boszormenyi-Nagy's contextual approach: multidirected partiality; constructive entitlement, and destructive entitlement. You will also find discussion of important social learning concepts such as minimal goal level and the psychological situation, as well as discussion of how psychodynamic concepts are used in this model.

This section continues with a chapter that provides a broader perspective on clinical work and on many of the personal and professional issues that arise in this sort of work. Some of the topics in Chapter 3 include learning to think like a pediatrician, getting comfortable with single session treatment, consultative roles, collaboration with other professionals, and parents as coaches and co-therapists. This chapter also addresses issues important in all clinical work, learning to be aware of your feelings, to use your feelings to help your patient, and yet not to be misled by those feelings, the problem of counter-transference.

In Chapter 4, we move from the seminar room into the therapy room and examine what is involved in helping children of various ages to open up about their concerns, in establishing a relationship with them, in gaining an understanding of their functioning, in deciding when psychological testing is needed, and in those instances when it is appropriate, assigning formal diagnoses.

Chapter 5 brings the material from previous chapters together into a unified framework that addresses how cases are conceptualized in this model and how this leads to treatment planning.

Chapter 6 looks at one of the complex issues clinicians who want to be flexible in treating children and families run into: What to do when parents' individual issues and concerns become the focus of treatment.

Chapter 7 introduces Section Two and is comprised of general issues that apply to clinical work across the age range covered in this book: sensitivity to cultural diversity, the potential value of play therapy, decisions regarding frequency of therapy sessions. Chapters 8 through 10 proceed developmentally, providing specific techniques for addressing equally specific problems of children from 4 to 14, and beyond. Chapter 11 treats problems that present at varying ages including selective mutism, pervasive developmental disabilities, and adjustment to physical disability.

The final section of the book is comprised of only one chapter, perhaps the most important chapter in the book, "Your Own Therapy Model." Theory is essential. Technique is a necessity. But theory and technique will only take you so far until they are integrated in a way that feels right, makes sense, and reflects who you are as a person.

As you read this book, you will learn:

- How to apply the technique of multidirected partiality to support every person in a family.
- How to reassure an anxious parent.
- How to engage very young children.
- How to determine when a parent needs individual work and how to engage him or her in this process.
- That one of the most important things you have to offer your patients is yourself.
- That confronting an adolescent about inappropriate behavior may be a powerful way to be partial to him.
- A simple biofeedback technique any clinician can use with $12 worth of equipment.
- When to let a parent decide on the frequency of visits and when to set an agenda.
- When and how to invite other people to participate in therapy.
- When to refer for a medication evaluation.
- How to talk with parents of children with PDD.
- Which kinds of issues and problems are likely to respond to medication and which are not.

This book presents a model of practice that focuses on taking each person in a family seriously, even the very youngest child. It invites you to join me as I interview children as young as 4 years old, both with their parents and by themselves. The chapters that follow show how a therapist can be an advocate for a child, even a very angry child, and for his parents, acknowledging both parents and child and slighting neither. It teaches you that thinking about individuals, whether children or parents, is not inconsistent with thinking systemically. It also teaches you that having a conceptual model does not mean that you should treat it as dogma. If you believe, as I do, that protracted individual work with children under 13 is usually not as effective as family work, you may still be willing to try it with an unusually verbal and mature child, and you may discover, as I have, that there are always exceptions that prove the rule.

ACKNOWLEDGMENTS

My ideas about therapy with children and families, especially about how to integrate differing theories in a way that enhances our abilities to help our patients, have been influenced by studying with, working with, and consulting with many people. Chief among these have been some remarkable psychologists and teachers: the late Ronald Mack at Cornell University; Amerigo Farina, George J. Allen, and Julian B. Rotter at the University of Connecticut; Pauline B. Hahn and Elliot G. Mishler at Harvard Medical School; and Ivan Boszormenyi-Nagy at Hahneman University.

My thinking about therapy generally and therapy integration has benefited immeasurably from discussions and collaborations with colleagues and friends: Jodie Ambrosino, Stephen J. Barcus, Stephen N. Berk, Deborah Bernstein, Nathan Blum, William C. Carey, Vincent Gioe, Judith Grunebaum, Julia C. Hayes, Linda Heller, Kathy Hirsch-Pasek, Rosalind Kaplan, Phillip C. Kendall, Peter Keller, Samuel Knapp, Linda K. Knauss, Leonard Milling, John Parrish, Paul Rappoport, Lawrence Ritt, and Andrea K. Shapiro.

In writing my previous books, I have been fortunate to have worked with, and learned from, gifted editors: Debra Fink at Professional Resource Press, Susan Munro at W.W. Norton, Cynthia Vartan at Henry Holt, and Tom Miller at John Wiley & Sons. This book has had a longer gestation than anticipated and has benefited from the patience, support, encouragement, and expert guidance of a wonderful editor: Tracey Belmont. Lynn Seligman, my literary agent of many years, was tireless in her commitment to finding the best possible home for this project. I have learned a great deal about parenting and childhood from Ariel and Matt Goldenthal.

These acknowledgments would not be complete without mention of Natalie Landro, who has been a constant source of friendship, support, and sound advice. Even when I wondered if this project would ever be completed, she believed in it.

SECTION ONE

Preparation

CHAPTER 1

Psychodynamic and Social Learning Concepts and Techniques for Working with Children and Families

Le coeur a ses raisons que la raison ne connaît point. [The heart has its reasons of which reason knows nothing.]

—Blaise Pascal (1623–1662)

In the course of a day, I may see a 5-year-old boy who refuses to use the toilet, insisting instead on wearing a diaper prior to having a bowel movement; a 21-year-old young man with Asperger's syndrome; a 7-year-old girl who is having difficulties adjusting to her school situation; a college student with a history of depression and a current substance abuse problem; a 12-year-old boy with social skills problems and significant parent-child conflict; a selectively mute 9-year-old girl; and a married couple in conflict about how best to help their anxious child with obsessive-compulsive tendencies or their child with pervasive developmental disorder (PDD). This sort of range of presenting problems and family issues is typical for a clinician with a practice in child and family therapy, and it calls for a different kind of model from that which suffices for colleagues whose practices are restricted to adults or even to adults and couples.

There are many competing models available, and many have at least one appealing feature, interesting strategy, or useful technique. How is a savvy clinician to formulate a model that gives him or her the freedom to incorporate these characteristics without ending up with a smorgasbord of unrelated techniques? This is the problem that has preoccupied me since my first days as a grad student. It is the problem that led me to learn to use psychodynamic, behavioral, and family therapy concepts and techniques. And it is the problem that led to the integrated model I present here.

Range of Convenience

The integrated model for therapy with children and families is a model with a clearly defined range of convenience. It provides a framework, with related strategies and techniques, that will be helpful to clinicians and others who work with children, adolescents, and their families. Although other kinds of professional activities, such as couples therapy, consultation to family businesses, and long-term intensive individual psychotherapy, have much in common with treating children and families at the highest levels of abstraction, they call for different sets of strategies and techniques, and so for different intervention models. Some readers may find it interesting to extrapolate from what is offered here to these other kinds of professional activities, but this is not my intent. As an aside, I believe that one potential pitfall for any model of psychological intervention occurs when its adherents try to apply it far more widely than was originally intended, rather like trying to use a socket wrench as a hammer. It's possible, but it will take far longer than it should, and the chances of banging your thumb are higher, as are the chances of bending the nail and denting the picture frame, windowsill, or cabinet top.

The Model

The integrated model is three models in one: an overall general and moderately abstract model; a more specific set of strategies and techniques for addressing externalizing problems, especially among younger children; and a parallel set of strategies and techniques for addressing internalizing problems at all ages. The overall model is composed of assumptions, values, and guidelines and offers a general approach to problems and a general therapeutic stance. Each of these features is discussed in detail, some in this chapter and some in the next.

Assumptions

I offer these assumptions largely without empirical justification and with the expectation that they are sufficiently familiar and sufficiently widely shared as to be relatively noncontroversial:

- The therapist-patient relationship is, if not the entire therapy, at least its most crucial component.

- Historical factors are important. Whether the case concerns a 2½-year-old whose parents are concerned about speech development, the oppositional 8-year-old with a single mother, or a depressed 15-year-old, we have to learn as much as we can about the child's history and the family history. Part of the reason for this is that family history figures significantly in our current understanding of a number of disorders, including obsessive-compulsive disorder, eating disorders, mood disorders, and substance abuse disorders. A second reason is that early experiences, among them traumatic experiences, figure prominently among the factors that are involved in the development of a sense of self. A third reason for being aware of family history is that it profoundly affects the capacity of parents to change how they see themselves and their children and their capacity to bring true caring, sensitivity, and consideration to the very challenging task of parenting. And the fourth reason, one about which I'll have much more to say later, is that knowledge of history is crucial to applying the useful contextual therapy concepts of *constructive* versus *destructive entitlement.*

- The patient is more important than the theory. The integrated model always takes second place to what the patient presents, what the patient needs, and what will help the patient. The guidelines I offer are just that: guidelines, not rules. They are meant to be modified as needed and replaced as needed. A therapist who strives to be consistent to the model, or to work "purely" within the model (whatever that means), is unlikely to be doing good therapy.

- Issues typically thought of as "purely physical" are important. The integrated model is not reductionistic: It does not try to reduce psychological phenomena to biological phenomena, biological phenomena to biochemical phenomena, and biochemical phenomena to phenomena responding only to something that can be dispensed by a pharmacist. It does, however, recognize the importance of nutrition, exercise, and rest, not only to physical health but to psychological health as well.

- Developmental issues are important. Developmental issues are front and center when we see children with learning problems and mental retardation. In other cases, the developmental issues are more subtle and involve social learning, fears of independence, and issues of identity. For many clinicians, the adjustment of manner and style to accommodate the needs and capacities of children from 2 to 16 are automatic and intuitive.

- Individual differences matter. Until fairly recently, this assumption was so widely accepted that stating it would have been superfluous. All personality theorists started with this as the most basic of assumptions. Psychological tests, whether of intelligence, other cognitive skills, or personality, are designed to be measures of individual differences. Among family systems therapists, some of this has, I fear, been forgotten. Interest in and, to a certain extent, concern for individual differences has been supplanted by interest in and concern for systemic differences. Family typologies have supplanted individual typologies. This is not altogether a good thing. Some psychodynamic approaches may have erred by going too far in the direction of purely intrapsychic therapies and by promoting approaches that seemed to be based on the notion that everything important occurs between one's ears. The first generation of family therapy researchers and theorists (e.g., Bowen, Haley, Minuchin, Bateson) may have felt that they needed to make a clean break from the psychoanalytic tradition in which most of them were trained if they were to draw clinicians' attention to their new models of family interaction and family communication. Much was lost, though: the appreciation of individual differences in intelligence, personality style, and personal history, in goals, in values, and, of course, in emotional difficulties.

- It's always worth trying the simplest and quickest interventions first, especially if the patient is very young and if there is a clear target problem on which one can bring a straightforward intervention to bear. I've always liked the metaphor of Occam's razor and see this model as incorporating an analogous perspective on therapy: The simplest intervention that works, not merely the simplest intervention, is the *best* intervention.

Integrating Three Models of Therapy

There is considerable variation in the way the term *integrative therapy* is used (e.g., Garfield, 1994; Goldfried, 1980, 1982; Norcross & Goldfried, 1992). Perhaps the clearest is that used by Stricker (1994), who defines *theoretical integration* as "an attempt to understand the patient by developing a super ordinate theoretical framework that draws from a variety of different frameworks" (p. 5). This book represents my attempt to achieve this goal by bringing together three seemingly disparate streams of thought about children, adolescents, and parents; their relationships; the behavioral, emotional, and interpersonal problems that occur in families; and how psychotherapists can most helpfully intervene. The three streams of thought on which I base this model are the psychoanalytic theory and practice developed by Freud and generations of his colleagues and students, social learning theory as formulated by Julian B. Rotter and his colleagues, and the contextual model of Ivan Boszormenyi-Nagy and his colleagues.

My solution to the problem of how to help children and families presenting a diverse set of problems rests on a primary assumption: Solving problems of childhood and adolescence is best done when one is equally comfortable with cognitive, behavioral, family systems, and psychoanalytic approaches. This assumption has a corollary: Clinicians who can integrate these approaches will function more effectively. This is what I set out to do here: to integrate psychodynamic, behavioral, cognitive, and family systems concepts in a way that is most useful to clinicians working with children, adolescents, and their families. To do this, I draw on a flexible behavioral model, Rotter's (1954) social learning theory; a flexible family systems model, Boszormenyi-Nagy's (1987) contextual theory; and Freud's psychoanalytic theory. I draw from these three approaches in different ways. Rotter's social learning theory explains the cognitive and behavioral mechanisms that lead children, adolescents, and their parents to make choices. Boszormenyi-Nagy's model provides a framework for considering four sources of information about those things that affect children, adolescents, and their families. It also draws our attention to the broader ethical nature of clinical work. The explicit goal of contextual therapy is to help people be more balanced in their relationships with those closest to them, give more spontaneously and freely of themselves to those in their families, and to state their own needs and wishes in a spirit of open dialogue. The role of psychoanalytic theory and psychoanalytic psychotherapy in my model is to provide a counterbalance to the behavioral and cognitive approaches of Rotter and Boszormenyi-Nagy. I draw on psychoanalytic ideas that speak to the child's developing sense of an autonomous self, psychological development more generally, the importance of unconscious motivation, the value of helping patients of all ages gain awareness of their emotional lives, the importance of the therapeutic relationship, and the importance of therapists' intuitive understanding of their patients. I incorporate Anna Freud's (1946/1964) insights regarding child treatment, especially her recommendations on engaging young children in treatment.

Therapists who work with the full range of issues and problems that confront children, adolescents, and their families need a model that addresses cognitive, behavioral, and emotional issues and can be applied to narrow behavioral issues (toilet training, sleep problems, tantrums); to emotional issues related to school achievement, adolescent identity, and social concerns; to parent-child conflicts, school achievement issues, and family relationship issues. Helping families also means being able to address the concerns of cooperative parenting as well as parents' individual issues that affect and are affected by their children. Any therapeutic model has to have a way of helping patients of all ages know what they are feeling, tolerate what they are feeling, and make informed decisions about what to do with those feelings. A useful model will have something to say about the therapist-patient relationship, including issues related to both transference and countertransference. A useful model will also address a problem that plagues those who treat more than one person in a family at a time: considering the impact of their interventions on each of these people, even when the people are temporarily at war. These three models complement each other to form an integrated and practical model that makes this possible.

In this chapter and the next, I offer brief synopses of the two sources that are likely to be less familiar to readers (social learning theory and contextual therapy) and, based on my belief that all readers will have some familiarity with Freud's work, an even more brief synopsis of some aspects of psychoanalytic theory and practice.

Integrated therapy for children and families is a model designed to help clinicians conceptualize and select interventions from whichever of the three component models fits the child, family, and situation best. The interventions themselves vary considerably depending on the kind of problem the child presents, the child's age and developmental level, and the ability of the child's parents to engage in treatment and to help their child.

Of the many ways to categorize children's problems, one of the simplest and most useful is to consider whether the child's presenting problems are primarily externalizing (tantrums, oppositional behavior, aggression, noncompliance, rule violations, etc.) or internalizing (anxious or depressed mood, social anxieties, chronic worry, sleeplessness, etc.). Some concepts are useful in treating all of these problems and situations, but in different ways depending on the particulars. One example of a concept that is useful in all treatment cases is the contextual principle of *multidirected partiality*, choosing interventions with awareness of their impact on each person they may touch.

The technique of multidirected partiality has to be used in one way with a shy, self-doubting, and somewhat dysthymic 7th-grade girl and in a very different way with an aggressive, oppositional, and defiant 7th-grade boy. Successful treatment of both children requires the development of a strong therapeutic alliance and a trustworthy relationship. In both cases, the therapist should strive to be as multidirected as possible. In both cases, it will be helpful to think about the extent to which the child and parents are relying on destructive entitlement. When we leave the level of these abstract treatment principles, things begin to diverge. The treatment of the internalizing girl will exemplify the adage "the relationship is the therapy" to a much greater extent than will the boy's treatment. It will be far less directive, more interpretative, and more exploratory. Depending on how verbal she is, significant amounts of time may be spent in individual sessions, with her parents' involvement being adjunctive. A classically trained psychoanalytic psychotherapist would be comfortable observing these sessions.

In contrast, the boy's treatment, in addition to attention to emotional and interpersonal factors, will involve some sort of direct behavioral intervention, probably including teaching his parents how to more effectively use reinforcement contingencies to manage his behavior. He will rarely be seen individually. Rather, the therapist will see him with his parents and may see them without him to provide further coaching. This treatment will be highly directive. Parents will receive instruction on how to use what contingencies they have available to regain some control over his behavior. Efforts at understanding the root of his challenging behavior will depend as much on learning about its antecedents and consequences as on uncovering his thoughts and feelings. If he were 5 or 7, even more attention would be paid to parenting techniques.

Integrated therapy offers a general set of principles and more specific sets of guidelines, one for internalizing problems and one for externalizing problems. This chapter provides a preview of these guidelines, and later chapters fill in the details. Included in the externalizing category are various behavior problems (challenging behaviors, toileting problems, enuresis, encopresis, tantrums, bedtime problems, so-called compliance issues, preschoolers with challenging temperaments, etc.). Some of these problems are more characteristic of younger children, usually preschoolers through 10-year-olds, and others occur more frequently among slightly older children. The treatment of moderate to severe Conduct Disorder often requires more structure than outpatient therapy can provide and is outside the range of convenience of this model, although support for parents dealing with this issue is not. Among internalizing problems are specific fears, general anxieties, relationship concerns, self-worth issues, identity issues, adolescent adjustment issues, and mood problems.

Because nothing can be that simple, a third option exists. Not infrequently, externalizers have internalizing problems, too. When the externalizing problems are mild or sporadic, it may make sense to focus on the internal conflicts that precipitate the behavioral outburst, school refusal, or noncompliance. When the behavioral problems are persistent, frequent, or more intense, this approach is not likely to succeed. This is what can seduce well-meaning but naïve therapists into believing that given enough empathic understanding and time, insight will obviate the undesirable behaviors. As Ann Richards said in her keynote address at the 1988 Democratic National Convention, "That old dog won't hunt." It makes more sense to work with behavioral contingencies and situational variables (e.g., school setting) to gain control over the unacceptable behaviors, and then to help the child come to grips with his or her inner turmoil. The way I expressed it to a boy I had been seeing weekly for over a year and with whom I had a strong relationship was something like this: "I know you're in pain and have been badly hurt, and I want to help you with that, but I can't when there are these constant crises of you screaming at your mom and threatening her."

Having roughly categorized problems as either primarily externalizing or primarily internalizing, the next consideration is the child's age. Externalizing problems of very early childhood almost invariably respond well, and often very quickly, when parents are provided with more effective parenting techniques. My belief is that we are obligated to resolve children's problems as quickly as we can. A particular therapist may be fascinated by the nuances of child development or bored with them. Either way, he or she ought to be trying to resolve the problem with sleep, tantrums, or toileting as quickly as possible. Patients are not research subjects. The goal is not to learn about child development from them, but to help them as quickly as possible, without resorting to depth psychology, if possible. Typically, this means relying on reassurance, education, coaching, and behavioral techniques—all of this guided by the general principles set out in the overall model. Very young children may be passive recipients of their parents' new skills, or they may be directly involved in therapy.

The treatment of internalizing problems, and problems characterized by both internalizing and externalizing components, has to be adjusted similarly in accordance with a child's age and developmental level. Dennis, whose case I discuss in Chapter 2, was an 11-year-old with the verbal abilities of a 5-year-old. His disruptive behaviors were the direct result of his frustration in trying to communicate and his parents' lack of appreciation for how significant was his delay. In treating him, I addressed his emotional upset and wishes by using language that he could understand and asking only for very simple responses.

A Few Words about the Language of Psychoanalysis

Some of the language of psychoanalysis suffers in translation. Many people have found it confusing and difficult to decipher into plain English. I rely on three sources to effect a translation: John Dollard and Neal Miller, Anna Freud, and Erik Erikson. Dollard and Miller (1950) wrote a landmark book that provides tremendous help to clinicians who want to learn from what psychoanalytic thought has to offer while maintaining a commitment to clear expression. Their work is important to all clinicians, whether their focus is the treatment of adults (as was theirs) or children, adolescents, and families (as is my interest). Unfortunately, their book is little read today; it is deserving of more attention. In brief, their goal was to frame psychoanalytic hypotheses about human behavior, as well as psychoanalytic techniques, in a more readable, and potentially researchable, language. Quoting from the introductory chapter: "We have attempted to give a systematic analysis of neurosis and psychotherapy in terms of the psychological principles and social conditions of learning" (p. 9). In this process, they note that "the concept of 'pleasure' has proved a difficult and slippery notion in the history of psychology" (p. 9). For this reason, they replace "pleasure principle" with "reinforcement." They go on to note, "The same is true of the idea that the behavior that occurs is 'adaptive,' because it is awkward to have to explain maladaptive behavior on the basis of a principle of adaptiveness" (p. 9). In the remainder of their introductory section, Dollard and Miller sketch out the way they will be recasting the concepts of ego strength, repression, transference, and conflict behavior into a clearer language, one that is more apparently tied to what was known about learning and cognitive processes.

In this spirit, and with appropriate credit to Anna Freud and Erik Erikson, I offer the following perspective on *psychosexual development.* For the casual and even not so casual reader, the idea of infantile sexuality may be either shocking or simply ungrounded in reality. If one reads this differently, it begins to make sense. Here is what I believe Freud, at least Anna Freud, is saying. As a child develops, the way he or she experiences and relates to the world and the people in it changes. These changes are not only cognitive (as discussed by Piaget, his students, and their students); the changes are also profoundly emotional and physical. The youngest—infants and very young children—experience the world and relate to their mother and other nurturers through their mouths. They must take food in through their mouths or starve. The mouth is the route to emotional connection as well: Food is love. As children grow, they begin to develop a sense of individuation from their mothers and to simultaneously develop the capacity to use their mouths in another way: to bite. Traditionally, when babies begin to bite the breast, mothers begin to think about weaning them: It is a sign that the baby is becoming, in a small way, independent and that he or she is ready for a tiny bit of distance. Psychoanalysts give this stage in every child's development a name, *the oral stage,* which they then subdivide into two aspects: *oral incorporative* (i.e., eating) and *oral aggressive* (i.e., biting). In psychoanalysis, these names for early childhood stages are used in speaking about later personality, emotional, and behavioral issues. Erikson refers to this as the stage in which the psychosocial crisis of basic trust versus basic mistrust first arises. So, when a 14-year-old girl fluctuates between being dependent, insecure, and clingy, constantly seeking reassurance and nurturance; and being sarcastic, verbally offensive, verbally aggressive, and moving away, one may speak of the adolescent as moving between oral incorporative and oral aggressive ways of relating to her parents. One may also speculate that this young person continues to be conflicted about aspects of her relationship with her parents that first occurred when she was nursing and that we are seeing her struggle to remain close and yet to move away into more independence at the same time.

During the second or third year, children begin to have some bowel control; in psychoanalytic terms, this is referred to as *the anal stage.* The newfound power enables them to choose to please their parents by having a bowel movement, to disappoint them by refusing to have a bowel movement, or perhaps to anger them by having a bowel movement at an inconvenient time or in an inconvenient place. The psychoanalytic literature writes about these alternatives as *anal-retentive* and *anal-eliminative* tendencies, emphasizing their biological and physical aspects. Psychoanalytic literature uses these terms to characterize emotional and behavioral realities as well as personality patterns. Erikson recasts the issue in psychosocial terms as one of a stage in which the important crisis is that of autonomy versus shame and doubt. For Erikson, the issue is whether children begin to take pride in their productions and gain a sense of being in control of their body or whether they begin to be preoccupied by a sense of having committed some infraction. So, children or adolescents who choose not to do their homework or chores may be spoken of as anal-retentive, and those who are very messy in their habits or in their room as anal-expulsive.

The next stage in development is referred to in classical psychoanalytic literature as *the phallic stage* and by Erikson as the stage centered on resolving the crisis of initiative versus guilt. This is followed by the stage of *latency* (in psychoanalysis), or industry versus inferiority in Erikson's psychosocial scheme. In Erikson's theory, the central psychosocial crisis of adolescence is that of identity versus identity confusion.

Psychodynamic Psychotherapy

Psychoanalysis as originally described by Sigmund Freud consists of three elements: a body of clinical lore, a theory of personality development, and a model of treatment. Anna Freud's (1946/1964) little book has much to offer any therapist who works with children. I write about her techniques for engaging children in treatment in Chapter 8.

The influence of psychoanalytic thought is so pervasive as to defy summary. Suffice it to say that all forms of therapy that have emerged since Freud have been either developments of psychoanalytic thought or reactions to it. In my work and in this model, a model that seeks to integrate diverse strands into one cable, the two most visible contributions of psychoanalytic literature are the theory of psychosexual development as formulated by Freud and expanded on by Erikson, and the psychoanalytic attitude toward individual human beings and toward the work of psychotherapy. Of those who have written about this, I have been most influenced by Anna Freud's book, by Guntrip's (1971, pp. 175–196) discussion of psychoanalysis and psychotherapy and Schaeffer's (1983) writings on the analytic attitude, and by a recent and very readable book by psychoanalyst Elio Fratarroli (2002). With the exception of Anna Freud, these writers do not concern themselves explicitly with the issues that confront the child therapist, and yet their ideas about the therapist (they would say the analyst) and the patient are relevant to the model I'm presenting here. This is true in part because my model is very much concerned with parents as active participants in the treatment of children, in part because the treatment of adolescents has much in common with the treatment of adults, and in part because these psychoanalytic writers speak to the uniqueness of each human being in a way that others, even those who agree with the position, do not.

The writings of psychoanalysts draw our attention to a number of important issues: what a therapeutic relationship is, how therapists can manage their own feelings, the role of personal therapy, how to use our own reactions to understand what is going on with patients, and how to help people get deeper into their emotions. All this is essential for working with parents and adolescents, and also with young children, although in a different way, as it helps us rely on intuition and connecting with children. Social learning theory provides an interesting framework for understanding how people make choices and is especially useful when trying to understand how adolescents make choices that may seem not to be logical.

Behaviorism and Social Learning Theory

Behavior therapist or not, one must recognize that behavioral principles, both classical and operant, explain much behavior. Pavlov described experiments in which dogs, after being exposed to a previously neutral stimulus (a bell) that was paired with a conditioned stimulus (food powder) a sufficient number of times, began to emit the conditioned response (salivation) to the neutral stimulus (the ringing bell) alone. Thus, the previously neutral stimulus becomes conditioned and is referred to as the conditioned stimulus. This is, of course, why it is called conditioned learning or classical conditioning. This was a powerful discovery.

Thorndike's (1911) law of effect states that behaviors that are followed by a reinforcing event will tend to occur more often in similar situations, eventually taking on the characteristics of a habit. Although Thorndike was not interested in what internal experiences might go along with this, even therapists who are very interested in internal events should remember this law, especially when working with young children and challenging behaviors. This single idea helps explain why young children engage in some of the behaviors that distress their parents so. The practical effect of this is that the behavior at hand becomes much more likely in the presence of the stimulus that signals a reinforcer in the offing than otherwise.

B. F. Skinner expanded on Thorndike's work when he developed his model of operant conditioning, a model of understanding and modifying behavior that has an important place today in the treatment of mentally retarded children and developmentally delayed adults in the form of applied behavior analysis. Skinner was opposed to theorizing and to postulating any cognitive activities that might mediate an organism's choices. As Rotter (1982) puts it, a theory of cognitive motivation does little to explain the behavior of rats, or of pigeons for that matter. It is essential, however, if we are to understand the behavior of people.

Rotter (1954) is not a behaviorist per se, but a research-oriented personality theorist who built on the work of Hull in developing a general theory of personality that predicts how people will make choices based on what they expect will be the result of those choices, on how much they value a particular possible outcome relative to other outcomes, and on how likely they believe that desired outcome is. Rotter puts this into a general equation: $NP = f(FM + NV)$, where f is function, NP refers to the need potential, FM is freedom of movement, and NV is need value. This equation may be off-putting to some readers, but before you flip the page, take a minute to consider what Rotter is saying: If we want to know if a child will be likely to follow his mother's instructions (what the child's need potential is for instruction-following behavior), say, following his mother's instruction to wash his face, brush his teeth, and get ready for bed, we will stand a better chance of knowing whether or not he will do this if we know what he expects will happen (his freedom of movement) if he follows the instructions and how important that thing he expects to happen (the need value) is to him. So, if he expects that quickly brushing his teeth will mean that his mother will read him his favorite story, and if he loves being read to, the odds are better that he will brush his teeth than if he expects that brushing his teeth quickly will mean only that he has to go to bed sooner, something he would rather avoid. That is all that Rotter is saying, and it's hard to argue with. Rotter is not saying that these factors (expectancy, reinforcement, and reinforcement value) are the only ones involved. He is saying, rather, that the child's behavior is a function of these factors and one other: *the psychological situation.*

The concept of the psychological situation is an important contribution to Rotter's model because it draws our attention to two issues that are easy to overlook. If we are to understand how reinforcement really works for a child, we need to understand what events and objects are reinforcing to the particular child, and to what extent they are reinforcing. We need to know the unique way that our particular patient responds to potential reinforcements. We need to know how likely this particular child believes it is that he or she will receive the desired reinforcement in response to particular behaviors and in a particular psychological situation. The adjective is important. It is not enough to take a situation into account (e.g., preschool, home, playground). We need to know something about the psychology of the situation for that child (e.g., a situation involving unstructured activity with peers, a situation involving the need to follow instructions from an adult, a situation involving competing for parental attention with a sibling). The emphasis on understanding the child's subjective experience of situations, of reinforcers, and of the relative value of potential reinforcers provides a framework for constructively and creatively using more narrowly behavioral interventions. The emphasis on the child's subjective experience and how he or she subjectively values reinforcers can, in conjunction with contextual and psychodynamic considerations, also help to explain seemingly inexplicable behaviors. Chapter 11 applies this concept, in conjunction with contextual and psychodynamic considerations, in the clinical vignette of a 4-year-old boy who was so enraged by the favoritism his parents seemed to bestow on his older brother that he intentionally soiled himself and played with and smeared his feces, all the while pretending to enjoy it. The distress this activity caused his parents, and the attention that resulted from it, made it worthwhile—made it reinforcing.

Of course, the formula says nothing about how a therapist may help parents and children. Rotter's theoretical writings do not provide specific guidance for therapists; instead, Rotter focuses on concepts that have implications that creative clinicians can use to develop helpful interventions. For example, Rotter defines a *minimal goal level* as the goal above which a person subjectively feels successful and below which he or she feels unsuccessful. His theory goes on to say that people who set their minimal goal levels too high will expereince (subjective) failure repeatedly. The result will be that their expectancies for (subjective) success will drop markedly, and so will their interest in trying those activities in the future. It is not too much of a stretch to see how this applies to many situations in which we would like to help parents help their children take on a challenge, whether that challenge is academic, social, or athletic. It also has clear implications for working with an underachieving high school student who believes that if she can't be sure of getting an A-plus, there is no point in trying, as anything less will feel like a failure to her.

Social learning theory has implications for guiding parents in their choice of behavioral techniques to use in parenting, in bringing disruptive behaviors under control, in toilet training, in encouraging a selectively mute child to begin to speak in public, and in addressing many other problems examined in Section 2 of this book. Most important, it puts behavioral considerations into a social and subjective context, one that explicitly draws our attention to understanding how children experience events and situations before we try to intervene behaviorally.

In the next chapter, our attention will turn to Boszormenyi-Nagy's contextual therapy and to the contextual concepts that will be most useful in working with children and families.

Anticipating Chapter 2

Although the integrative approach includes a family therapy approach, it emphasizes the thoughts and, above all, the emotional lives of individuals, in contrast to the emphasis on the family as a system. Thinking of families as systems can be very useful. It is important to remember, however, that these systems are made up of people who have thoughts, feelings, and complex inner lives. Individuals are systems, too, not just cogs in a systemic wheel.

Failing to see each individual's personal concerns, feelings, thoughts, wishes, hopes, past hurts, and disappointments can lead one to make major errors when conducting family therapy sessions as much as they can when working with an individual. Children, as well as adults, differ from each other in important ways. Some of these differences, such as ego strengths and weaknesses, character structure, ego defenses, and coping style, are emphasized by the psychodynamic tradition. Other important individual differences reflect difficulties in life that are experienced by people as individuals. Even in an approach that tries hard to focus on resources rather than on pathology, it must be recognized that some people with whom we work have very significant individual emotional and psychological difficulties; when a child has diabetes, cystic fibrosis, or cerebral palsy, or when a parent has lupus or has suffered a stroke, this condition needs to be recognized, acknowledged, and addressed.

CHAPTER 2

Contextual Concepts and Techniques for Working with Children and Families

Happy families are all alike; every unhappy family is unhappy in its own way.

—Anna Karenina, Leo Tolstoy

Background: Contextual Therapy

Contextual therapy represents a model of human experience, family life, and therapy whose goals are widely admired, whose assumptions are widely endorsed, and whose concepts are widely borrowed. Neither experienced therapists nor educators argue with the belief that one must understand a child's or a parent's past and current family relationships if one is to be able to help that child and that parent. Neither do they deny that issues of fairness and loyalty are central to life and to close relationships.

But many who have an interest in practicing contextual therapy, and many others who would incorporate into their work contextual concepts such as constructive and destructive entitlement and treatment approaches such as multidirected partiality, worry that these ideas are shrouded in mystery. Practitioners of all stripes who have attended my workshops and seminars have often told me that they find contextual ideas to be "wonderfully philosophical," frequently adding that they find the concepts difficult to turn into action. Occasionally, colleagues have asked me how I can talk with children about such abstract and seemingly philosophical ideas as fairness. There is no need to speak in philosophical terms, however, because children understand what it means to be treated unfairly, just as adults do.

My professional experience includes work in the public sector with disadvantaged multiproblem families with very disruptive young children; in a tertiary care children's hospital with children with developmental delays, chronic medical

---

This chapter contains material that appeared previously in *Doing Contextual Therapy* (Goldenthal, 1996).

conditions, life-threatening illnesses, and traumatic injuries; and in private practice with children from privileged backgrounds. I have found contextual ideas useful in all of these settings and with these varying populations. Contextual principles always consider the impact of therapy on all the people who might be affected by them, to help people (children and parents) look for opportunities to give to each other and to acknowledge each other's efforts to give, and to focus on resources for building trust rather than on uncovering pathology.

Nevertheless, in practice, a great deal of variation exists in how this model is implemented across settings and populations. In my experience, although the precepts of contextual therapy are helpful in many areas of professional practice, they are too abstract to be immediately useful. They need to be tied to specific intervention strategies and techniques. Many problems of childhood, such as sleep problems, tantrums, toileting issues, fears, school avoidance, and selective mutism, require the use of both psychodynamically oriented and behaviorally derived interventions, none of which is incompatible with the contextual model, but few of which are explicitly included in it. The contextual therapy literature has not focused on issues such as the role of emotion and emotional expression, how and when to be directive, and how to use behavioral interventions. Books on contextual therapy have little to say about problems of early childhood. Neither has much in the contextual tradition been published about childhood problems that originate within the child rather than between child and parents. In fact, some who follow the contextual model may argue that no such problems exist, believing instead that all childhood problems reflect parents' and grandparents' unresolved issues.

This book reflects my experience that procedures and techniques associated with approaches as divergent as behavior therapy and psychodynamic psychotherapy can be usefully combined to help my young patients and their families. The task of how best to formulate cases inclusively and in a way that makes the role and function of these various techniques explicit has occupied my thinking since the publication of *Doing Contextual Therapy* (Goldenthal, 1996). Additionally, I have found that certain adjustments to the contextual model as represented in the writings of its developers and proponents (myself included) make it more readily teachable and understandable and perhaps more directly applicable to certain specific problems of childhood. For example, empathetically siding with a preschooler may mean that the therapist actively participates in fantasy play in which the young patient is a wild animal.

In the next section, I offer a brief overview of the general structure of contextual therapy and define some of its major concepts. Subsequent sections and chapters provide much more detail about how contextual concepts are applied to a model that specifically targets problems of children and their families. Those who wish to explore the conceptual framework and intellectual foundations of contextual therapy in more depth will want to read the works of Ivan Boszormenyi-Nagy and his earliest collaborators (e.g., Boszormenyi-Nagy, 1987; Boszormenyi-Nagy, Grunebaum, & Ulrich, 1991; Boszormenyi-Nagy & Krasner, 1986; Boszormenyi-Nagy & Spark, 1973). Those looking for a brief theoretical overview of the approach may also find the work of Goldenthal (1993, 1996) of interest.

Why Contextual Therapy?

I came to study and use the contextual approach in my practice after being confronted by a number of problems that I believe many clinicians who work with children face. One of these problems is how to conceptualize therapeutic work in a way that combines what we know about individual psychological functioning with what we know about family systems. Until fairly recently, these questions were represented by two warring camps that rarely communicated. Fortunately, this is much less true today, but the problem of how to integrate them remains.

Another problem facing many clinicians is how to establish working relationships with all family members who are involved in the child's life. Whether we call it a therapeutic alliance or rapport or something else, it is a crucial aspect of our work and can be difficult to accomplish when working with a family in which there is disagreement, tension, and conflict—in other words, the kind of families who seek therapy. In the following pages, I discuss one way of handling this very difficult task and even go a step beyond by taking into account other people we never actually see in the therapy room but who are probably going to be affected by what goes on there.

Finally, all therapists are faced with the problem of finding a way to make sense of the unfortunate reality that people who genuinely care about and love their families—their spouses, their parents, and above all their children—still at times find themselves in situations where they have done something that has caused hurt to the people they care about the most. We must try to make sense of this in a way that will help us to promote growth and caring in families. These questions confront us particularly strongly when we work with families with young children or adolescents because of the need to be able to support parents in their personal growth while helping them learn to better support their children's growth.

Contextual ideas offer a way of making sense of this difficult facet of life: that parents, who are the greatest source of love and support for their children, are sometimes responsible for their children's suffering. It helps therapists meet the difficult challenge of establishing working alliances with the people whose actions have caused injuries to others, simultaneously helping those who have been injured to voice their grievances and risk reengaging with those who have wronged them.

Contextual Therapy Goals

At the highest level of abstraction, the goals of contextual therapy are to help those who seek therapy to make fundamental changes in the ways they think about relationships and in the ways they act in those relationships with the aim of moving toward greater balance. For example, parents can be helped to find ways to ensure that their own needs for love and intimacy are met in ways that do not harm their children, ideally in ways that enable them to be more responsible and responsive parents to their children.

Contextual therapy aims to help people change in ways that facilitate their abilities to acknowledge each other's positive efforts. Whenever the therapist acknowledges a person's positive efforts or past injuries, he or she does so with the intention of facilitating similar acknowledgment of efforts and contributions among family members. The therapist's acknowledgment is a catalyst for further growth, not an endpoint. Beginning with the first meeting, the therapist looks for ways to give credit to people in order to help them give credit to each other. As people begin to do this, both the one acknowledged and the one who does the acknowledging benefit. The contextual approach is not blind to the existence of pathology both within and among people, but its emphasis is on optimizing resources and catalyzing growth.

The Importance of Considering Fairness

The contextual model emphasizes fairness as a major theme and issue in all close relationships. It takes seriously the obligation to help children and parents talk with each other in ways that help each person to state his or her own feelings and to hear the other person's side. This has obvious applicability to all forms of parent-child conflict, as we shall see in detail later. By highlighting the issue from the first, the therapist helps each person (whatever his or her age) think about and discuss what is fair and unfair.

It is extraordinarily difficult to define a concept like fairness, although it is crucial in all relationships. There are some things about which there is widespread agreement. Infants and the very youngest children deserve love, nurturance, and protection. They deserve to have trustworthy parents who do not use their children to meet their own personal unmet emotional or physical needs. Children also deserve to be free to love and show their love for both parents, whether those parents are happily married, unhappily divorced, or have never been married. Similarly, adults can rightfully expect that their relationships will balance out over time—that they will receive in fair measure what they have given.

Fairness issues and their implications are paramount in the contextual approach and dictate therapists' activities from the very beginning. They provide the foundation for the relationship between therapists and clients. They govern decisions about questions to ask, and they guide thinking about what may have caused problems and what may be done to ameliorate them. They provide a context for understanding and integrating patterns of family communication and power transactions, historical information (both personal and intergenerational), and psychological issues. Observing, thinking about, and helping people think and talk about fairness provide the overall principle that creates the possibility for an integrative framework. The overarching concern with fairness leads to a model that can be incorporated with concepts, procedures, and techniques from any other therapeutic model as long as they are consistent with helping people to enhance the quality of their most important relationships. This openness is essential to the inclusion of contextual therapy in the integrated model.

The Importance of History

Helping families to move forward often depends on understanding not just their present difficulties, but also their past experiences, particularly those that caused them pain and injury. We seek information about people's prior experiences not because we wish to become archaeologists of the mind, but because we want to understand them, especially the ways they have been hurt, so that we may help them develop new ways of experiencing and relating. To be partial to parents as well as children we need to know about the things that have hurt each of them earlier in their lives. In the language of contextual therapy, we need to know about their personal histories of experienced unfairness and injustice. Some aspects of people's histories are strictly individual, some refer to their families, and some apply to members of their race, gender, or cultural group.

This emphasis on understanding personal history shares much with other approaches that think about family issues over an intergenerational time frame including the psychodynamic family therapies of Ackerman (1966) and Framo (1982), as well as the multigenerational approach of Bowen and his colleagues (Bowen, 1966, 1978).

Integrating Individual and Family Systems Issues

A third defining feature, and one that differentiates the contextual approach from many family systems approaches, is that it provides a framework for integrating concepts and techniques from diverse models of individual and family development, functioning, and therapy. Contextual therapy is based on the assumption that many personal and interpersonal problems will benefit from interventions that increase people's capacity for achieving greater balance in their most important relationships. It enthusiastically endorses the use of any and all techniques likely to benefit people, as long as they are consistent with this goal; it seeks to be inclusive rather than exclusive (Boszormenyi-Nagy et al., 1991). For this reason, and despite its many historical ties to the family therapy movement and its leaders, the label "family therapy" does not adequately reflect the scope of this approach. Contextual therapy is a good fit for an integrative therapy (e.g., Garfield, 1994; Goldfried, 1980, 1982; Norcross & Goldfried, 1992). Although there is considerable variation in the way the terms are used, Stricker's (1994) description of *theoretical integration* as "an attempt to understand the patient by developing a super ordinate theoretical framework that draws from a variety of different frameworks" (p. 5) is one of the best.

Contextual therapy's emphasis on ethical considerations is also important. The fundamental defining goal is to help people be more considerate in their relationships with those closest to them, to give spontaneously and freely of themselves to those in their family, and to state their own needs and wishes in a spirit of open dialogue.

Other family systems concepts find their place in this model as well. These systems concepts include patterns of communication among family members, triangulation, coalitions, boundaries within the family, boundaries between the family and the environment, family roles, and the potential for scapegoating, as well as issues of interpersonal power and control. Therapists' observations of these phenomena during sessions and family members' reports of how they communicate and interact with each other receive careful attention in the contextual approach.

Limitations of Individual and Family Systems Approaches

Although this integrative approach and the so-called classical family therapies, or family systems therapies, overlap to a certain extent, significant differences between them also exist.

Other important individual differences reflect difficulties in life, such as disabilities, chronic illness, and enduring losses that are experienced by people as individuals.

Developmental Issues

When treating children, the need to pay attention to individual psychological issues takes on added significance. It becomes especially important to assess and attend to developmental issues as discussed by Anna Freud and Erik Erikson. Many of the children who are brought into therapy by their parents are having difficulties of one kind or another in school. In addition, parents may sometimes have specific questions about learning disabilities or hyperactivity.

Some family therapists believe strongly that such school problems must reflect family issues, or perhaps parent-child issues. Although this is sometimes the case, it is not always so. Before leaping to the conclusion that parents are to blame for a child's problems, it makes sense to pay attention to each child's cognitive strengths and weaknesses and his or her emotional and interpersonal style. We also need to be alert to developmental disabilities. In some cases, informal evaluation, perhaps limited to asking some questions and observing the child or talking to teachers on the telephone, is sufficient. In other cases, formal psychological or neuropsychological evaluations as well as continuing collaboration with other professionals such as educators and pediatricians may be needed.

Four Dimensions of Contextual Therapy

The concerns with fairness, the psychological functioning of individuals, patterns of family communication, structure, and power, and learning about personal history are interrelated.

These concerns may be grouped into four dimensions: *dimension I: objectifiable facts* treats issues of individual and family history; *dimension II: individual psychology* includes what I have been referring to as individual issues; *dimension III: systems of transactional patterns* encompasses family systems variables; and *dimension IV: the ethic of due consideration or merited trust* treats fairness issues.

These terms may appear to describe four independent sets of concerns and issues. Instead, these dimensions attempt to capture four highly overlapping and interconnected aspects of people's lives. In clinical practice, many of the questions we ask about history and much of what we observe about family transactions have clear implications for understanding the capacity of family members to see each other's needs and hurts. Concern with issues of fairness provides the glue that holds this integrative framework together. Like individual psychodynamically oriented therapy, contextual therapy is interested in people's inner psychological functioning. However, it differs in its emphasis on interpersonal realities and its search for interconnections between fairness issues and psychological issues. If psychodynamic therapy can fairly be said to focus on feelings, contextual therapy can be said to focus on fairness. Like other family systems therapies, contextual therapy is interested in patterns of family interactions, communication, structure, and power issues. It differs from the strictly systemic therapies in that its major interest is in relating these features of family life to fairness issues.

Multidirected Partiality

Therapists who utilize contextual therapy concepts try to consider the welfare of everyone whose life is likely to be affected by what happens during, and as the result of, therapy—even those they may never meet, for example, estranged or separated spouses, parents who no longer live with their children, and adults' cut-off siblings, parents, or grandparents. This concern for others who are likely to be affected by whatever changes are made as the result of therapy applies to individual as well as family therapy. Adult patients often have a spouse or adult partner, they sometimes have children and siblings, and they always have parents. All of these people and more will be affected by what happens in therapy. Indeed, even children and grandchildren who are not yet born will be affected profoundly by these changes.

Contextual therapists are committed to being partial to each of these people and are prepared to support them when necessary. But being partial to one person does not eliminate the need to be partial to others; therapists must be aware of each of these people and be prepared to be partial to each at different moments in therapy. Unilateral partiality, advocated many years ago in traditional child guidance clinics, whereby one worker took the child's side and another the parent's side, is not recommended. Neither will complete impartiality or therapeutic neutrality work for our purposes.

The contextual approach emphasizes a multilateral or *multidirected* partiality that guides us to carefully consider each person's previous experiences, especially those that involve being exploited or otherwise subjected to unfair injury, as well as current needs and feelings, and to lend our therapeutic weight to the person whose past injuries or current efforts to give to others call for our support the most at that moment. This does not mean that we always or frequently side with one person against another or against all others (although we may do this at times); rather, it means that we are prepared to do this to help people to speak their minds, to give to each other. Among contextual therapists, "giving" has its own connotations and refers to instances in which the "giver" temporarily places his or her needs on hold to try to meet a need of the "receiver." This kind of giving occurs when a parent listens for the tenth time to a child's story of how he completed a new Lego kit in record time, gets up at 4:30 in the morning to drive a child to hockey practice, or puts off purchasing a new car so that private school tuition can be covered. Giving also occurs when parents overcome their natural inclination to be laissez-faire, to their children's detriment, and learn to be more authoritative, to their betterment. In general, contextual therapy directs therapists to help family members acknowledge each other's efforts and to achieve more balanced relationships. We need not and should not strive to be equally partial to everybody at the same time; we need not strive to care equally about everyone at a specific moment. Rather, we strive to be open to the possibility of lending our therapeutic weight to each of the people who will be affected by the therapeutic process, those who are in the therapy room and those who are not.

The meaning of this concept can be broken down into components. In general usage, *multi* refers to many; *directed* here means "aimed toward"; and being *partial* means favoring someone or something, as in "I like all ice cream, but I am partial to anything with chocolate in it." Thus, multidirected partiality involves aiming (i.e., directing) one's favoritism (partiality) in multiple directions, or, in the case of therapy, toward multiple people, not all at once but selectively.

In one of my earlier books, I described my work with Dennis, a mildly mentally retarded young child who had great difficulty expressing himself. At times, I spoke for him; at other times, I directed his parents' attention to his strengths or his positive efforts. In each instance, I was motivated by a wish to increase each person's capacity to give to the others in the family. In part, I chose to be partial to Dennis out of concern that he might stop trying to achieve and to contribute to his family if someone did not acknowledge his giving. I also hoped to model how one may acknowledge a child's efforts, even if those efforts are not always successful.

Cases throughout this book contain similar examples following the principle of multidirected partiality by being partial to one person at a time. I do not do this in a predetermined manner; neither do I intentionally side with one person or another in order to unbalance a family system. Decisions about whom to support at a given moment are always based on clinical judgment about who has been harmed the most in the past in ways that interfere with their abilities to speak up for themselves or to respond with consideration to what another has to say. And each decision is made with full awareness that in the next session, or perhaps in the next moment, I may be encouraging another family member to talk about his or her needs, aspirations, hopes, or injuries, pushing another family member to consider a partner's or child's concerns more carefully. Multidirected partiality guides the therapist to consider each person's perspective and then to decide who needs our partiality at that moment.

Techniques of Multidirected Partiality

How can a therapist actually be partial to each person who will be affected by what happens in therapy? Many clinicians are familiar with the techniques that move multidirected partiality from being an interesting idea to a powerful therapeutic tool (see Table 2.1). The basic techniques have been described in detail by Boszormenyi-Nagy et al. (1991). In brief, the most familiar technique is empathy. All therapists experience and express empathy in response to clients' pain, loss, anxieties, and life difficulties. Multidirected partiality is no different in this regard. To stifle one's natural human response to another's past or present suffering is unlikely to be therapeutic in any sense. To share these feelings and validate another's pain are as important here as in any therapeutic relationship.

Multidirected partiality also involves acknowledging the unfairness of what has happened in a person's life. If empathy can be thought of as acknowledging a feeling, then being partial

Table 2.1   Multidirected Partiality Techniques

1. Empathy.
2. Acknowledging experienced unfairness in the past.
3. Fostering patients' (especially parents') efforts to give credit to others (especially their children).
4. Helping people of all ages see the impact of their actions on others.

might be thought of as the next step: First we recognize and acknowledge the depth of a person's feeling, then we help the person to identify what was unfair in how he or she was treated. One of the important implications of thinking about fairness in relationships is that it gives us an opportunity to help people identify those times when they have received unfair treatment from others. The point of our focusing on the concept of fairness is not to say that life should be fair, but to recognize that life can be unfair and to acknowledge the lasting hurt that unfairness can sometimes cause.

In attempting to be partial to each family member, the therapist may encounter situations in which it is difficult to side with a person's present behavior, for example, in the case of a parent who is being abusive to or neglectful of young children. In such cases, it is useful to explore the past injustices that led to the parent's inability to see the harm he or she is causing the children. This process allows the therapist to be partial to the person without endorsing his or her present actions.

Being partial involves more than being empathic and acknowledging the unfairness in a person's past. A third technique is helping people to give those they are close to (as well as themselves) credit for the efforts they have made to be helpful to others and to acknowledge their own positive contributions to those who are most important to them. Working with families also requires that the therapist draw other family members' attention to actions that deserve credit. Therapists may do this in a general, open-ended manner by asking something like "Do you see anything positive about the fact that your son is willing to tell you what kind of school he would prefer to attend, even though it might not be your first choice for him?" They may also call attention to possibilities for giving credit in a very focused and almost directive manner: "I don't know if you see it the same way that I do, but it seems to me that your daughter would like to be helpful to you and that she cares about you a great deal."

A fourth and essential aspect of being partial in a multi-directed way involves helping people to see the impact of what they say and do on other people, especially those in their families. In contextual language, this aspect of multidirected partiality is often referred to as "holding people accountable." This can be the most difficult and challenging of the techniques we have discussed. It can also be the most crucial. In a session with an older teen and his mother, who was an active alcoholic during the teen's childhood but is no longer, a therapist may ask: "Do you think that your son may have been hurt in some way that you did not intend during that time?" In asking this question, the therapist tries to point out the imbalance in the mother's relationship with her son; in holding her accountable for her actions, the therapist opens a door for her to work toward greater balance (i.e., a more fair relationship). The goal here is not to criticize or humiliate; neither is it to rearrange the family hierarchy or to shift the balance of power; it is, rather, to foster the growth of a more balanced relationship.

From Past Hurts to Future Possibilities

Earlier in this chapter, I talked about the problem of understanding how people who care about each other can still hurt each other or stand by while others are hurt. One's own pain is always much more real than another's pain. And if one's own pain is of sufficient magnitude and immediacy, then the pain of the other may not be real at all; it may be invisible. People who have been terribly hurt, especially during childhood, are particularly prone to this inability to see the distress of another person. When people have received little caring or consideration for their own pain, the risk of being insensitive to others' distress, even to the distress of their own children, spouse, or parents, is great. More than that, there is always the risk that such individuals will justify hurting others or being unmoved by the suffering of others based on their own past injuries.

From the contextual perspective, these people have accrued so much *destructive entitlement* and rely on it so heavily that they have become blind to the impact of their actions on others. This concept is both complex and central to the approach and so we shall return to it repeatedly.

What is destructive entitlement, and how could anyone possibly be entitled to be destructive? Perhaps the clearest way to illustrate this apparent contradiction is to consider young children who have been diagnosed with a debilitating illness. There is no sense in which such youngsters can be said to have brought the illness on themselves, no sense in which they deserve the illness, no sense in which it is fair. On the other hand, it is clear that these children are entitled to some recompense for their suffering and loss, are entitled to have someone take responsibility for helping them deal with their anger, are entitled to a better life, and are entitled to be insensitive to the relatively minor misfortunes of others. The following case illustrates destructive entitlement.

-------------------- **CASE ILLUSTRATION** --------------------
Dave

Some years ago, a mother brought Dave, her 9-year-old son, to see me. Dave had sickle cell anemia, a chronic, life-threatening, genetically transmitted illness that causes frequent painful and frightening crises that often require hospitalization and blood transfusions. He was referred to me for treatment because of his highly disruptive behavior at home and at school. He was hyperactive, impulsive, and inattentive in school and was physically aggressive both at home and in school. He had threatened to hit his sisters, his mother, and his father. He had also been suspended because he had threatened to hit his teachers and principal. He had talked about wanting to die and had tried to climb out a third-floor window at school. His parents were completely distraught, and his school had run out of ideas, plans, and options.

When I first met Dave, he was very angry. In our first meeting, this little boy said, "I don't like this planet. It isn't fair." And of course, he was absolutely right; because of his illness he was *entitled* not to care about how his behavior might bother or inconvenience other people.

Reliance on destructive entitlement may be seen in a person's lack of sensitivity, caring, or concern for others, for their needs, feelings, hopes, and misfortunes. Parents who rely on destructive entitlement are also particularly insensitive to the ways their actions affect their children. Everybody occasionally does things that hurt others; this may not represent destructive entitlement, but only human frailty. People who rely predominantly on destructive entitlement in relating to others, however, have experienced so much pain and injustice that they have become blind to the harm they cause others.

By way of contrast, some people have experienced great personal loss, personal injustice, and even personal tragedy in their lives and are still able to be sensitive to others and to consider how their actions will affect other people. Examples of this sort of transformation of personal tragedy are evident in all spheres of life. Consider, for example, the physicians and medical researchers who specialize in research on a disease process or in developing new treatments for a condition that might have led to the early death of their mother or father, or perhaps a condition from which they themselves suffer. Organizations such as Mothers Against Drunk Driving and those advocating the control of handguns vividly reflect how some people are able to respond to personal tragedy in positive ways. These are people who typically express their motivation by saying that they are doing this work so that other families will not suffer as they have. By anybody's standards, these individuals have experienced injustice in their lives. Like Dave who suffered from sickle cell anemia, they have every right to be less than sensitive to other people's life difficulties. They have every right to be preoccupied with their own troubles. We would not be surprised were they to rely on their destructive entitlement in dealing with other people. We would not be surprised were they to use their own past hurts and injuries to justify being insensitive to others, perhaps even harmful to others. And yet, these people are not insensitive to others. They are instead remarkably giving in their relationships with other people. Some of them have devoted their lives to helping others. These people have much accrued destructive entitlement but rely on its opposite, *constructive entitlement*, when it comes to their relationships and to all facets of their lives. Such people, those who seem invulnerable to the numbing and compassion-blocking effects of personal loss, have almost certainly had significant relational inoculations early in their lives. They may have had an especially nurturing and loving extended family who fostered their capacities to care about other people. Or there may have been one family member, a parent or grandparent, or even a close family friend whose guidance, protection, and care was sufficient to counterbalance difficulties and deprivations in childhood and later.

People who can see the future as having possibilities not presented by the past are more likely to rely on constructive entitlement. These people, in contrast to those characterized by an inability to give to others, have preserved their capacity to care about others, to be considerate of others, to be sensitive to the pain of others, and, above all, to give to others. Whereas those who rely on destructive entitlement seem to be blocked in their capacity to give, these individuals seem to have avoided these blockages. In the language of social learning theory, these people appear to have greater "freedom of movement" with regard to their ability to give. The other group has a markedly constrained freedom to give. The hurt of the past has led them to give up that freedom. It has led them to replace the question "How can I enhance my own worth by being helpful to others?" with the worry "I have to think of myself first."

Unwilling Caretaking

One of the most dramatic and frequent ways in which children are harmed is by being forced to care for an adult in a way that undermines their own development into healthy adulthood. This occurs earliest and with the most devastating consequences when young children are made the unwilling caretakers of their parents, such as when a teenage girl must be the primary source of emotional support to her mother following her parents' separation. In the language of contextual therapy, this state of unwillingly becoming a caretaker is referred to as *destructive parentification,* or, more simply, *parentification.*

There is a distinction between the concept of a parental child as originally used by Minuchin (1974) and the destructive using of a child that exemplifies destructive parentification. Merely having some parent-like roles (e.g., babysitting for younger siblings) does not necessarily constitute parentification in the sense in which we are using the term. A parentified person, whether child or adult, is called on to act like a selflessly giving parent. In the case of a parentified child, this most often means that the child becomes the parent to his or her own parent. The teenage girl of the recently separated mother who stays home every Saturday evening because she worries that her mother will be lonely and depressed is acting as if she were the mother and her mother were the child. In a couple, the parentified person is explicitly or implicitly required to care for the other as a parent would. This occurs frequently when one parent assumes all responsibility for the children. Of course, all close relationships involve a measure of taking care of the other, but there is a dramatic difference between relationships in which this caretaking balances out over time and those in which one person does all the giving all the time.

Acknowledging Efforts and Sacrifices

Earlier, I mentioned the emphasis on helping people to acknowledge their own positive efforts and those of others as one of the defining features of contextual therapy. Acknowledgment plays an important role from the first minute of the first session and takes several forms. In a first family session, for example, when a therapist asks whether a temporarily scapegoated adolescent may have been trying to be helpful despite appearances, or whether this person may try to be helpful at other times, the therapist is inviting other people in the family to acknowledge the adolescent's positive efforts to give something of interpersonal value to them.

The second form of acknowledgment involves acknowledging the injustice (unfairness) that has occurred in someone else's life. Examples include both acknowledging how one's own actions have harmed another and acknowledging the unfairness of having been born with a disability or chronic life-threatening illness. Acknowledging that another has been harmed, or that another has given generously, is one indicator of a person's ability to act based on constructive rather than destructive entitlement.

Acknowledge the loss of identity and hope to an adolescent who is no longer permitted to play hockey because of a serious injury. People's most unpleasant, insensitive, inconsiderate, and angry statements and actions often reflect imbalances in their lives. They have been hurt, they have been exploited, they have tried to be helpful, and they have received no acknowledgment for either their pain or their good efforts from those closest to them. To a scapegoated person, one who has experienced only blame, acknowledgment from those who matter the most often has striking and salutary effects. A seemingly simple statement of appreciation for trying to help, or one of sympathy for struggling to overcome an injury, can make a world of difference. It is not unusual to see people's attitudes shift in a few moments from being aggressively confrontational to quietly receptive when they hear such acknowledgment from other family members.

The Place of Contextual Concepts in the Integrated Model

The integrated model has been influenced by contextual therapy in making its focus the child in his or her family environment and in considering every aspect of the child's life in conceptualizing cases and in developing and implementing treatment. It is a model with a clearly defined range of convenience. It provides a framework for practice, with related strategies and techniques, that will be helpful to clinicians and others who work with children, adolescents, and their families. For many problems, the model provides all that is necessary by way of psychological intervention. For other problems, such as alcoholism, substance abuse, and conduct disorder, it can be helpful in conjunction with or following appropriate inpatient or residential treatment.

CHAPTER 3

Twenty-Three Basic Principles of Working with Children and Families

To improve is to change; to be perfect is to change often.
—Winston Churchill (1874–1965)

Beyond Conceptualizing

Having a conceptual model is not enough. As my friend Linda Knauss, who directs internship training at Widener University, shared with me, graduate students and others interested in increasing their skill repertoire have plenty of theoretical models from which to choose. By the time students are halfway through their training program, whatever sort of training program it is, they have become familiar with two or three theoretical approaches and have learned a great deal about one of them. It's not theorizing, but the real-world implementation of the model that challenges them. The principles in this chapter will help you translate conceptual principles into action. They function as part of the bridge between the conceptual model and the very nuts-and-bolts chapters of Section Two of this book.

Working as a child and family therapist, whether it defines your professional life completely or is one of several professional roles you fill, is no easy task. It can even be a challenge to explain the role to those in closely related fields such as pediatrics. After trying out several responses to the question "What do you specialize in?" I now respond that my professional life is analogous to that of a family doctor who sees patients of all ages while maintaining a strong commitment to pediatrics. The perspective of this book is that a therapist who works with children will of necessity work with the child's family and will then be, if not a family therapist, then a therapist for families. This distinction is important because "family therapy" often connotes therapy geared toward family change, therapy in which the entire family is the target of therapy, and therapy that eschews a focus on an individual's problems as the focus of treatment. Therapy for families, in contrast, accepts the notion that it is possible, and sometimes desirable, to treat one person in a family and that it is possible and sometimes desirable to accept that individual's perspective on his or her problem as valid and important.

Eclecticism and Psychotherapy Integration

"Eclectic" is derived from the Greek *eklektikos,* meaning "picking out." The original eclectics were Greek philosophers who incorporated into their thinking concepts from many other philosophical systems. Eclecticism can be very appealing to therapists who work with children and their families. Very young children's behavioral problems often respond best to straightforward behavioral interventions. Parents of school-age children need help with parenting skills and often with marital issues as well. Parents of children of all ages bring their own life traumas and difficult experiences with them and to their parenting efforts, and so need individual attention as well.

All of this may suggest that eclecticism represents an ideal approach for the practical-minded clinician. The freedom to pick and choose from among the hundreds, perhaps thousands of interventions that have been developed for each case seems ideal. The quandary is deciding how one does the picking and choosing. It is one thing to say to oneself, one's colleagues, or one's students that the idea is to choose the best intervention for that particular patient at that particular time for that particular problem, to paraphrase Gordon Paul (1969). It is quite another thing to pick that choice out of myriad possible choices. Such a process could easily be daunting in the extreme. Imagine meeting a new patient and having to choose from behavioral, psychoanalytic, cognitive, family systems, and other approaches and then to make choices about which of the possible interventions offered by each approach to use at each point in therapy. One would almost certainly experience emotional and intellectual gridlock.

One solution to this quandary is to have an integrative framework that facilitates flexibility while providing a set of practical decision rules and an overall model. One need not have a repertoire consisting of every possible therapeutic intervention. The idea is to develop a repertoire that is large enough and varied enough to suit the range of patients you are likely to see in your practice. For example, I have considerable familiarity with relaxation techniques but only a rudimentary knowledge of advanced hypnotic techniques. This suits my practice, as I am fairly regularly called on to help children learn to relax but have not yet needed to hypnotize patients.

Eclecticism has gotten a bad name in some circles for being the product of sloppy thinking. The argument against eclecticism goes something like this: A rigorously trained therapist will use a single and highly focused approach to treatment. He or she will have been trained in a unified and coherent treatment model, with its own constructs, its own strategies, and its own techniques. The model will be well suited to treating a specifiable range of problems experienced by patients of a specifiable age range. The model will also have generated a body of research on its propositions, its methodology, and its efficacy.

This is a nice argument, and an appealing one. For practitioner, teacher, and supervisor alike, thinking about how a first interview should be conducted, how to formulate questions and responses, how to formulate a treatment plan, and how to decide who should be in the therapy room is facilitated if one has a single coherent model. But if the only alternative to eclecticism is rigid adherence to one model, one is truly on the horns of a dilemma. What is the clinician who wants both flexibility and a coherent model to do?

Fortunately, there is a third option, one that offers the flexibility of eclecticism and the intellectual coherence of a single model. Every child and family treatment case requires the same ingredients at the beginning: careful assessment of child and family issues, reassurance for both child and parents, collaboration with schools and pediatricians, and initiation of a treatment plan. Cases differ only in how much of each ingredient is needed.

The 23 items that follow are intended to be guidelines that will help you implement the integrated model on which this book is based.

1. Learn to think like a pediatrician.

There are many reasons you should learn to think like a pediatrician. First, and perhaps most obvious, many of your youngest patients will come to you via a pediatrician's referral. To be maximally helpful to them, you need to understand how a pediatric practice works and, most important, how a pediatrician works. If you want to continue to receive referrals from the pediatrician, you should understand how he or she thinks about diagnosis and treatment and what kinds of information he or she would like to receive from you. If you use a standard consent form to share information in your practice, be sure that it is completed at the first visit so that you can discuss the patient with his or her pediatrician without delay.

There are several very good reasons for a psychologist to learn to appreciate the ways that the most expert pediatricians approach their job. One is that the best pediatricians have a highly informed, and yet very practical, attitude about their young patients. They may be active as researchers and teachers, and yet, when in the office, they focus on the child and the family. They take one problem at a time, considering the possibility that they are interrelated, but not assuming that they are. When a pediatrician is told that a 7-year-old has a temperature of 103, a sore throat, and a limp, he or she doesn't look for an underlying pathology that will explain all the symptoms. Rather, the pediatrician treats the sore throat and fever as one condition and checks the child's foot and ankle to see if there is a sprain or other physical problem that accounts for the limping.

2. Therapy is for the patient, not the therapist.

Therapy has one purpose: helping patients. Conducting research, validating your theory, and learning about child development are secondary. Any of these things may happen along the way, but they are not what therapy is about. The reason people come to you is to get help for their children, for themselves, and for their families. If, in the process of helping them, you learn that your model is a good one, that's fine. If, instead, you learn that it's more important to diverge from your model than to adhere to it, so much the better. If you enjoy your work, that's very good, too. This principle is essential for therapy to do what it is supposed to do: help people. The early first-century Jewish teacher and scholar Hillel is often quoted as saying that all of the Torah can be summed up in one sentence, "Treat your neighbor as you would be treated," with the addendum that "all the rest is commentary." The parallel here is that there is only one principle of therapy: Keep the patient's welfare uppermost in your mind; all the rest is commentary.

3. Personal therapy is essential.

The people who develop reputations as great, not merely competent, therapists have been in intensive therapy themselves, and many consider ongoing therapy to be essential to their maintaining a high level of professional functioning. If you aspire to join this select group, you should give serious consideration to finding a therapist with whom you can work long enough and deeply enough to learn where your areas of vulnerability are. This is important so that you can work with patients in an uncontaminated way. This does not mean that you must "solve" all of your own problems, whatever that means, but that you know what your problems are so that they do not intrude into your work. Even with personal therapy, you will inevitably run into a problem that brings up unresolved issues in your own life. If you find this affecting your work, you should either immediately get supervision or additional therapy for those issues, or refer the patient to a colleague. Personal therapy will also help you know yourself, your values, what is most important to you, and what kind of patients you are comfortable working with. I was recently asked if I would be interested in providing consultation and therapy to an outpatient dialysis unit for adults with end-stage renal disease. Having seen children and adolescents with this condition as part of my work at Children's Hospital of Philadelphia, I was intrigued. But, on further thought and reflection, I realized that I was not the right person for this particular assignment. Therapy will also help you make every intervention consistent with who you are.

A colleague teaching at a large research university shared his concerns with me about a local therapist who attracted many students as patients by dint of his halo of successful practice, self-promotion, fancy leather office furniture, and arrogance. The unexpressed promise was "Follow me and you, too, will have a successful practice and make lots of money." That he had hired one of his ex-patients to work in his practice before she completed her dissertation only increased his appeal. But he was more interested in having acolytes than was good for his patients.

There's nothing wrong with having a famous and well-published therapist, but credentials and fame do not bestow clinical skill on their owner. It's far more important to find someone who understands clinical work and who can help you understand yourself than it is to find someone famous, hoping that a bit of her prestige will rub off on you. It won't. Worrying about that will interfere with your getting out of therapy what you are getting into it for: self-knowledge. It also doesn't matter much whether the therapist you select shares your theoretical orientation or not. It does matter that the therapist is not the least bit rigid and that he sees his role as being helpful to you in whatever way he can. Stay away from therapists who refuse to answer questions, give advice, or provide suggestions about a difficult case you are treating. For some readers, this list of failings may call up characteristics of psychoanalysts, but it shouldn't. There are first-rate analysts who are also very flexible, who would regard a refusal to answer a question as an example of rudeness, plain and simple, and unwillingness to offer specific help as a breach of their therapeutic contract. There are also rigid and standoffish social learning, cognitive-behavioral, and family systems therapists. Choose the person, not the school. Accept recommendations from your mentors and colleagues, but when it comes down to it, make up your own mind.

Some graduate programs recommend personal therapy; some require it; some are laissez-faire on the issue. You are fortunate if your graduate program is, or was, one of those that encourages this sort of personal exploration. But whether this was part of your training program or not, find a therapist.

Personal therapy is also a great way to learn to manage your own anxiety. Someone once said that in therapy, it is often true that one person is quite anxious and that things go far better if that person is not the therapist.

4. Patients are people, not sources of data.

One of the risks of having a conceptual model is that of investing in it so much that you are more interested in your theory than you are in your patients. If you catch yourself wondering "How can I apply my theory in this case?" think again. As important and practical as a good theory is, it loses its value when you value it more than you do your role as helper.

5. See your patients through a clear lens.

Seeing your patients as a source of data is similar to seeing your patients as a reflection of yourself. It is easier than you might think to fall into this trap, because patients will inevitably present issues that are not so very different from those you confront in your life. Some of these are hot buttons indeed. When a colleague of mine was in the middle of a divorce with a complicated custody situation, she avoided seeing children whose parents were in the midst of similar situations. On the other hand, having been through that, and having worked on it in her personal therapy, she is better able to understand and help these children and their parents than she was before.

By way of contrast, another case involving divorce, children, and custody issues shows how egregious examples of bad treatment can arise when therapists are not aware of their own conflicts. As we often do, I learned of this particular example of bad treatment from a patient, who called me after he had discontinued treatment with his previous therapist. The patient, a teacher in his late 30s and in the midst of a divorce, had been in treatment with his previous therapist for over a year. When he told her that he was considering seeking primary custody of his young son, the therapist reacted with great emotion: "How dare you take a child from his mother?" My patient told me that he responded that he was not trying to take his son from his mother, only to have the little boy reside with him and visit his mother twice a week, instead of the more usual pattern of residing with the mother and visiting the father. My patient explained that he and his son had an unusually strong bond, that his wife had acknowledged that he was the more nurturing parent, and that he thought this would be best for his child. My patient also told me that he asked his previous therapist, "Would you ask that same question of a woman who told you she wanted to be her child's primary custodial parent?" My patient told me that he began to realize how much his therapist had been caught up in her own feelings when she made the same statement again several weeks later, apparently not remembering his response, which he then repeated to her.

From this story, it is clear that my patient's previous therapist was temporarily unconscious, an unconsciousness only penetrated when the patient asked for the second time, "Would you say that to a woman who wanted custody of her child?" When a therapist is unconscious to this extent, the odds are high that something about her patient's concerns touched a highly vulnerable and unexamined area of her life. If I had been her supervisor or her therapist, I would have asked her about her own divorce, about her custody arrangements, and, most important, about her feelings when her patient was experiencing something that was so close to home for her. I might well have suggested that she consider referring her patient to someone else. There can be no guarantee that you will never find yourself reacting from your own past traumas as this therapist did, but personal therapy can be a helpful innoculant.

6. There's not a moment to lose.

When treating problems of childhood, the quickest treatment that resolves the problem is the best treatment. And when treating very young children, the quickest treatment can be quick indeed. The notion that therapy must take years and involve a thorough review of family history can seriously interfere with your ability to help. Your pediatrician does not insist on doing a cardiogram and EEG when you bring your child in with a red ear and a fever, and you would quickly find a new doctor if she did. So, too, you can successfully treat a 5-year-old anxious about his first day of school without a complete family history, and you ought to try, because the longer you spend getting background information and addressing his mother's leftover childhood anxieties, the longer you delay his school entry, only worsening his fear. Do what you can now to get him to school, and then see if his mother would like your help with her anxieties, both past and present. Later, I present such a case that I treated in less than an hour.

This is not a great way to build up a caseload of long-term patients. Neither is it a great way to have interesting and dynamic cases, but it is what is needed. Treatment must be tailored to the problem, not to your preference. Every treatment case doesn't have to be the equivalent of a training analysis.

7. Give patients all the time they need.

Take the time the problem calls for. This may seem to contradict what you just read. It does not. A 5-year-old who still refuses to use the toilet, with kindergarten starting in 2 months, presents a problem that allows you very little time. It's your obligation to do what you can as quickly as you can. A 14-year-old boy with serious interpersonal problems who is just beginning to grapple with his profound unhappiness and his deep need for parental support is on a very different kind of time line, as are his parents. To rush them is to miss the depth and subtlety of his problem. To rush them is to fail.

Children on the verge of adolescence and in midadolescence need time, and great gobs of it, before they are even ready to deal with their most pressing concerns, and so must not be rushed. This principle and the one that immediately precedes it are not contradictory: Therapy shouldn't be thought of as either long term or short term but as long-enough term. If this sounds antithetical to the goals and procedures of so-called managed care, and if I sound hostile to those goals and procedures, there's a reason for that. It is, and I am. You, the therapist, should be the person managing the care of your patients. You, the therapist, should be the person who decides, in concert with the child and family, how often to meet and for how many weeks, months, or years. Whenever these decisions are left to an organization that profits more from less treatment, regardless of need, the patient will suffer. Whenever decisions are made by people who are evaluated based on how well they have controlled costs, the patient will suffer. My practice consists in large part of patients who have come to me after a managed care failure; this is not coincidence. Anytime therapy is successful for a patient with managed care, that is pure happenstance.

8. Appreciate each child's and family's complexity.

The simplest presenting problems are more complex than they appear. Even something as seemingly straightforward and compatible with a purely behavioral intervention as encopresis must be understood in the context of the particular child's temperament and medical history, family history, parents' personalities, and cultural issues. As you will see in the case examples of treatments for encopresis, these factors guide treatment decisions as much as, perhaps more than, the diagnosis.

9. Keep diagnosis in its place.

It's easy to get carried away with diagnosis. Diagnosis needs to have a purpose, and when it has a purpose, it's worth doing. The purpose may be to select the right medication, to obtain the highest insurance reimbursement allowable for that condition on behalf of your patient, to accurately assign a patient to the correct group in a research protocol, or to make decisions about necessary consultation or referrals. It's unusual for a nonmedical therapist to be the first to diagnose a brain tumor, mononucleosis, or astigmatism, but it has happened, and these are important diagnoses. Similarly, nonmedical therapists who see patients weekly are sometimes in the best position to make the differential diagnosis between unipolar and bipolar mood disorders. Diagnostic issues regarding children's intellectual capacity and cognitive strengths and weaknesses are important for educational planning, decisions regarding supplemental services, and remediation. As the child's and family's therapist, you have access to information crucial to the success of treatment. Your training may permit you to do some formal psychological testing, but whether it does or not, and whether you choose to do this or not, you may be the first to gain insights into developmental issues that others have missed.

Not all of these diagnostic distinctions are useful. Some diagnostic decisions are essential, and some differential diagnoses, such as between attention-deficit/hyperactivity disorder and mental retardation, make huge differences in treatment planning, educational placement, and family education. Other diagnostic distinctions are useful as well. For example, you really ought to know what questions to ask to determine if a child's encopresis is secondary to constipation. It's very easy to mistake early-onset bipolar disorder in an adolescent with attention-deficit/

hyperactivity disorder plus oppositional defiant disorder; the distinction is of the utmost import in both the short term and long term. In other words, a complete history is an important part of preparation for treatment.

On the other hand, some diagnostic distinctions are of only academic interest, as they do not affect treatment in any way. It is worth considering whether a youngster who has trouble making friends is a bit "different" or has mild Asperger's syndrome. But it is not worthwhile obsessing over this particular diagnosis, as there is no specific treatment for mild Asperger's syndrome. It makes more sense to identify specific problems and then see what you can do to help the youngster with each of them, while bearing in mind the possible diagnosis. Of course, if he has non-mild Asperger's, the situation is different because diagnosis may make specialized educational services available to your patient.

Those who treat children and adolescents psychopharmaco-logically as well as psychologically need to make more subtle distinctions in order to decide which SSRI will be prescribed, for example. The same is true for nonprescribing therapists when they are the first to identify the need for medication. Such distinctions inform their choices regarding medications in important ways. For therapists who do not prescribe medications, these distinctions have less meaning and less importance. Unless you need to identify target symptoms that you are going to address psychopharmacologically, this kind of diagnosis is often of limited usefulness.

As I write this, my psychological colleagues around the country are eagerly pursuing legislation that would permit them to prescribe some psychopharmacological agents. Some therapists may be able to focus on adjusting dosages and administration time, being alert to potential drug interactions, making the continuous trial-and-error decisions that are routine when treating children and adolescents. For many other therapists, including this one, it is probably in the patient's interest to have a therapist who does not have that distraction.

10. Learn from your patients.

If your way of working remains unchanged from year to year, or worse, from decade to decade, something is wrong. Innovations grow out of observation and openness. Those once innovative models become calcified when innovation ceases, especially when openness to new data ceases, and your most important source of new data is your patient. The best conceptual model is constantly changing and growing in response to what you learn from your patients. You may have had the most renowned teachers, the most brilliant supervisors, and the most insightful peers. You will still learn your most important lessons from your patients.

11. Appreciate the importance of Jedi training.

Fine-tune your intuition. Know what you are feeling, and why you are feeling it. Learn to tell the difference between feelings and intuitions that reflect something about your patient, and those that only reflect something about you. If the heading of this principle is a mystery to you, rent or buy the *Star Wars* movies and discover how powerful an ally intuition can be and what it can do for you and your patients.

12. Be clear about the difference between statements your patients make that are about you and those that are about your patients.

If your 17-year-old patient regularly says, "I think I told you this before," do not lapse into defensiveness and explain to her that you can't possibly be expected to remember everything all your patients tell you. Rather, realize that she is showing you how much she frets that she may inconvenience you by repeating herself.

13. Rise above your education.

Unless you graduated from a remarkably open-minded training program, you were indoctrinated with a number of biases, both pro and con. Even the wisest of your mentors had biases without which you will be better off. My dissertation advisor, a wonderful man to whom I shall always be indebted, fervently believed that those who were investigating possible genetic, biological, and neurochemical factors underlying serious psychopathology were headed up a blind alley. You may have been taught that behaviorism is rigid and formulaic and that it neglects relationship issues, that psychoanalytic ideas and procedures are antiquated and foolish, or that family systems work is haphazard and chaotic. All of these statements are false. My advice is this: Whatever you were taught, remember all the useful things and get rid of the various axes your professors and mentors were grinding.

14. Find another place or, even better, several other places to meet your own needs.

One important avenue is through regular formal or informal peer supervision. Another obvious recommendation? Perhaps, but one that bears repeating, especially in the era of managed care and "do more with less" psychotherapy.

15. Promise little. Deliver much.

When parents are overwhelmingly anxious, it's natural to want to reassure. But reassurance that verges on promises of "cure" can put you in a very awkward spot, to say the least. There are times to promise results, but they are few and very far between.

16. Learn to trust your own judgment and intuition.

This is another one of those aspects of therapy that are easy to write about but hard to do. Those who come to this work from a psychoanalytic background have an advantage, as one of the major purposes of the training analysis is to develop self-understanding. But there are many roads to Rome and many ways to learn to fine-tune one's clinical intuition to the point of knowing which feelings say something about the child, parent, or family and which are more reflective of your own issues. Especially when working with children and their families, the risk of slipping one's own agenda into the therapy is significant. This is even more true for those who have the temerity to advise parents regarding parenting without meeting the children. I have, on more occasions than one would have predicted, been told by parents that their therapist (almost always a therapist who sees only adults and who has never met their child) disagrees with my approach to their child's treatment and believes that something else is indicated. Other adult therapists may strongly advise their patients regarding such issues as child custody without ever having met their children. This is not a good idea. The requirement to be able to make this distinction is important to every therapist, not just to those with psychoanalytic training. Here I only wish to highlight the importance of this; the how-to will come later.

17. When faced with very challenging clinical situations, remember that you aren't obligated to make things perfect, but that you are required to try to improve things.

This is another one of the ways in which treating children and families differs from the treatment of adults. It's much easier for the child and family therapist to start to believe that every problem has a solution and that every symptom has a cure. Those who treat severely mentally ill adults know that cure is unlikely and see their role as providing long-term care, rather like the work of a rheumatologist whose patients have severely debilitating arthritis. The cure doesn't exist for Asperger's syndrome any more than it does for arthritis of the most severe sort. But much can be done to help the child suffer less and be more functional.

18. Offer criticism gently. Offer strong criticism very gently.

This recommendation contains several implications. The first is that criticism is sometimes necessary. Therapists do not always have to agree with their patients. With all respect to Carl Rogers, we ought to do more than reflect what patients are feeling and saying. There are times when we must point out flaws in patients' thinking.

19. Take everything your patient says seriously.

Taking children seriously is fundamental to good parenting. Taking seriously what children tell us and what parents tell us about their children is equally fundamental to good therapy.

20. Learn about each patient's culture.

Cultural sensitivity and cultural awareness has been a part of every graduate program's curriculum for decades. This is a good thing, but it has not gone far enough. To rise from the ranks of competent therapists to that of great therapists, one must be sensitive to not only each patient's culture, but to the particular way patients' cultures affect them and their unique reflection of their cultural backgrounds. Learn also about the microculture of each patient. It is important to be sensitive to cultural differences among major ethnic and racial groups, such as African American, Native American, Asian American, and Latino. It is important, but it is not enough. It's also important to be sensitive to differences among members of those broader cultures. Hispanic culture in Cuba shares much with Hispanic culture in Puerto Rico, but it is not identical to it, and the Chicano culture of the American Southwest differs from both of these. We must also be sensitive to differences among groups that are sometimes seen as homogeneous. Although we don't usually think of them this way, White Anglo-Saxon Protestants (WASPS) are a minority culture with mores and ways of doing things that are all their own. For non-WASP therapists, the emotional reticence and understatement of the WASP parent of a profoundly depressed and potentially suicidal adolescent can very easily be mistaken for lack of caring. Doing so would be unfair to that parent and could easily lead to irreversible therapeutic errors.

As clinicians, we are always dealing with individual differences, not with groups, and so should be as acutely aware of the differences among individuals within groups as we are of differences among groups. Every group is composed of many subgroups that may be invisible until one increases one's awareness. I learned not to be too quick to apply what I thought I had learned about cultural differences from two Italian American families I worked with soon after completing my training. The father in the first family told me that he grew up in a typical Italian home, which he went on to describe as very emotional and loud. The father in the second family also told me that his childhood was very much influenced by growing up in a typical Italian home, which he described as being very strict and as headed by a very stern and authoritarian father. If two Italian homes can be this different, or at least make such different impressions on those growing up in them, it points to the wide variations within cultural groups as well as between cultural groups. To many outside of Judaism, for example, American Jews appear to be a homogeneous group, but this is very far from true. Values and beliefs regarding parenting and adolescent dating practices, for example, differ widely among various Jewish groups. Orthodox Jews, for example, will work closely and comfortably with both men and women but would not be comfortable shaking hands with a member of the opposite sex. It's important to be aware of this to avoid making a person uncomfortable. It's also important to be aware that for an Orthodox family, teenagers holding hands is potentially upsetting.

Being sensitive to cultural issues means far more than withholding judgment about parenting practices or family composition. It also means being ready to learn from patients. For example, Hispanic cultures value relationships in a way that is foreign to many non-Hispanics and from which many psychotherapists could learn a great deal.

21.   Allow yourself to be aware of how you feel about your patients.

Some schools of psychotherapy and family therapy postulate an ideal therapist-patient relationship, including a right and wrong way for therapists to feel about patients. Some advocate neutrality; others endorse unconditional positive regard. In the real world, therapists will experience real affection for some patients and, believe it or not, genuine dislike for others. It is crucially important to not keep these feelings a secret from yourself. Disliking a patient does not mean that you can't help him or her. In fact, the realization of a patient's unpleasantness can be an important key to helping that patient. It's just as important to be aware of positive feelings for a child or parent. Don't miss an opportunity for a truly healing therapeutic relationship because you are working hard to maintain neutrality or to keep therapeutic distance.

22.   Develop a way of working that is true to yourself.

Rigid people who become psychotherapists—not a great idea to begin with—generally do best within rigid systems of therapy. Authoritarian people who become psychotherapists do best when they work within authoritarian systems of therapy. Conversely, flexible therapists who eschew authoritarianism, or who are simply uncomfortable being authoritarian, generally do best when they have the freedom to operate within a flexible system.

23.   Don't be too careful.

Sometimes it's best to relax and let things happen as they will, to shoot from the hip. If you have followed the other recommendations, done your personal therapy, and are working to be aware of your own issues, you don't have to plan every intervention. Just as clinging too tightly to your theory can make it difficult to see what is really going on with your patient, so, too, can clinging too tightly to a protocol make it difficult to be a real person or to establish a real relationship.

CHAPTER 4

Beginnings: First Sessions with Children, Adolescents, and Families

Well begun is half done.

—Aristotle

Beginning therapy with children and their families involves the therapist in several simultaneous and overlapping functions: assessment, diagnosis, treatment planning, early interventions, and relationship building. It is better not to think of these as either stages or phases. Although the linear nature of language forces me to write about them sequentially, and forces you to discuss them sequentially with your patients, they are in fact more simultaneous than they are sequential. All these functions are active at the same time; it is more a matter of the extent to which you decide to focus attention on one or the other than it is a matter of choosing one instead of the others. It is important to maintain flexibility in deciding which of these beginning functions to emphasize at any point in therapy, including your first meeting with patients.

In this chapter, I present a case of a young boy with encopresis. Jake has been referred by his pediatrician. His mother worries that if this problem is not resolved her son will not be permitted to begin kindergarten the following September. I offer the case by way of illustration of how you can incorporate social learning, contextual, and psychodynamic concepts of this integrative model into your assessments and how issues outside of the presenting problem can crucially figure in your decision making and eventual outcome. I discuss the specifics of treating encopresis in Chapter 8.

Begin with the Relationship

There can be no therapy without a strong relationship between you and your patient. This is true of therapy with individual adults, and much more true of therapy in which children are the focus of attention. Despite her psychoanalytic training, with its emphasis on the need for the patient to develop both positive and negative transference and to form a transference neurosis, Anna Freud (1964) makes the point that in therapy with children, one wants to diffuse negativity and keep the relationship only positive. You have no choice about whether or not to consider the relationship as you start with a new patient: You must think about the relationship. The choice, rather, is how you consider your relationship with your patient and how you choose to proceed with that in mind.

With some patients, you may need to begin with a formal assessment process, but most patient families respond better to a beginning that emphasizes establishing a relationship while gathering enough information to know what their concerns are. For these families, assessment must play second fiddle to relationship building. When parents seek psychological help for their children and their family, they are rarely looking only for a technical fix, for the psychological equivalent of a front-end alignment. Parents of very young children are often looking for technical guidance: how to reduce sibling conflicts, how to increase cooperation, how to teach children to use the toilet. But they need this guidance to be tailored to fit their personalities, their family, and their children, and they want to know the *why* of their children's behavior as well as the *what* of it. They need to know that you are not reading from a cookbook, but are responding to them in the context of a human relationship, even if that relationship lasts only 50 minutes. The decision about how structured and formal to be in a first session depends on a number of factors.

Decision Making in the Assessment Phase of Treatment

There are many choices to be made as you begin treatment. Fortunately, there are several useful rules of thumb. These rules are independent of each other: A separate decision needs to be made about each rule. Don't worry that the decisions you make about one rule may negate decisions you previously made about other rules.

Child's Age

The need for structure in a first interview is inversely related to the age of the child. With your youngest patients, you won't know what to do until you obtain some kind of developmental history. It won't take very long, and parents expect it. So, unless there is a compelling reason to do otherwise—and the subsequent items in this section may on occasion give you such a compelling reason—take a complete developmental history soon after greeting your patient and his or her parents. There are many ways to do this. I've included the questions and the order I use as Appendix A.

The Nature of the Presenting Problem

The case I present in this chapter involves a young child, an anxious mother, and a focused problem (encopresis). When a young mother brings her very young child to see you because she is worried that he will never learn to use the toilet, she will likely be reassured when you ask her a number of detailed questions about her child's early development and toilet training. Similarly, she will be reassured if you ask her to complete a questionnaire such as Levine's (1996) ANSER system. The reason for this is that she fears that her child has a very unusual and possibly incurable condition, and your steady questioning conveys certainty and that you have done this a hundred times before and know exactly where the road is leading and how long it will take to get there. The placebo effect by another name is operating. She has been referred by her child's pediatrician and is expecting a medical-model first interview. Because you will need this developmental and physical health information, there is no reason not to get it directly and quickly.

I was consulted by the parents of a teenager who had been a premature infant who spent 11 months in a neonatal intensive care unit. After her mother told me these two facts, adding that the teenager had been in special schools her whole life, I chose not to ask further questions about her development during that first meeting. There were several reasons for this: Her parents planned to bring a copy of a recent comprehensive neuropsychological evaluation to their next appointment; there was no question that their daughter had developmental delays; the issue that was pressing on them was their daughter's intense unhappiness and equally intense oppositional behavior. My immediate task was not to determine what was going on developmentally but to find some way to connect with the unhappy and angry teenager and her equally unhappy, frustrated, and worried parents. It would have taken hours to obtain a complete developmental and medical history.

Assessment and Diagnosis

When you are meeting for the first time with a child and his or her parents, you are faced with a number of diagnostic and assessment questions. Some concern the child as an individual, some concern the parents as individuals, and some concern the family with its various relationships.

It is all too easy to base a diagnostic impression on insufficient data. One good way around this potential pitfall is to have a protocol that specifies the areas to be covered in initial meetings. In the beginning, it may be helpful to follow this protocol step-by-step, as if it were a pastry recipe or a laboratory procedure. Later, as you get used to it and as its goals become part of your natural way of working, it will become largely automatic. The idea is to touch on the important factors whose attention we are drawn to by the three theoretical models that compose the integrative approach.

The four-dimensional contextual model provides a natural jumping-off point for the development of just such a protocol. Each of the four dimensions, *objectifiable facts, individual psychology, systems of transactional patterns,* and *the ethic of due consideration/fairness,* has important implications for assessment. The dimensions are abstract, making for easy synthesis with the other two models that make up the integrated model. They are inclusive, rather than exclusive or restrictive. After you have used the approach for some time, you will likely no longer think of the dimensions as distinct. In all likelihood, you will not be thinking of the four dimensions at all when you are in your office with your patients. They will become integrated into a flow that will operate in the background, allowing you to focus on the nuances and the all-important nonverbal channels of communication, about which I'll have much more to say in a bit.

Let's take a look at a typical case to see how using the notion of a four-dimensional assessment can be put into action and how one may choose to make the whole assessment process subservient to the need to engage in relationship building.

CASE ILLUSTRATION
Jake

Imagine that you receive a call from the distraught mother of a not quite 5-year-old boy, Jake, who is soiling every day. She and her husband have consulted a number of medical and nonmedical specialists in several cities and received widely conflicting advice. The pediatricians in one city told them that the problem was purely physical, that Jake had been constipated; they would do a clean-out, and then he would be fine. A team of specialists in another city told them that their son had a subtle but significant developmental disability. A psychologist at a renowned medical center told these worried parents that the problem was purely behavioral, that Jake was being oppositional in refusing to use the toilet and that a new behavioral plan would resolve the problem. Mrs. Smith sounds both anxious and angry as she tells you this in a rush in the office. She is anxious because she fears that her son will not be permitted to start school in the fall if this problem is not resolved. She is angry because all the other doctors promised results and failed to deliver. "Nobody can do anything about this!" she insists.

You begin this meeting, one in which you know that you will eventually have to do some sort of assessment, not with questions about developmental or family history, but with reassurance. The most important thing is to let Mrs. Smith know that you understand what she and her husband have been through, what they are worried about, and, not least, that you have the expertise in treating young children with encopresis for which they have been looking.

If, at this point, you are thinking, "Wait, I don't have expertise in treating encopresis," you have several choices: You can decide in advance that you will refer such cases out; you can arrange to have a pediatric psychologist or a developmental-behavioral pediatrician on standby to provide consultation and possibly case-specific supervision; or you can get some training in treating this disorder.

You begin by listening, and listening with great care, not just to what is being said but to how it is being said and, equally important, to what is left unsaid. Within minutes, Mrs. Smith shares her distress over what she feels is her husband's lack of support for her and his tendency to hold her responsible for parenting and to blame her for any parenting difficulties that arise. She begins to cry as she recounts various examples of how she has been disappointed by her husband's responses to parenting issues, making it painfully clear that her son's encopresis is her smallest and most readily fixable problem. You realize that she is showing you a level of emotional distress that will not be much diminished if your only response is a detailed description of how you're going to treat her son's encopresis. Neither will she experience much reassurance if all she hears is a vague, though heartfelt, expression of concern. Bland therapeutic neutrality won't do much for her either. She needs reassurance that her distress as a mother and as a woman will be understood and addressed. This need not be, and should not be, anything fancy. A simple statement such as "You have an awful lot going on right now" is sufficient.

She again brings up her frustration about receiving so much conflicting advice regarding her son's encopresis (one expert saying that the problem is purely behavioral, the other that it is purely physical). You rely on your intuition (a crucial clinical skill that will receive much attention in later chapters) and realize that this is not the time for you to wax philosophical: "On the one hand . . . and on the other hand." Rather, Mrs. Smith needs you to take an expert stance. So you say, quite simply, "They're both right. It's physical *and* behavioral, and as soon as we get both aspects on track, he'll be fine."

What you have done in this imaginary, but realistic, scenario is given priority to the need to meet Mrs. Smith as a person, to be real and supportive, while temporarily giving less priority to taking a history and the other steps in assessment of her, her marital relationship, and her son's encopresis. Although you have emphasized the relationship function and de-emphasized the diagnostic function, you have still learned a great deal about Mrs. Smith, her family, and potentially about some of the factors that are responsible for her son's encopresis. It is evident that things are stressful at home. If little Jake is like most 5-year-olds, he feels this tension. There is not a parenting issue in the world that is not worse when parents are fighting. Neither is there a parenting issue that is easily resolved when one parent is anxious and depressed. Treating encopresis might well provide a model for the way these variables interact. Given a solid partnership between the parents or among the adults who are parenting the child, a parent who is either relatively free of anxiety or who can bracket off the anxiety in order to create an anxiety-free parenting space, and a child who is gastroenterologically intact, there is nothing easier to treat and hardly anything that can be successfully treated more quickly. Uncomplicated encopresis (uncomplicated by other physical conditions) is one of the very few conditions for which the experienced therapist can offer a guarantee of success—not instant success, but success nonetheless. On the other hand, when encopresis occurs in the context of marital discord and a parent who is emotionally overwhelmed and overextended, treatment becomes difficult indeed.

So, not 15 minutes into this first interview, you have obtained a lot of information about family transactions and about Mrs. Smith's current emotional functioning. You have reassured her that you will be able to help and that her child will learn to use the toilet. You consider your protocol for initial assessments and decide to gather more information regarding Jake's developmental history (the dimension of objectifiable facts) and other aspects of his current functioning (the dimension of individual psychology) next.

Developmental History

If you're going to work with children, you must make it a habit to include some kind of developmental history as an absolute, never-leave-out part of your initial session or sessions. Even if Jake was referred by your very good friend and trusted colleague, the area's top child psychiatrist, general pediatrician, family doctor, or developmental pediatrician, take your own developmental history. Even if the problem is very circumscribed and you are anticipating resolving the presenting problem in one session, you should ask the essential questions about pregnancy, labor, and delivery as well as about developmental milestones and significant medical history.

There are probably as many ways to take a history as there are graduate programs, internships, residencies, and fellowship programs. Some therapists like to mail questionnaires such as

Levine's (1996) ANSER system to parents prior to the first visit. Some therapists use these or similar forms in the office, handing them to parents during the first visit and requesting that they be returned the next time. There are undoubtedly advantages to this standardized procedure: The therapist is sure to cover all the important topics, there is some time saving, and some patients may reveal more information on a form than they would face-to-face. There is also a downside to all this efficiency. A very rich source of information, the nonverbal, is completely missed. And, even more important, the information is provided outside of the therapeutic relationship. The use of questionnaires and checklists fits the needs of a very busy clinic in a teaching hospital, where cases must be quickly screened and triaged. It also suits developmental pediatricians, psychologists, and child psychiatrists whose practices are restricted to evaluations of one kind or another. But for a therapist who must have a solid relationship in order to be helpful, there is no good substitute for putting in the time to get the information you need the old-fashioned way: from the person who has it, in a face-to-face conversation.

So take a developmental history. Were there any problems with pregnancy, labor, or delivery? Is the child she brings to you today her first child? Her first pregnancy? Did the child go home with mom after the usual time period? Has he ever been in the hospital overnight since or been seen in an emergency room? Has he ever had a seizure with high fever or otherwise? Has he ever had an injury to his head that produced loss of consciousness? Does he have allergies? Does he take medication? When was his last well-child visit? Who is his pediatrician? When did he first sit up and walk? When did he utter his first word? His first two-word phrase? How is his appetite? And, of course, ask about toilet training, whether or not that is the presenting problem.

The child's developmental history becomes much more complicated if he or she has a positive medical history such as multiple surgical interventions or hospitalizations. Here again, it is extremely important to rely on your finely tuned intuitions. Some parents may need to recount every medical visit and hospitalization so that they can be sure you "get it," that you really understand what it has been like for the child and the family. Other parents may prefer that you gain your information from reports and summaries they provide to you.

The Presenting Problem

It is very important to learn as much as you can about the presenting problem, that is, the problem as the child's parents see it. From your perspective, and perhaps from Mrs. Smith's, too, the true problem is her profound unhappiness. Nonetheless, the presenting problem is to be ignored at your peril. It's one thing to acknowledge that she has other concerns that are as distressing as those surrounding her son's encopresis. It's quite another thing to say, or even imply, that her "real" problem is with her marriage, relegating her son's encopresis to the realm of pseudo-problems. It does not matter that you may be right; if you leap into an intervention like that one too quickly, you will not have the opportunity to help either child or parent.

Be sure you know as precisely as possible what the presenting problem is. The more potential embarrassment you sense in parent or child, the more direct you will want to be. "Let's talk about the soiling. How often does it occur? What does his stool look like? Is it solid? Runny?" You need to be comfortable asking those questions because you need the answers if you are going to address this problem adequately. There is a huge difference between how one treats a constipated child who has streaks of fecal material in his underwear and a child who is already taking so much stool softener that his stool is completely liquid. Do not assume that parents are using words as you would. When parents tell you that their child has diarrhea, they may mean that he moves his bowels frequently or that he has very loose stool, or both.

After you are satisfied that you understand in detail what the presenting problem is, take as much time as you need to learn about the history of that problem. When did Jake first begin soiling? Was he ever toilet trained? Has he ever used the toilet? What interventions (medical or behavioral) have been tried before? What were the outcomes? If you feel a tinge of anxiety that your questions may come across like an interrogation, remember that this worry is much more likely to be about you than about them. Parents almost universally experience a questioning attitude as indicative of interest and professionalism. If the anxiety persists, it's better to say something (e.g., "I know I have a lot of questions, but I want to make sure I understand this as well as possible") than to stop short with only an incomplete understanding of their concerns.

Family History

When you have obtained a basic developmental history and basic information about the history of the presenting problem, it's time to turn your attention to family history. There are, as with most things, at least two schools of thought about how best to obtain this information and, indeed, about how much of it is needed. One approach is "Get all the information now, every bit of it, because you never know what may be significant until you hear about it and now is the best time." Some may be tempted to call it the shotgun approach, but this is not really accurate. A more apt metaphor would be that of a fishing net, cast wide to capture as many fish as possible. Advocates of this approach often simultaneously advocate using a genogram format to record the information you obtain and to guide follow-up questions. This approach has some advantages. Genogram-driven information gathering and recording can be standardized; it is quite teachable; it does ensure that a great deal of information will be gathered, at least some of which is sure to lend itself to formulating interesting hypotheses about the case; and genograms themselves can readily be presented at case conferences, quickly displaying a great deal of information and sparking interesting discussions.

If this first approach can be characterized as "maximal information gathering—leave no stone unturned," the alternative approach might be thought of as the "minimalist—just enough information to begin treatment" approach. In contrast to the casting of a wide net, this approach relies on a few careful casts. The minimalist interviewer, rather than asking for an accounting of every relative, asks something like this: "Has anyone else in the family had a problem like this?" or "Is your concern about your son related to anything you or anyone else in your family has experienced?" The clinician might then follow up with more focused questions, such as "Are there any stresses affecting Jake or others in the family?" Another question that can be surprisingly useful is this one: "What about your child concerns you most?" Mrs. Smith's response to this question may well have been "That he'll grow up to be like his father," a response that tells far more than even the most comprehensive genogram ever could.

This second, fly-fishing approach has one advantage and one disadvantage. The advantage is that it tends to fit better into a natural flow of conversation and to foster the development of your relationship with your patients. You ask a question, your patients respond, you share an observation or perhaps ask another question. The conversation flows. This can happen in the context of a more comprehensive family history as well, of course, but it is a bit trickier. The disadvantage is the same disadvantage that occurs in fly-fishing: The pool you pass by may turn out to be the one with the bigger fish living in it. The risk diminishes with experience, and one can, of course, always return to that pool, but the chance of missing something is unavoidable. Of course, it's also unavoidable with the wide net approach. It's best to make this choice based on who you are and who you wish to be as a therapist. Which approach would you prefer, if you were the patient? Which one would be more comfortable for you? Which approach would increase your confidence that the person sitting opposite you is truly interested and can help with your problems? The answer to these questions is also the answer to the question of which approach you should choose. It's worth trying each approach and more than once. Be aware of how patients respond to each approach; discuss the pros and cons with colleagues; above all, be aware of your inner experience as you try each approach.

Assessing Individual Differences

One of the most important courses I took in grad school was taught by Julian B. Rotter, the eminent psychologist perhaps best known for developing the concept of expectancies for internal versus external locus of control of reinforcement. The course was called something like "The Construction and Validation of Personality Measures." I've never constructed a test myself, nor do I plan to do so. What was so valuable about this course was its emphasis on individual differences as worthy of serious study and attention. If individual differences are worthy of serious study and attention in the academy, how much more serious attention are they worth in the consulting room?

That aspect of the diagnostic function that contextual therapists refer to as the dimension of psychology does simply this: Like the psychoanalytic approach, it draws the therapist's attention to the individuals in the office, to their particular and unique intellectual strengths and weaknesses, to their emotional features (both immediate and longer term), and, above all, to as comprehensive an understanding of their personalities as possible, including their strengths, values, areas of vulnerability, and those areas in which they are seeking growth. The number of individual differences that a clinician may wish to consider is limitless, reflecting more than 100 years of research and scholarly work. When one makes a note that a parent seems depressed, or anxious, or defensive, one is making a judgment that this patient is relatively higher on this particular individual difference variable than the average person. Similarly, when one has the impression that a child is more reticent, less responsive, less engaged, more verbal, more active, or more fearful than is typical of his or her age, one is assessing each of these individual differences.

Assessment Techniques and Methods

There are two distinct challenges here. One is to assess the child; the other is to assess his or her parents. You have several options for assessing the child and far fewer options as to how you will assess the parents. Just as some therapists find questionnaires and parent report forms of various types useful in taking a history, so, too, do some therapists find other paper-and-pencil forms useful in assessing children on individual difference variables relevant to their presenting problem and to the therapy. The majority of these are general behavior rating scales (e.g., the Achenbach Child Behavior Checklists). Some focus specifically on attention and activity level (e.g., Conner's Parent and Teacher Rating Scales, Barkley Home Situations Questionaire, Barkley School Situations Questionaire). A few focus on mood (e.g., Children's Depression Inventory). The Personality Inventory for Children is a 275-item forced-choice test designed to reflect cognitive, behavioral, and emotional issues that is completed by parents and scored by hand or computer. Interpretation of these instruments of course presumes knowledge of both normal development and developmental psychopathology.

These instruments can be especially useful when used in conjunction with other instruments as part of a psychological screening or a comprehensive psychological or neuropsychological evaluation. They are of limited usefulness to a therapist whose goal is to develop both an understanding of a child and his or her family and a relationship with them that will foster positive change. A therapist who pays attention to what a child says and does, who learns how to talk with children about their feelings and experiences, and who pays attention to his or her own responses to these children will learn more that is immediately useful as therapy begins than he or she would by beginning with testing. As therapy progresses, questions about intellectual functioning, cognitive abilities, or school placement may arise that are best answered through the use of psychological tests.

Diagnosis

Diagnostic decisions should have clinical usefulness. If a differential diagnosis, say, in a 5-year-old, between attention-deficit/hyperactivity disorder (ADHD) with social skill deficits and very mild pervasive developmental disorder (PDD), will not make any difference in your treatment, in your recommendations regarding parenting, or in your recommendations regarding educational placement, it is not worth making the differential. If, on the other hand, the differential diagnosis for a 14-year-old is between ADHD with mood disordered features on the one hand, and Bipolar Disorder on the other, and the latter will lead you to discuss a change in medication with the child, his parents, and his physician, it is not only worth doing but essential, even if extraordinarily challenging.

In the beginning, the more important aspect of diagnosis involves the interpersonal dimension. How does this child or adolescent relate to you? Does he or she understand what you or the parents say to the child? Can the child accept your interest in him or her, or does it make the child unbearably anxious? Can the child talk about his or her inner experience? How capable is your patient of empathy? These are the diagnostic issues that will help you decide whether to see a child individually in addition to—or rarely, even instead of—the child's family, how often to see the child, and how best to approach treatment. Your own reactions form an equally important part of diagnosis. How do you feel when you anticipate seeing this particular child and his or her family? How do you feel when they are in your office? Many years ago, I saw a 10-year-old boy at 4:00 each Wednesday afternoon. No matter how much coffee I had that day, or how well I slept the night before, I always felt sleepy during his appointments. It wasn't until many years later that I learned, through work with other patients, that I was responding to his emotional muteness, his burying his feelings so deeply that there was nothing for me to identify or work with. He was trying to be there and not be there at the same time.

Psychological Testing

It may seem odd to have a discussion of psychological testing in a book about therapy, and it may seem odder still to have this discussion of psychological testing in a chapter devoted to beginning therapy. There is a reason, however, and here it is: You cannot and should not rely on your referral sources, parents, or children's schools to provide sufficient information about a child's intellectual capacity and cognitive strengths and weaknesses. I have seen many children whose low grades had long been attributed to lack of motivation who in fact had significant learning issues or low ability. As the child's therapist, you become the central person in coordinating his or her educational planning and overall treatment. Your patient may have been seen by many specialists, each of whom assumed that someone else would have picked up on learning issues if they were present. Often, this does not happen, especially if the child or family is in crisis. When there is a crisis, professionals focus on resolving the crisis. If the crisis is that the child is severely depressed or is acting up wildly, consideration of cognitive assessment is often delayed or forgotten. So, when you first meet a child and learn that he or she is doing poorly in school, ask whether psychological testing has been done, and if it has not, alert the family that it may be something you will need to do or arrange to have done in the future.

To Test or Not to Test

When the therapist is also a psychologist, the question arises as to whether you or someone else should do any needed psychological testing. The question is parallel to that which might confront child and adolescent psychiatrists: Who should prescribe medication? I would guess that in a survey of 1,000 psychiatrists, the answer from 990 of them would be that the psychiatrist who provides psychotherapy should also prescribe medication. And this is the right answer for psychologists, too. If you are a psychologist and have established a relationship with the child, you are in a good position to ensure that the child's performance during your assessment accurately reflects his or her true ability to acquire and use information. Put your training to use and do the testing yourself. Both before and after your formal assessment, take the time to explain to the child's parents what psychological testing can and cannot do. A short piece for parents on this topic is included here as Appendix B and may be reprinted for your patients.

Toys

Every child psychologist has some toys and games in the office, but I've found that the best toys are the ones that parents and children bring with them. After trying various alternatives, my custom is to have a few things in the office: several board games, a chess set (even very young children love moving the pieces about), a small wooden toy airplane, and crayons. Five plush "Wild Things" creatures and a green monster from the *Monsters, Inc.* movie serve as decoration on my windowsill when not being played with. I do not consider myself a play therapist (this issue is discussed in more detail in Chapter 7); nonetheless, these toys serve a number of functions. They give young children something to do during times when I am talking with parents or with older brothers and sisters. They provide an opportunity to see how children gain access to the toys they are interested in: Do they ask me or their parents? Do they impulsively approach and grab? Do they shyly circle about, hoping that an adult will notice their interest? When scheduling a first appointment with a child under 6, I always suggest that the child bring a few favorite toys, especially creatures or other toys to which the child has given personalities. This is especially helpful with shy children and children with selective mutism (discussed in detail in Chapter 8). If you have room for a small dollhouse or a big box of Legos, by all means keep those handy as well.

Greetings

Even if you anticipate that most of your work will be with the child's parents, you must establish a connection with the child right away. It doesn't matter so much how the child responds to you as that you initiate contact with him or her. When you walk to the waiting room, introduce yourself to the adults, then bend down and extend your hand in greeting to the child. If the child is bilingual, and if you know only a few words in Spanish or French or Korean, greet the child in his or her native tongue. Once you are in the office, you need not keep the focus only on the child; in fact, you should not, because he or she may become uncomfortable.

The Magic

If you are just beginning to work with very young children, and by this I mean children under the age of 5, you may be unsure how to connect with them. There is a magic, to be sure, but it is a magic that can be learned. If you are a parent, you perhaps have some advantage, but I have to add that some of the most gifted child clinicians I have taught were young childless grad students.

When first meeting young children, remember to *feel* while you are thinking. Trust your instincts. This may begin to sound like a mantra in this book, and it is. Being aware of your feelings and intuitions, knowing what they mean and what to do about them is a central feature of great therapy. Don't devolve into a lot of superficial chitchat with the child. Speak to him or her from the most real part of your person. Be willing to be silly and to quite literally get down to his or her level. Make sure your office is arranged in a way, and that the carpet is thick enough, so that it is comfortable for you to sit on the floor from time to time.

Summary

This chapter presents some of the issues that confront therapists at the very beginning: putting patients at ease, connecting with very young children and their parents, gathering information about the child's and family's history. It is worthwhile to keep multiple perspectives in mind, including the four contextual dimensions as well as psychodynamic and behavioral perspectives. Intuition is important, as is learning to trust your feelings, even while engaged in the largely cognitive activity of history taking. The next step is to integrate the information you have gathered, nonverbal as well as verbal, into a three-dimensional understanding of your patient and his family. Chapter 5 shows how the integrated model is used to do this, illustrating the process of doing so with a variety of cases, including several each with encopresis and selective mutism.

Case Formulation with the Integrated Model

A theory is the more impressive the greater is the simplicity of its premises, the more different are the kinds of things it relates and the more extended the range of its applicability.

—Albert Einstein

I began this book with consideration of a new therapeutic model at a fairly abstract level. The second section of the book is less abstract and far more concrete, focusing on what to do when presented with particular, and sometimes tricky, clinical situations. This chapter and the next one serve as segues between the abstract first section and the concrete and practical second section. I show how the integrated model works as you begin a treatment case and how the model helps the therapist consider all the factors and variables that are important in children's and families' lives. I struggled over the title for this chapter. The term "case formulation," like its cousin "case conceptualization," has always seemed to me an odd verbal construction with no clear meaning. I believe that what we really mean when we talk about formulating or conceptualizing a case is deciding how best to think about the patient, his or her problems, and what we ought to do about it. This chapter demonstrates how the three perspectives that make up the integrated model are combined to facilitate thinking about cases and deciding what to do about them.

The premise of the integrated model is that every child case has contextual, behavioral, and psychodynamic elements and that each of these traditions and perspectives has something unique and valuable to offer; that every case has features and issues that fit into each of these three conceptual models. Developing a conceptual model for a new child and family case involves putting concepts from each of these three models to work. This is as true of cases that respond well to very brief, highly focused, behaviorally oriented interventions as it is of cases that require long-term and open-ended exploration of experiences and feelings. Rather than thinking of some cases as "behavioral cases," others as "contextual cases," and still others as "psychodynamic cases," we are going to think about every case as having elements of all of these perspectives. In some cases, for example, our old friend the encopretic 5-year-old, we may talk extensively with parents about behavioral interventions, and the same may be true in the case of an aggressive young child. But, even while this discussion of antecedents and consequences, of reinforcement contingencies and time-out is going on, we will talk with parents about the way the child's aggression echoes his grandfather's aggression and of the crucial importance of helping the little boy become fully aware of his resentment of his little brother, even while he loves him. In thinking about the case, we will not choose among the three perspectives; rather, we will incorporate all three in our thinking so that we can incorporate all three in our planning and interventions.

This reflects the construct point of view that I learned from Julian B. Rotter 25 years ago. Psychological theories, including theories of treatment, are useful because they manage to capture an aspect or several aspects of reality. They don't have absolute truth, however, and none has a monopoly on the one and only correct way to represent reality. It makes no more sense to argue that children's problems are always due to unresolved internal conflicts and have nothing to with their reinforcement histories than it does to argue the reverse. It makes no more sense to argue that children act up only when they have been parentified and not because their aggression sometimes leads to positive outcomes for them than it does to argue the reverse. Each of these explanations has value, and each illuminates an important aspect of reality, and so it makes sense to combine theories in ways that capture more aspects of reality and give us more ways to help people. The following sections illustrate how these three perspectives are integrated at each step of the way toward developing a conceptual map for a new case.

Gathering Information

The first step in developing a useful conceptual model for a case requires gathering information relevant to the key concepts of the integrated model. Mapmakers (at least pre-GPS mapmakers) spend a lot of time walking around and measuring distances and directions before they sit down to create a map. Therapists similarly have to spend a lot of time gathering information before they are ready to create a conceptual map. There are three kinds of important information: history, the presenting problem, and the therapeutic relationship, which is itself composed of three kinds of information: the quality of the child's way of relating to the therapist, intuitions about the patient, and nonverbal information.

History

In the integrated model, taking a history means paying attention to issues that each of the three component models typically emphasizes. Some of these kinds of information are important to all three models. Other kinds of information are considered to be secondary by one or more models and emphasized by others. The integrated model attempts to achieve a more comprehensive perspective on the patient and his or her family by including as many of these issues and sources of information as possible. The contextual perspective, like all family systems approaches, emphasizes family history, especially events that may have led parents to a greater than normal reliance on destructive entitlement. This tends to include such things as having been hurt directly by their parents' actions or failure to act, as well as being the victim of acts, blame for which cannot be placed on specific people, such as losing a parent to illness when one is still very young. Contextually, therapists will want to learn about the childhood experiences of parents as a way of understanding them and their parenting. The contextual perspective also draws our attention to issues related to family loyalty. For example, if the presenting problem is disruptive behavior in school, the contextual perspective encourages asking questions about whether either parent, or perhaps another family member, may have had similar experiences in school. The contextual perspective also makes explicit what may be only implicit in other traditions: the value of engaging every family member in the history-taking process and, more generally, in the therapeutic process. This can sometimes very quickly reveal patterns in family communication or in the ways people are credited and blamed in the family.

The behavioral perspective draws our attention to additional antecedents of the presenting problem: developmental history, school history, and the natural history of the presenting problem. An important contribution of the behavioral perspective is to encourage incorporation of a pediatric perspective with its interest in the details of physical development, past and current medical conditions, allergies, hospitalizations, and medications, as well as the child's early experiences with feeding, sleeping, and early temperament.

Psychodynamic thinking figures importantly in history taking in the integrated model. As it often does in this model, it serves to draw our attention to a most important aspect of children's and adults' lives that neither the behavioral nor contextual approaches addresses explicitly: emotion. The historical data points overlap with those of behavioral and contextual interest. The difference is in the way these data are used. For example, both psychodynamic and contextual understanding of a patient, whether child or adult, requires knowing about ways your patient may have been hurt in childhood. So a patient's loss of a parent due to accident or illness when the patient was very young is noteworthy from both perspectives. Contextually, such a loss is considered to be a potential source of destructive entitlement and may affect how capable one is of caring for others. The emotional experience of loss and hurt is assumed but not explicitly explored with the patient. The addition of psychodynamic thinking to the model emphasizes the traumatic nature of losing one's parent at an early age, the potential arrest in emotional development such a loss may precipitate, and the need to discern the extent to which your patient (child or parent) can know his or her own feelings about this loss, both then and now.

More broadly, the integrated model's interest in psychodynamics means that we are interested in our patient's relationship history. A 10-year-old girl who experienced adoption, followed by the divorce of her adoptive parents and then the death of her mother from breast cancer has experienced the trauma of loss multiple times. She has, to be sure, also experienced unfairness and has accrued a great deal of destructive entitlement. Beyond that, she has lost her primary love relationship at least twice. Awareness of the potential for her to rely on destructive entitlement helps explain her anger and apparent selfishness. Awareness of her terrible losses points the way to helping her heal her capacity for connection and intimacy and also points to the need to do so. With children of school age and older, the psychodynamic aspect of the integrated model directs us to listening carefully and to observing carefully to understand and to help our patients become aware of their feelings about their relationships with parents and siblings.

Presenting Problem

The three perspectives are equally complementary when we consider the presenting problem, whether it is externalizing or internalizing. When the child presents with an externalizing problem, the behavioral perspective is helpful in providing a structure for detailed interviewing about antecedents and consequences. When does the problem usually occur? Under what circumstances does it never, or hardly ever, occur? How do parents, other adults, and other children usually respond when this behavior occurs? If the problem is aggression, the behavioral perspective guides us to ask very specific questions about the target behavior's appearance: time of day, amount of sleep the child had the day before, weekday versus weekend, the social situation at the moment when the behavior typically occurs.

Equally specific information about the way parents respond is essential. Do they react emotionally or in a controlled way? Do they punish the child? If so, in what way?

All these specifics and more are important to nail down the target behaviors and to evaluate what works and what does not. Sometimes, happenstance favors us as well. Parents may not have a babysitter for an 11-month-old younger brother and so bring him to the office with their 5-year-old. Their descriptions of how the 5-year-old sometimes "accidentally" bumps into his brother come to life as he demonstrates his tumbling skills just a bit too close to his brother. This gives you an opportunity to see first-hand how the aggression unfolds and also an opportunity to provide guidance to his parents regarding how best to respond. When such an event unfolds in the office, it also illuminates our understanding of the child and his family in ways that complement the behavioral perspective. Observing the 5-year-old's body language as he selects a spot to show off his somersaulting, one detects very subtle cues that it is not by accident that he chooses a path that comes within an inch of his little brother.

The 5-year-old approaches to tell you about his toy, and as if on cue, his brother crawls over and begins to babble in your direction. Here is where your intuitive and empathic understanding of your patient's emotional life comes into play. You intuitively know that his "accidental" bumping is in reaction to the way his very cute younger sibling is stealing the stage. You speak to the toddler, quietly and gently, so that both the 5-year-old and his parents will hear. "Hold on there," you say, "you've got to wait a minute. Your brother and I are having an important conversation." Perhaps you continue as if *you* were the 5-year-old: "Boy, is this ever annoying! A guy can't even talk without being interrupted!" All of this is in not much more than a whisper (you don't want to frighten the toddler or his parents). And throughout, you are monitoring the reactions of the parents. Of course, you don't do any of this in a first meeting and not until you have a very solid relationship with both parents.

One contribution of the psychodynamic perspective to evaluating the presenting problem is its emphasis on intuition and emotion. Another important contribution is its sensitivity to possible symbolism or metaphor in presenting problems. Several years ago, I saw a selectively mute 5-year-old boy whose family had many secrets as the result of a problem of some import with the Internal Revenue Service. They were highly selective about whom they would trust, and so was he.

Thinking contextually about the presenting problem means thinking about how the current problem may reflect a retelling of an old family story. There are several possible variations on this theme. A child's problem may arise from loyalty to a parent or parents, in the way that an adolescent's substance abuse mirrors his father's alcoholism. Problems with anger and aggression may arise directly from the child's having been parentified or having experienced unfair treatment in another way.

The contextual aspect of the integrated model also brings up the possibility that a child's symptom or problem may be the result of the child's attempt to keep a pathologically damaged and battered family system afloat. What at first looks like a child's unprovoked disruptive and noncompliant behavior may represent his attempt to prod his depressed mother from her half-slumber on the sofa. Or it may be his way of pushing her to provide more active parenting. In other words, it may be a sign of his having been parentified. The inclusion of behavioral thinking in the integrated model means that we will be sure to ask such questions as these about the presenting problem: How does the problem present itself? When did it begin? What happened recently that led to this appointment?

You should not have preconceived plans about which of the three components of this model will guide your initial explorations. Comforting as it can be, both emotionally and intellectually, to have a fixed plan, such an approach is antithetical to the goals of this way of doing therapy. Here, it is important to let the child and his or her parents show you where to start. The extent to which the child or adolescent is positively inclined toward therapy and his or her capacity to tolerate the anxious feelings that always arise in therapy is crucially important. This means that in addition to having knowledge of the child's presenting problem, you must have a feeling for the child and a feeling about the problem. This requires tuning in to your emotional response to the child and the family. And it requires being able to tolerate a degree of ambiguity and uncertainty that would not have been as large a part of your professional life had you opted for engineering or accounting. Of course, your personal receiver must be tuned first so that you can tell the difference between static you are generating as the result of internal short circuits and genuine emotional tones coming from your patient.

Find a Useful Analogy

Developing a conceptual map for a case is a lot like developing a new theory. Whether you think of yourself as a theoretician or not, whether you are actively involved in publishing in professional journals, whether you have presented or intend to present at professional meetings, every time you begin work with a new child or family case, you are developing a new and very particular theory. This theory is not a grand theory of personality development. It is the opposite: a highly ideographic theory about this particular child and his or her siblings and parents at this particular time and with special reference to this particular problem or set of problems. Your special theory about this child represents how all the ingredients of the particular child's situation fit together.

Find a way of organizing your thoughts that works for you. If you are a visual learner, a flow chart, decision tree, or genogram may work well. Another visual option is a pictorial representation of the nomological network for the particular case, with circles containing relevant concepts linked by arrows showing which constructs or variables influence which other constructs or variables, the clinician's equivalent of a path analysis. If your natural style of thinking and learning is verbal and linear rather than visual and simultaneous, do it the old-fashioned way and write an informal narrative. The important thing is to have a method that facilitates your thinking about the case and does not impede it. I spent quite a bit of time constructing genograms before I realized that I was working so hard to get the drawing right that I missed what was going on in the room. When I switched back to note taking and verbal memory, things went much more smoothly.

In treating very young children, contextual and psychodynamic issues sometimes appear to fade into the background as you learn about the behavioral parameters of presenting problems from parents. This is not a problem, but in fact is a plus. Parents need reassurance that you understand children in general, their child in particular, and their child's problem even more particularly. For most parents, the first step in this reassurance is your demonstration that you know the right questions to ask about the presenting problem. Not only do you need to know the parameters of the problem, but your asking about them demonstrates your expertise and therefore offers reassurance. Parents do not have readily available means to assess a child therapist's expertise, and letting them see how you think is one of the things you can do to help them see that you know what you are doing. Asking questions about antecedents and consequences, about developmental history and physical health, though necessary, is far from sufficient. You must connect with the child and the family in a way that has some emotion in it.

Developing your model for this particular case begins as you gather information about the family, especially about how they are relating to each other and to you. You may want or need to refine your understanding later, in the quiet of your office, on the drive home, or in discussion with senior colleagues. But it begins the moment you meet your patient. Is your expertise being sought because parents are primarily concerned that their child or adolescent is in emotional distress? Is your expertise being sought primarily because the child's or adolescent's behavior is causing the parents to be distressed? Are parents aware of how their issues overlap with those of their child? How open are they to talking about these issues? You may come to view the core problem differently from the way the child's or adolescent's parents do, but it is still essential to be able see it from their perspective. Begin with the variables that will help you determine whether you are faced with an emergency or near-emergency. If the child or adolescent is in imminent danger of causing self-harm or harm to someone else, all theoretical considerations and niceties go out the window, and safety is the only variable of concern. After you determine that the child or adolescent is not at imminent risk, you can focus on other problem variables. How acute is the problem? Is this something the parents have been concerned about since school began 6 months ago, or did they notice a dramatic change in their child's mood or behavior 2 days ago?

Try to avoid the urge to decide in advance which of the three source theories will take the lead in the initial case formulation and in an initial treatment plan. Every case has elements that are best captured by social learning formulations, others are best captured by psychodynamic formulations, and still others are best captured by contextual formulations and concepts. For every case, you must consider the most basic and objective factors, the facts or existential realities of the contextual model, beginning with the child's age and physical health status and history. In the integrated model, we assume that even circumscribed problems presented by very young children that appear to be amenable to purely behavioral interventions may well reflect both psychodynamic roots and family context issues. The most expedient initial approach to the child's presenting problem may well turn out to be one grounded in behavioral principles. A treatment plan largely utilizing behavioral interventions may be most likely to lead to rapid and successful resolution of initial presenting problems for these very young children. At the start of treatment with very young children, rapid progress on the behavioral front has a number of advantages and very little downside as long as one remembers that children's problems are infrequently as simple as they initially appear to be.

Behavioral problems have a way of multiplying. Children who soil themselves several times a day soon experience peer rejection. Children whose aggression toward siblings leads to subtle parental rejection of favoritism often develop self-esteem and mood issues. Quick and direct attention to such problems often leads to very rapid initial progress. Successful treatment of the behavior problems of very young children often appears to be purely behavioral, especially if the child has a developmental delay. In fact, it always involves all three components of the integrated model. When apparently purely behavioral interventions work like magic, the magic comes from careful attention to emotion, to relationship, and to the child's family. Without the specific behavioral interventions, treatment would take much longer. Without the contribution of contextual and psychodynamic perspectives on the family and the therapeutic relationship, many parents would not be able to accept or carry out the behavioral interventions. This is often the secret behind those amazing one- or two-session treatment successes.

CASE ILLUSTRATION

Consider three cases of 4-year-old boys who are not yet using the toilet on a regular and predictable basis and who will be starting school within 6 months. Each boy is brought to your office by his mother. All three mothers express concerns that if this issue is not resolved, their son may not be admitted to the school they have selected for him. So far, the three cases are, if not identical, very similar.

Now consider the three mothers. The mother of one boy is a general surgeon. She is by nature decisive. She is used to people respecting her expertise and taking her advice. She sees you as a peer, a specialist in your own field whose expertise she is seeking. Other than a fairly brief explanation of the issues involved in treating toileting problems and a response to her question about how many such cases you have treated, little overt preparatory work is needed. All or nearly all that needs to be communicated about your relationship with this parent can be communicated directly and verbally. You can focus on the reinforcement contingencies that may be maintaining the toileting problem and how to manipulate them to lead to the desired change.

The mother of the second boy is more anxious. At age 9, her nephew still soils on occasion. When she calls for an appointment, she tells you that she is afraid her son will follow this course. Although you know that treating his toileting problem will require the same behavioral interventions you delivered—or taught the surgeon to deliver—to the first child, you must address this mother's anxiety first, and you must do so explicitly. So, even before a face-to-face meeting, you more directly reassure her than you did the first mother. You explain that as long as her child has received a clean bill of health from his pediatrician, she can be assured the problem will be resolved. You guarantee that as long as she can work with you, this problem will be resolved before school starts in September. Her ability to acknowledge her anxiety tells you that she is open to your help. When you meet her and her son several days later, all the nonverbal cues tell you that aside from her considerable anxiety about her son's toileting, she is largely a healthy parent and will work with you well. Observing this, you proceed quickly to the same sort of behavioral interventions described in Chapter 8.

The third mother presents a different picture. She is a bit overdressed for a doctor's appointment. Her clothes are a bit too revealing and her makeup is overdone. More important, every nonverbal communication channel indicates that she is profoundly uncomfortable emotionally, that she is not truly in her body. You feel just a tiny bit anxious with her, as if you had to be sure of doing and saying exactly the right things. Unlike the other two mothers, she very quickly denigrates her husband. He has never been there for her. He is an absent father. He does not take his son's problem seriously. He does not take an active role in family life. She is also highly critical of other doctors she has consulted about her son's toileting issues. None of them really understood the problem. The implication is clear: "You understand it so well. Perhaps you will be the one to help me." She is tearful, both about her son's toileting problems and about her unhappy marriage.

The whole picture: the tearfulness, the too tight and too revealing clothing, the makeup, her criticism of other doctors and of her husband, is oddly seductive. Although there is nothing overtly sexual about her behavior, she communicates a sort of angry seductiveness in all the ways I've just listed and in every aspect of her nonverbal communication. The result of this nonverbal communication is that she has created distance between her and you. You feel a wish to back away from her, from engaging her therapeutically, and, of course, from challenging her in even the most gentle way. You find yourself noticing this nonverbal communication exactly because it feels incongruent with the problem about which she has sought your help. It is also oddly congruent with her son's problems. Unlike the surgeon who dashed over in between patients, still wearing her lab coat, or the mother of the other little boy who was dressed in the very casual way of a very busy and overworked mother of two young children, this mother has dressed for the occasion. But why? What is she telling you about herself? She is quite literally spilling out of her clothing. She is leaking. Just as her little boy is unable to contain his stool and to let it go in the socially sanctioned way, she is unable to contain herself. The information available to you from these nonverbal sources is extremely valuable, and you will be using it in formulating each case. That doesn't mean, however, that you will talk about your observations with every patient family.

Bearing in mind that contextual and psychodynamic factors are also at play, try to resolve the problem using one of the various empirically validated treatments, or if this is not possible, at least a treatment that is logically related to the empirically validated treatments, all of which are based on social learning principles to a greater or lesser extent. If the behavioral approach works to reduce or remove the target behaviors that were of original concern, you may find that other issues are left. You can then discuss with the child and parents whether or not there are other issues that they would like help with.

For example, you may be able to help a single mother rapidly gain control over her oppositional 5-year-old in just a few sessions. Since she began her first consultation with you by talking about how overwhelmed she is feeling and how it exhausts her to care for her son by herself, you may, as you wrap up the behavioral phase of treatment, ask her if she would like to continue therapy herself, if that would be helpful to her. If she chooses to do so, the remaining two-thirds of the integrated model, the psychodynamic and contextual, will become much more prominent. Illustrations of this sort of process appear in the chapter on parents as patients (Chapter 6).

In cases where the empirically validated treatments either can't be applied, or fail, or are not accepted by parents or child, one must rely relatively more on the less directive aspects of the integrated model: the contextual and psychodynamic aspects. In a word, when treating your youngest patients, be directive and focused and rely on empirically validated, behaviorally derived treatments whenever possible. While doing this, however, you will be aware of broader and deeper issues: fairness, family history, parents' and siblings' emotional reactions to the young child's behavior, family stresses, anxieties that parents may have about the child's future, and, of course, their relationship with you.

Nonverbal Communication

One can find references to nonverbal communication in psychodynamic literature beginning with Freud's original writings, most famously in the following statement: "No mortal can keep a secret. If his lips are silent, he chatters with his fingertips; betrayal oozes out of him at every pore" (Freud, 1905, p. 94). It is possible that Freud's seemingly magical dream interpretations were in part the result of an extraordinarily acute sense of his patients' body language, gestures, intonation, and facial expressions. He may have intuitively incorporated these sources of information into the interpretation of patients' dreams.

As you conduct your interview with the child and his or her family, pay careful attention to the rich source of nonverbal information that is available to you. Just as you must learn about the child's developmental history, the history of the presenting problem, family medical and psychological history, and school history, you must equally learn about the emotional life of the family. Often, this is learned better from observation than from direct questioning. Yogi Berra was right when he famously said, "You can observe a lot by watching." Nonverbal channels of communication are often rich in the information a therapist needs. Just as a dog's sense of smell gives him, but not his master, huge amounts of information about the world, so too can nonverbal information give you a fuller, deeper, and more sensory experience of your patients and their emotional lives. The verbal channel consists of words only. Nothing of verbal information is lost when a conversation is transcribed and printed out. There you can read questions and answers, you can discern the difference between a person who speaks a lot and one of few words, and you can tell if someone is clearly guarded, clearly hostile, or clearly refusing to engage in conversation. But the verbal channel is susceptible to the influence of education, culture, and intellectual ability in ways that don't always serve the clinician's purpose. It's too easy to make much of a person's choice of words when it reflects educational level or reading habits more than feelings and relationships.

Every other kind of information available to you as you interview a patient is nonverbal: facial expression, gesture, posture, gait, and vocal qualities such as intonation, pitch, and inflection. There are many resources available for those who wish to become students of nonverbal communication. For the clinician, however, these resources are of limited usefulness. In the midst of a diagnostic interview or treatment session, you are unlikely to think, "Hmm, it looks like the facial muscles associated with surprise are being brought into play along with those typically used to uplift the corners of the mouth in a smile, so perhaps my patient is surprised to be smiling, or perhaps the smile is not genuine." Neither are you likely to consciously analyze a facial expression, note that while the mouth is smiling, the eyes are not, and so to conclude that the smile is merely social as opposed to a spontaneous expression of happiness. And there are very few clinical situations in which it is wise to remark about a patient's nonverbal behavior, as Fritz Perls did in the first "Gloria" movies: "Are you aware of your smile? What are you doing with your feet now? Are you aware that your eyes are moist? What is that with the foot? Do that more!" This sort of finger pointing is much more likely to be experienced as a power play than a desire to help. Patients don't like it, and it rarely helps. Perls was perhaps trying to dramatize aspects of his approach for the film. In clinical practice, however, such statements are not likely to produce much therapeutic movement.

Notice your patient's nonverbal behavior and use your observations in your work, but do not share every observation with every patient each time you observe something interesting. The idea instead is to heighten your sensitivity to all the information about your patient that is available to you, the verbal as well as the nonverbal. Even from a diagnostic perspective, such information can be crucial.

The treatment of selective mutism is discussed in some detail in a later chapter. Here, I wish to use this condition to illustrate the importance of nonverbal communication. Consider two 4-year-old boys, neither of whom speaks to anyone outside their immediate family, with the exception of speaking to other children, but only if no adult is present. One boy sat in therapy sessions with his arms crossed, would not get out of his seat, a frown on his small face, refusing to smile or to indicate agreement or disagreement by head shake or nod. The other boy smiled, sat on the floor playing with his Legos, allowed me to play with him a bit, and by the second or third session was giggling, climbing on the furniture, and making growling noises to accompany his play with a furry creature from *Monsters, Inc.* Both boys met diagnostic criteria for selective mutism, but the treatment of the second boy was on the fast track compared to the first boy's treatment.

There are two routes to understanding what people of all ages are communicating nonverbally: the analytic and the intuitive. The analytic approach involves studying each nonverbal signal or cue and deciding what it means. It is the approach taken by those whose professional work centers on investigation of the facial expression, gesture, and posture. The intuitive approach is better suited to the needs of clinicians and to the realities of clinical work. Even if you have made a study of nonverbal communication, you do not have time to step back from the therapeutic relationship to analyze and synthesize all the available data. Even if you were able to stop the clock, stepping back from your relationship with your patient is the last thing you should be doing. An intuitive response is what is called for: a rapid, nearly automatic integration of all those sources of data (facial expression, voice characteristics, gesture, posture, gait, etc.). The value of this sort of intuitive understanding applies to children, adolescents, and their parents. The more guarded the person and the less self-aware, the more this kind of information will help you. Reading books and articles about nonverbal communication is primarily useful as a way of heightening your awareness of how important these things are, not as a way to learn the code by which you can translate every gesture or facial expression into verbal language.

Children between the ages of 5 and 10 who show primarily externalizing problems such as aggression, oppositionalism, and high degrees of sibling conflict also respond well to interventions that involve helping parents understand the effect of reinforcement contingencies and use those contingencies to alter their children's behaviors. But for these behavioral techniques to work, much attention must be paid to the child's emotional life by bringing in contextual and psychodynamic considerations. When working with parents of school-age children, you will want to explain to them from the first that addressing the behavioral issues will be a necessary but not sufficient part of treatment, that to really help their child, you and the parents will need to help the child know what he is experiencing about himself and his family that leads him to be difficult or aggressive.

Even when children have developmental delays, all three perspectives will enrich your understanding of the child and family and result in your being able to offer more help. Working with some children with developmental delays may mean emphasizing behavioral interventions. It's important not to take this too far, however. The long case that I presented in *Doing Contextual Therapy* (1993), which involved a 10-year-old boy with a measured IQ between 50 and 60, focused on his strengths, on acknowledging his desire to be independent and to help his parents, and on losses (of his relationship with his father and his best friend). Acknowledgment of his desire to be more independent, not changes in rewards and punishments, was in the foreground throughout. In this treatment case, I acknowledged his struggle to find ways to express himself, but having done that, I did my best to de-emphasize his limitations. Instead, I focused on acknowledging his positive intentions, his desire to be helpful to his parents, and their commitment to him. Sensing that he truly wanted to show these signs of independence, I felt that providing him with an alarm clock so he could assume responsibility for getting himself up and ready for school in the morning would be more effective than an artificial reinforcer. Those who are interested in a detailed description of this case will find it, along with transcripts of sessions, in Goldenthal (1996).

Sharing Your Formulation with Parents

Parents want to know what you are thinking and what you plan to do to help their children. They do not want to be left in the dark. Depending on the child's age, they may be willing or even eager to have you meet privately with their son or daughter. This does not mean that they do not want to know what is happening or where you are headed. I will discuss the nuts and bolts of privacy issues later. Here I focus on how to begin treatment in a way that makes sense to you, to the child, and to his or her parents.

This business of talking to parents about the presenting problem, what you are thinking about it, and what you have in mind to do about it is often a major stumbling block for beginning therapists, and for experienced therapists as well. It is also one of the times in treatment when the integrated model can be most helpful. This is because the idea that children are best helped when one addresses particular behaviors, alternatives to those behaviors, family relationships, and deeper feelings makes perfect sense to parents, to older children, and to adolescents. Even when parents ask for help with what appears to be a purely behavioral issue, they most often want help with the *why* as well as the *what*. Sometimes this is explicit, as it was with the parents of three squabbling boys. These parents quite clearly told me that they needed help getting their family life under control. They just as clearly told me that they wanted to get to "the deeper causes" of their boys' conflicts.

I encourage you to let parents and families in on your thinking. The way you do this will depend on the family, on the child or adolescent, and on the problem. With an aggressive preschooler, you may say something like this: "We need to help Robby know what he is feeling and to learn other ways to communicate about it. At the same time, we need to work together to come up with ways to control his behavior so his little brother is safe and so he doesn't get a bad rap among other children and adults." Here, in very straightforward and jargon-free language, you will have captured the essence of the integrated model and communicated it to parents. And you will have told them of the need to address feelings, language, understanding, and behavioral control.

This straightforward approach to discussing a treatment plan is equally appropriate when the patient is an adolescent. You may be starting work with a depressed 15-year-old who has begun to be self-injurious, scratching and cutting his arms and legs. Your discussion with his parents might be as brief as this: "Barry needs help integrating and becoming fully aware of his feelings. What he is doing now is using cutting when he can't tolerate his feelings. It's one way he is trying to deal with stress, including family stress. This can take a long time, so while Barry and I are working and exploring his feelings together, I am going to be clear with him that I would like to help him stop cutting."

Summary

Case formulation is a continuous process, and an iterative one. The therapist gathers information and develops a preliminary story about the child's or adolescents presenting problems, history, and family situation. With this preliminary formulation in hand, it becomes possible to construct an equally preliminary plan for beginning treatment. So, we begin, and in beginning learn more about the patient's problems and his or her ability to engage in psychological work. For our youngest patients, this means considering how able parents are to engage in psychological work. With adolescents, we consider how prepared they are themselves for this kind of undertaking.

CHAPTER 6

Working with Parents

The joys of parents are secret, and so are their grieves and fears.

—Francis Bacon

Any practical model for treating children and families needs to offer guidance about addressing adults' treatment issues in sensible ways. This chapter provides guidance for dealing with the most frequently arising situations that call on therapists to more directly intervene with the adults in a child's life.

So far in this book, the focus of therapy has been the child. Parents have figured importantly, but mostly as independent variables, as those who care for children and whose actions and relationships affect children. We have treated parents as therapy gatekeepers, as consultants, as informants, and as the caregivers who implement behavioral interventions crafted by the treating therapist. For the most part, I have not written about parents as patients, as people who suffer in their own right. Of course, this is a huge oversimplification of what really happens in therapy. The premise of the integrated model is that therapy works best when it is comprehensive and takes into account as much of the child's life as possible. The integrated model, influenced by contextual therapy, explicitly embraces an obligation to think about the impact of therapy on parents, as well as the goal of intervening in ways that help them as well as their children. But these two goals—carefully considering how parents affect children and how child therapy may affect parents—are incomplete.

There are cases in which working with parents means only establishing rapport, offering reassurance, and finding a balance that preserves the young person's need for privacy and provides necessary information to his or her parents. There are also cases in which one treats the parents first, in order to help their children. In addition to cases in which therapy proceeds solely along these lines, there are many other instances in which one must assess and treat parents' adult issues if one is to be truly helpful to the children. I do not regard this as a detour, but as an opportunity to help the family in another way.

There are four general clinical situations that call for this sort of work with adults. One occurs when you realize that a parent is experiencing significant emotional distress or has a level of character pathology that must be addressed before you can make any meaningful progress with the child. Another occurs when a parent has insights into his or her own functioning as the result of your therapy with the child and clearly asks for therapy for himself or herself. A third situation arises when a child is in crisis and the child's parent needs support beyond what is possible around the edges of treating the child. The fourth occurs when your adult patient introduces concerns about his or her children.

The varieties of therapy run along several continua, one of which reflects the patient's age. This particular continuum is anchored at one end by therapy for individual adults in which one never probes about children, and certainly never expects to meet the children. At the other end, it is anchored by a kind of child therapy in which at least 90 percent of the treatment is with the child alone, meetings with parents serving only to establish sufficient rapport to facilitate the "real therapy" with the child. Although there are cases at the extremes, most cases fall toward the middle of the continuum. Up to this point, we have concerned ourselves mostly with cases falling to the right on this continuum, those cases in which treating the child is primary and treating adults is secondary. This chapter emphasizes cases in which one must engage at least one parent, and perhaps both, in treatment in a more direct and intensive way for therapy to be successful.

The need to engage parents in this more intensive way takes several forms and can occur at several points in therapy. You may need to work so hard to engage a parent or to reassure him or her that a child is in safe hands that it feels like that parent is your patient, and you are right. You may begin working with a child on what appears to be a straightforward pediatric issue (for example, one of our by now very familiar toileting cases), only to discover that the case is far more complex than it appeared and that the child's physical problem is directly related to the child-parent relationship or the parent's emotional issue. You may be in the process of working productively with a child when a parent asks to see you individually. An adolescent may begin to refuse to participate in therapy or may participate so nonproductively that it only makes sense to work with his or her parents instead. The integrated model considers these to be special situations rather than contraindications.

What starts as a referral for child therapy may quickly turn into therapy for the parent. In some cases, much more direct therapeutic involvement with parents is necessary, often to the point that one is meeting much more intensively with the parent or parents than with the child or adolescent. A flexible child and family therapist may find himself focusing treatment largely, or even solely, on one or both parents for several reasons arising out of several different circumstances. Sometimes we begin with what initially sounds like straightforward, garden-variety, child treatment, such as encopresis, and find that the child's problem is the tip of a rather messy iceberg.

When a Parent Becomes the Patient

Parents can morph into patients in several different ways. The easiest transition, for both patient and therapist, occurs when therapy with the child or adolescent is going very well, and the parent is so comfortable with you and your style that he or she broaches the subject of seeing you individually, either instead of or in addition to the child. This can be a nearly ideal situation. You already have a relationship with the parent and the child. You can help the adult deal with concerns about the child and his or her parenting in ways that a therapist who had never met the child cannot. I have been present when discussions arise about possible ethical problems when one therapist sees more than one family member. In fact, there are no ethical problems. Treating a parent and a child is totally different from treating a person you have hired to build your house. It is not a dual relationship. Once you have clarified privacy issues, it can be very positive for both parent and child.

────────── **CASE ILLUSTRATION** ──────────

A case I've written about before in this book involved a woman who consulted me about her son's behavior and soon after bringing him for an initial consultation, began to make regular appointments in which she talked mostly about her unhappy marriage. The extent to which her depression, the lack of cooperative parenting, and ongoing marital tension would impact any efforts to treat her son's encopresis became very clear at the second or third family appointment. Becoming aware of an increasingly intense odor in the office, I asked both parents if they thought that one of them should perhaps take their son to the bathroom. Mother's reply was discouraging: "No, it's too late, he's already gone." I repeated my suggestion, adding that there was nothing to lose and that perhaps he had not yet soiled. I again encouraged one of them to take him around the corner, just in case. The father finally took the boy to the bathroom, returned several minutes later, and sat down with no comment. I asked what had happened. He replied that his son had had a small bowel movement in the toilet and that he had not soiled. I could hardly believe my ears. Here these folks had been all over the place to try to find a way to toilet train their son, who had never had a bowel movement in a toilet, and they had nothing to say to him about it. Incredulous, I asked several times to make sure I had heard correctly, and then responded as I would have expected them to: "Wow! That is so great! Unbelievable! In the toilet?! That's wonderful!" After this expostulation, I explained that if they wanted to encourage more similar toileting behavior, it was a good idea to show their son some enthusiasm so that he could see that they were pleased and excited. But there was so much marital tension and so much depression in both parents that they could not do so. Ultimately, this case could not move forward until both issues, the marital tension and the depression, were addressed at some length.

There are also cases that go in other directions: Parents call to arrange individual therapy for themselves, and it soon becomes clear that their major concerns are their parenting and their child's adjustment. Some people are uncomfortable about asking for therapy for themselves but will do so for their children. This may be because of anxiety or because they do not feel deserving enough but are prepared to request therapy for their child. When parents tell you this as directly as occurred in the case I am about to present, you can be fairly sure that things will go well.

CASE ILLUSTRATION
Cynthia, Robert, and Bobby

About 10 years ago, I received a call from Cynthia, the mother of a 4-year-old boy, asking for help. She began by telling me that he was out of control, that his preschool teachers had suggested that he might well be hyperactive and had encouraged her to call me. Nothing unusual in any of that. What was unusual was that not 5 minutes into this phone call, Cynthia said: "This is probably as much about me as about him. I've got a lot of baggage."

Cynthia and her husband, Robert, brought Bobby to see me several days later. He was clearly active, on the high side of the normal range, but not out of the normal range. I told Cynthia and Robert that I could not make a diagnosis of attention-deficit/hyperactivity disorder based on the history they provided and my observations. I learned that Cynthia's childhood had been traumatic, as she was frequently bullied both emotionally and physically by her two older brothers. She freely acknowledged that when her little boy became wound up and physically energized in the way that small boys do, she would sometimes become too easily upset and would over-react. Cynthia also acknowledged a lifelong struggle with de-pression, especially during the winter months. Therapy con-tinued with Cynthia individually and with the participation of Robert, but without her son, as everyone quickly agreed that his occasionally challenging behavior was best viewed as a de-pendent variable rather than as causal. His behavior only verged away from the active side of normal when Cynthia was especially impatient or critical.

Therapy continued for about a year. It included several brief discussions of parenting issues but focused mostly on Cyn-thia's lingering vulnerabilities from her difficult childhood, on the way that she and Robert communicated, and on helping her feel better about herself as a parent. During the course of ther-apy, I recommended that she give light therapy a try, believing that her depression was truly seasonal and one of the clearest cases of seasonal affective disorder I had encountered. The light therapy turned out to be a dramatic success. Cynthia went from what she referred to as hibernating from November to April to being able to function fully all year long.

Robert reluctantly acknowledged that she was sometimes overly critical and angry. He explained that he had not said anything before because he believed that it would not help mat-ters if both of them were irritable and that it was better for him to try to keep things calm at home. Surprisingly to him, Cyn-thia welcomed his being forthcoming about his feelings. The result was that she was even more motivated to change. Along the way, Bobby's behavior improved. Most important,

Cynthia's ability to tolerate his shenanigans and energy improved a great deal.

While working on the manuscript for this book, I received a call from Cynthia, who wanted me to know that she was doing well, and especially that her son, now 15 years old, was doing well with friends, with his studies, and with his musicianship; he had studied trumpet for a number of years and was now playing with a jazz band. Although 5-year-old Bobby spent only a very few hours in my office, from my perspective, he was as much the focus of therapy as was his mother. From the perspective of the integrated model, this is as truly child treatment as any case that appears in this book. I probably saw the child only five or six times. I spoke only a few times about parenting issues, and beyond doing a careful developmental and behavioral assessment of her son, focused almost solely on Cynthia's personal issues, many of which concerned her parents and siblings.

This is but one of the ways that a child and family therapist is called on to engage a parent in order to help the child and the whole family. There are options, of course. A therapist who has not received training in working with adults may choose to refer a parent like Cynthia to a colleague who specializes in treating adults. Therapists whose training and experience have been almost exclusively with children have a second option, and a better one. That option is to find a colleague or mentor who can provide consultation and instruction on the adult side of such a case. This will lead to multiple benefits: for the therapist, for the child, and for the parents. Referring to an adult therapist is not without risks: It may result in the parent's receiving conflicting input about what the child needs most.

Engaging the adults in a family can be simple or complex. It can be a one-time undertaking, accomplished in the first 15 minutes of a first visit, or it can be continuous. Your relationship with a child's parents can be cooperative from the beginning, or it may be adversarial. If adversarial, it can be productively adversarial or equally unproductive. The next cases I describe can't help but bring that famous Monty Python line to mind: "And now for something completely different."

A very different situation arises when a parent comes to your office alone requesting treatment and then mentions, as if in passing, that he or she has concerns about a son or daughter. This does not happen often, but it does happen. Unless your practice is strictly limited to treating children and adolescents, you are sure to receive requests for treatment from adults, perhaps even on occasion from adults who are not aware that you specialize in treating younger patients. I have even had adult patients talk about a concern regarding their children and then remark, "I know you probably don't treat children, but . . ." If you encounter this sort of assumption on the part of a patient, take the opportunity to provide some information about your practice. Not only does this make good marketing sense, it will also give your patient a chance to talk about his or her child in more depth. In my experience, the parent asking the questions has anxieties about the adequacy of his or her parenting as well as concerns about the child's current treatment (often, the child is already in treatment). In contrast to those parents who make a straightforward request that you provide treatment or evaluation of their youngster, these parents are conflicted, and the conflict comes across in many different ways. The most obvious, of course, is that they ask questions about their child, about whether you think the child should be in treatment or on medication or in a specialized educational setting, but do not accept your offer to see the child face-to-face. Consider the following dialogue, excerpted from a discussion with a father who had come to solicit my opinion of his child's problems and current treatment.

Recently Jerry, a man in his 40s, called requesting individual therapy for himself. Before his first appointment was over, however, he made it clear that one of his main concerns was Benjamin, his 8-year-old son, and not only that, his son's current therapy. Benjamin, the third of three boys, was at that time in therapy with a local psychologist who specialized in the behavioral treatment of obsessive-compulsive disorders, following a highly structured model. Jerry had originally called this psychologist because Benjamin had developed a significant hand-washing habit, resulting in red, raw, and inflamed hands, especially in the winter. Jerry was enthusiastic about the improvement in compulsive hand-washing behavior he had seen in Benjamin since they began to work with the local psychologist. What he was still concerned about was that Benjamin seemed to have what his father referred to as an anger problem. He was easily provoked into a rage by his older brothers and other boys at school and often acted this out in highly inappropriate ways. Jerry received some very reasonable parenting advice from the psychologist and was doing his best to be firm and consistent in administering consequences for inappropriate behavior, but he was not satisfied that this was, or would be, enough. He asked me what I thought of the treatment his son had been receiving.

I felt in an awkward situation. The treatment that Benjamin had received for his habitual hand-washing (whether it was truly compulsive was not at all clear from Jerry's description) had obviously been successful. I knew of this psychologist by reputation and had met him at a seminar I had given many years earlier. He had impressed me as a genuinely nice person, and sincere as well. I recalled that his background was in educational psychology and that he typically restricted his work to readily measurable target symptoms. My impression was that he had found his niche, that his treatment approach and area of specialization fit both his training and his personality. Based on what Jerry told me, it sounded as if Benjamin's psychologist was not especially eager to delve into the *why* of child and adolescent externalizing behavior, something Jerry was hoping for. All of this inclined me toward encouraging Jerry to seek another opinion on his son's anger after bringing his work with this psychologist to a conclusion. On the other hand, Jerry made it clear to me that Benjamin, who had objected to other psychologists they had consulted, liked this one a lot and felt particularly appreciative for his help in overcoming the hand-washing habit.

I experienced several long moments of indecision. Should I encourage Jerry and his son to hang in there with the psychologist both of them liked and who had helped in the past? Or should I tell him that I thought the psychologist had probably done as much for them as he could, that it sounded like it was time to move on to someone else for help with his son's anger issues? If I chose this path, should I offer my services? The choice was making me anxious in a way that working with children typically does not. I reflected on this anxiety and realized that it was not the decision of what to say, it was something about Jerry and the way he told this story that suggested he was feeling on the spot about what to do himself and that he would like to transfer that anxiety to me instead. This is one of the things that can happen when parents become more than informants or treatment expediters. It is also one of the times in treatment when knowing how to use your intuition becomes essential. I could not put my finger on exactly what Jerry was doing that was making me anxious, but I knew that there was something very different in the way I was feeling as he relayed his tale about his son's therapy from how I had felt many other times when parents told me of their disappointment in the treatment or evaluation their child had received, often at the hands of a managed care organization. The best answer I could come up with for myself was that Jerry was not being particularly direct.

He was not saying "Dr. X did this and nothing more, and we're not satisfied. What would you do? Do you think you have anything else to offer?" He didn't even ask me to see his son; he just wanted to talk to me about his son.

Then he told me a story that clarified things enough so I knew how to continue. The story was that he had felt awkward because he had attended a charity fund-raising event where he was seated at the same table as his son's psychologist. I also learned that Benjamin's psychologist had known ahead of time that his patient's father would be there and had neither discussed it with him ahead of time nor asked to be seated at a different table. At that point, I had two concerns. First, I was concerned about the child psychologist's apparent lack of concern about Jerry's possible discomfort that his attendance at this social function might engender. I began to wonder if part of Jerry's reluctance to ask me directly to see his son or to even ask directly how I might begin treatment with his son was because Jerry was anxious about initiating therapy in which both he and his son would be involved with me. I began to realize that Jerry might want my help in dealing with his feelings about his son and about himself as a parent, while maintaining the privacy of a one-to-one therapy relationship. This was an instance in which the child's presenting problem of occasional aggressive and angry behavior was fairly straightforward and might well have led to equally straightforward treatment but for his father's pressing need for treatment himself.

Ultimately, I chose to advise Jerry about the kind of therapeutic approach that would be likely to help his son, and not about who should provide that therapy. I explained my point of view, that behavioral interventions were necessary to curb his son's angry outbursts and that concurrent exploration of the why behind these angry outbursts was equally necessary. I gave Jerry some very abbreviated examples of how therapists can talk to children to help them identify and communicate their feelings. I did not offer to see Benjamin myself, and Jerry did not ask me to do so. Although one never knows how this sort of thing will go, this time it worked out well. Jerry talked with Benjamin's psychologist and asked him to consider taking a more exploratory approach, focusing on Benjamin's feelings and thoughts in addition to his behaviors. The psychologist agreed to try this, Benjamin was responsive, and therapy happily continued along a new track.

In any practice devoted to helping children and adolescents, one will inevitably encounter cases that are beyond one's ability to help in an outpatient office setting. For therapists working in settings that also provide residential treatment, a transition to a more intensive and more restrictive form of treatment can occur more or less smoothly. For those working in outpatient clinics or in private practice, the process is considerably more complex. Most parents are extremely reluctant for their child to be "sent away," whether this is to a short-term crisis hospitalization, a residential treatment center, or a boarding school with a strong therapeutic component, often referred to as an "emotional growth school." Almost all parents will try every other alternative first. Those who bring up the option of a residential placement after meeting with you two or three times are the exception. If a child's condition deteriorates to the point where this is necessary, the parents will need your support, and lots of it. This is not a time to be the hero and try to rescue the child by yourself. Neither is it the time to give in to the fantasy that being a good therapist means never having to say you've reached your limit.

In this model, every case involves the therapist in understanding a child's parents and in establishing a relationship with them. Cases that involve only two or three meetings, such as the first two toileting cases I presented in the previous chapter, don't give one much time to develop a deeper therapeutic relationship with parents. Nor is there need to do so. But even in these cases, there must be understanding, reassurance, and trust—in other words, a relationship. Develop a deeper relationship with the parents during their child's transition from outpatient to residential or inpatient treatment.

When recommending residential treatment, you may need to be far more authoritarian than is familiar or comfortable for you. The irony of having to recommend more restrictive treatment for a young person is that those families who are most committed to their child and working the hardest to help him or her are sometimes the families who will resist recommendations for residential treatment. Few families will enthusiastically greet a subtle hint that they might consider such a placement. During the weeks and months that you discuss this with your patient's parents, there will be better days, and perhaps even better weeks. The parents will try to convince themselves that things are getting better without such treatment. They will worry about what might happen to their child if they send him or her away.

The dynamics are similar to those that arise when parents receive their first recommendation that their child take medication to address emotional or behavioral issues. The more psychologically minded the parents, the more they see themselves as responsible for helping their child grow, and the more engaged they are in therapy, the less receptive they will be at first to such a recommendation. If your approach to this patient and family has been open-ended and collaborative, you may find that you have to be more forceful and directive. The feel of therapy may change temporarily, in large part because your recommendation for a more restrictive therapeutic setting is based on your recognition that you are not making progress with the child. During this transition, your therapeutic efforts must of necessity be directed more toward the child's parents.

Even after you inform them that you have done as much as you can for their child in the setting in which you work, your work with the family is far from over. Although your role as the child's therapist may have ended, the family continues to need your support. At times, this may take a very practical form, as when a child is ready to be discharged from a residential program and the parents ask for help in identifying an appropriate educational placement. At other times, they need you to help them remember that their decision to send their child to a residential setting was made reluctantly, only after exhausting other options, and in order to help him or her, perhaps to save his or her life.

And then there are the occasions when therapy with a child or adolescent morphs into therapy with a parent, quite apart from the child's therapy. Other than the very important knowledge of the child or adolescent, there may be little to distinguish this therapy from any other therapy with an adult. Once the therapy begins, it proceeds as does any other case of adult treatment, and thus is outside the scope of this book. But at the edges, at the beginning, at points when your adult patient's concerns for his or her children arise, things can be very different. At those times, the one difference, your knowledge of the child or adolescent, has a thousand ramifications.

Treatment Techniques for Resolving Specific Problems

CHAPTER 7

Applying the Integrated Model to the Treatment of Children and Families

But what constitutes an even greater difficulty is that in many cases the child itself is not the sufferer, for it does not perceive the trouble in itself at all; only the persons round it suffer from its symptoms or outbreaks of naughtiness. And so the situation lacks everything which seems indispensable in the case of the adult: insight into the malady, voluntary decision, and the will towards cure.

—Anna Freud, 1926

If the first section of this book can be thought of as taking place in the seminar room, the second section takes place in the treatment room, in my office, and in your office. The concepts and general principles of the integrated model have been defined. Now is the time to put them to work to address real clinical problems. The next three chapters present problems that are most likely to lead to referrals for preschoolers (Chapter 8), for school-age children (Chapter 9), and for adolescents (Chapter 10). Each of these chapters shows how you can apply the integrated model to specific clinical issues. Because the core concepts and techniques are applied differently with children of differing ages and with adolescents, each chapter begins with a presentation of the way the model approaches patients of their particular age range.

Working with each of these age ranges requires specific approaches and techniques. Some issues are common to all three age ranges, however. It is to these issues that I now turn my attention.

Play Therapy

It is often assumed, both among professionals and among the public, that therapy with very young children means play therapy. It is equally often assumed that play therapy involves a set of tools (e.g., dollhouse, sandbox, finger paints, water) and a set of techniques (interpretation) that have equal usefulness for all young children, regardless of their presenting problems. These assumptions about play and therapy have been influenced, either directly or indirectly, by the writings of Melanie Klein. Klein (1959) promoted the view that children's play should be interpreted psychoanalytically in the same way as the free associations of adults. She believed that the road to the child's unconscious was through his or her symbolic play. The job of the adult psychoanalyst is to observe and interpret an analysand's free associations. The job of a Kleinian child analyst is to observe and interpret the child's dollhouse play, sandbox play, and finger paintings. Just as many of Sigmund Freud's ideas have become part of our culture, so, too, have Klein's ideas become part of the culture of child therapy. Some equally well-established child analysts, Anna Freud (1946/1964) among them, rejected the view that a child patient's play should be subjected to the same kind of interpretation as an adult's free association, and so chose not to use play in the way that Klein advocated.

Another assumption of play therapy is that therapy works best when parents are excluded. From a traditional play therapy perspective, intensive work, privately conducted, is prescribed for even the youngest child. Parental involvement is proscribed, as is parental participation in, or observation of, play sessions. The integrated model rejects this assumption as a silly one. Our job is to help parents help their children, not to replace parents.

But there are other ways to use play in treating children. In the integrated model, play serves several useful functions. It gives very young children something to do while adults are talking, whether during a first interview or later. It provides opportunities to observe how these very young children engage their environment. Do they ask if they may play with a game from the shelf, or do they impulsively pull it down? It can provide naturalistic opportunities to observe parenting style. Do parents permit their children to grab things off your desk, climb on the furniture, and switch lights on and off, or do they set limits? Play provides a way for you to connect with children, whether that means a game of chess with a 10-year-old or a mock dinosaur fight with a 4-year-old. Play can also provide a way to help children distance themselves from a problem enough so that they can metaphorically "discuss" it. In a case that I present in more detail in Chapter 8, I used play with a 4-year-old and her plush toys to talk about problems she was having on the playground at preschool. But, from my perspective, none of this is "play therapy," any more than talking with an adult patient about a movie is "movie therapy" or offering her a cup of coffee is "coffee therapy."

Empirically Supported Treatments

Among psychologists, expressing skepticism about the value of empirically supported treatments, sometimes referred to as empirically validated treatments, is not so far removed from casting aspersions on Mom, Old Glory, and apple pie. How could anyone be opposed to using psychological interventions that have been shown in numerous well-conducted studies to be helpful to children and adolescents? It does not seem reasonable to ignore the evidence that shows their efficacy. Neither is it reasonable to fail to consider using one or another of these treatment technologies when you have a patient who has a problem for which such a technology exists. The reasonable question to ask then, is not "Should I consider using a treatment that has been found to have empirical support?" The reasonable question to ask is "Must I use *only* techniques that have been so endorsed?"

The Society of Clinical Psychology, Division 12 of the American Psychological Association, endorses a number of treatments for childhood disorders based on the availability of published papers on research using standard research methodologies designed to minimize external and internal threats to the validity of experimental findings. On their Web site (www.apa.org.divisions/div12), the Society presents information for parents about treatment for four childhood disorders: anxiety, encopresis, enuresis, and oppositional behavior. This Web site includes brief statements about available evidence regarding efficacy of treatments for these disorders. The treatments are cognitive-behavioral therapy (for anxiety), behavior modification (for encopresis), behavioral treatment (for enuresis), and parent management training (for oppositional behavior). After statements claiming that some evidence exists that indicates the efficacy of a specific treatment for a specific condition, the Division 12 Web site authors write this: "While other therapies may be helpful for the treatment of childhood (anxiety/encopresis/enuresis/oppositional behavior), they have not been evaluated scientifically in the same way as the treatment listed here." This is a totally reasonable, balanced, and accurate statement. Other treatments may well be helpful, even if they have not yet been evaluated or if they have been evaluated using different research methodologies.

Some psychologists have gone beyond the highly reasonable recommendation that all therapists become acquainted with these well-studied treatments and learn to apply them as indicated. These more radical psychologists believe that only these well-studied and published approaches should be used clinically, banishing all others to the dustbin of historical artifacts.

There are numerous problems with this argument. First, it assumes a very narrow definition of what empirical evidence is. The argument assumes that only treatment approaches that have been the subject of a certain kind of investigation (controlled experimentation using large sample sizes, randomized assignment, tests of significance, etc.) are worthy of consideration. Other approaches that have received intensive study of another kind, such as case studies, are not given equal consideration. Although qualitative research involving the intensive study of small samples through observation or interview is not excluded on principle, such research tends not to be included in the journal articles that are the basis for deciding to include a treatment on the "approved" list.

The second major flaw in arguing that only a restricted range of treatments be "authorized" by the American Psychological Association is that such an argument conveniently forgets that psychotherapy is far from being a mature technology on two counts: It is a new endeavor, and it is as much art as science.

The third flaw in the argument is that it assumes that treatments that have not yet received the attention of those who conduct controlled studies are not as useful or effective. I am far from the first to observe that the choice of which treatment in the lab to study is guided more by how easily one can operationalize its concepts in a way that facilitates data collection than by any other variable.

Another school of thought about empirically supported treatments promotes the idea that treatment should be standardized in the form of protocols or manuals. There are standard interventions in pediatrics for treating an inflamed ear, an obstructed bowel, and a fractured tibia. Shouldn't there be standard interventions for encopresis, for school avoidance, for social anxiety? The answer to this is both yes and no. It is possible to sketch out a protocol for some aspects of treating encopresis in young children. I offer one such protocol in Chapter 8, and others are available in the pediatric and pediatric psychology literature. But protocols or manuals that have been designed primarily to guide empirical research do not direct a therapist to a sufficiently subtle appreciation of a patient's nonverbal communication. Nor do they help a therapist use his or her intuitive understanding of a patient to guide interventions.

Meehl (1987) points out that there is nothing wrong with making clinical decisions or, by implication, using an intervention strategy "on less cogent evidentiary basis than we would in a research seminar" (p. 10). The problem, continuing with Meehl's analysis, "with some current clinical practices is Persistence in Approaches (whether diagnostic or therapeutic), despite clear *negative* evidence against their validity or efficacy. Restricting our treatment options for those for which there is 'empirical support' in the form of quantitative data, significant testing, etc. runs the risk of making the therapist 'an obsessional perfectionistic purist' " (p. 11). Continuing to follow Meehl's argument, it often makes sense to use an approach or intervention for which we have the support of clinical experience but not of research-generated quantitative findings. It does not make sense to use an approach or intervention that has been shown not to work.

Logically Supported Treatments

A therapist who wishes to apply a meaningful criterion to choosing which intervention to use and which to put in the "wait and see" file can do his or her own logical analysis of the various treatments currently on offer. Logicians tell us that true statements can be combined in such a way that they seem to, but do not actually, justify a conclusion. Such a combination of statements constitutes a logically fallacious argument. Examining the assumptions behind various treatment approaches may reveal logical fallacies that are not otherwise obvious. The principles of logic have much to offer an open-minded and yet hard-nosed therapist. Logical analysis asks one essential question: Is the conclusion logically justified by its antecedents? If we are willing to accept the antecedent statements as true, does that necessarily mean that the conclusion is true? Perhaps the most famous example of this kind of analysis is the following syllogism. "All men are mortal. Socrates was a man. Therefore, Socrates was mortal." Of course, this does not work the other way: "My dog is mortal. All men are mortal. Therefore, my dog is a man." The first two statements are true, but the conclusion is logically fallacious.

A logical analysis, especially when combined with personal observation, may encourage one to utilize a therapy technique in the absence of data from randomized trials. Some selectively mute children respond well to a playful atmosphere in the office. It seems logical that a child who smiles, laughs, and perhaps giggles is becoming more comfortable and is on his way to speaking more freely. To put this in syllogistic form: "To be cured of selective mutism, a child must speak. Speech involves pushing air over the lips and teeth to make sounds. Laughing involves pushing air over the teeth and tongue to make sounds. It is logical to be playful with children with selective mutism if this leads to their being increasingly willing to let sounds emanate from their mouths." Another logical example: "Adolescents want to feel the support and help of interested adults. They often do not want to talk to their parents about some issues. So it is logical that they will often benefit from speaking with an adult who is roughly of their parents' generation and who will offer them both privacy and understanding."

On the other hand, there is less apparent logic in treating aggressive young children by placing them in a free play situation with few rules and even fewer consequences. In fact, it is so illogical that it can be used to illustrate the utility of looking for logical fallacies as one way of considering whether a particular treatment is worthy of your adopting it. The argument involves a flawed syllogism: "Ignoring rules and expectations of adults is characteristic of aggressive children. The absence of rules and expectations is characteristic of unrestricted and unstructured play therapy. Therefore, unstructured play therapy is an appropriate treatment for aggressive children." The first two statements are true, but the conclusion is false. This is an example of a logical fallacy commonly referred to as the fallacy of the undistributed middle (i.e., the middle term of the syllogism refers only to some members of a category, not all of them).

In the chapters that follow, I refer to some intervention techniques for which considerable quantitative evidence exists to support efficacy, some techniques for which most of the evidence is qualitative and resides in case studies, and some techniques for which there is little published evidence of any kind but which has been useful in my practice, that is, which has clinical evidence. Each of these intervention technologies has a place in the integrated model.

Cultural Diversity

The essence of therapy lies in being acutely aware of each person's uniqueness and in helping each person appreciate his or her uniqueness. A comprehensive discussion of what makes each individual unique would require referencing nearly every adjective in *Webster's Unabridged Dictionary.* The therapist who works with children and adolescents must be familiar with child development and which issues, stresses, and accomplishments are characteristic of children at each age. The therapist must also be familiar with gender, racial, cultural, and class differences. Numerous seminars and workshops are available to sensitize therapists to differences among cultures and ethnic groups.

Culturally competent practice must go beyond acquiring new, albeit positive, stereotypes of cultural groups that differ from one's own. To be truly sensitive to cultural differences, one should develop a new way of thinking about differences among cultures and subcultures. I recommend taking or auditing a course in cultural anthropology at a local college or university. Such an educational experience can help one begin to think about culture in a new way—not as a static group defined by equally static rules, but as an evolving, yet cohesive, living system. Studying anthropology can also help one become interested in learning more about cultural differences from the people who are most familiar with them: your patients. One can learn surprising things.

Recently, the European mother of a very shy young boy I was treating told me how he had made a new friend at school whom he had described as "chocolate, like you, Mommy." To my eyes, this boy's mother's skin tone was no different from my own somewhat olive complexion. And yet, as I learned when I asked her about this, in her home in northern France, nearly everyone is very fair, and so her somewhat darker skin tone makes her stand out in a crowd. As our discussion continued, she referred to herself as of mixed race because her mother was French and her father Moroccan. And so I learned from her that not everyone from France who speaks French has the same cultural identity. It is the subtle, nondramatic differences among cultural groups that are often the most important. The obvious differences can be learned from books; these make the most dramatic illustrations and are the ones typically mentioned, but the all-important microcultural differences that make families unique must be learned from your patients.

Some generalizations are helpful. It is helpful to know that in Latino families, a grandmother's opinion on matters of child rearing and parenting is given great weight and must be treated with great respect. Of course, the therapist who is happy to apply the principle of multidirected partiality will already be doing everything he or she can to include each family member in important discussions. One must go beyond this sort of generalization, however. That is where the benefits of intellectual curiosity come into play. The best source of knowledge about the particular and specific culture of an African American, Italian American, Latino, or Hasidic family is the family itself. People are happy to teach us about their culture, including the microculture of their home. All we have to do is ask, and the best way to ask is directly.

It is also important to be aware of differences among groups not typically thought of as minorities and not typically discussed in continuing education on cultural diversity. For several years, a developmental pediatrician and I teamed up to evaluate children with possible learning and attention issues. After an interview with parents of several medically involved children, I was shocked by the absence of complaints of fatigue, frustration, the lack of availability of child care, or problems with schools that one typically hears and that are totally normal. I commented on this to my colleague, who said, "You don't complain, you offer it up." I learned that in religious Catholic families such as my colleague's and the family we had seen together, hardship is often perceived and experienced in a way different from other cultural groups. I had learned an important lesson in cultural sensitivity despite the fact that everyone in the room had more or less pale skin and spoke only English and were born in this country. Cultural differences exist among people who look and sound the same. So it is important to consider each new family one meets as possibly being culturally different from oneself, whether they come from the other side of the world or next door.

I am a middle-class White American Jew, so I thought I was on fairly familiar ground when Sam, a middle-class White American Jew, called my office to talk about conflicts among his children and related parenting issues. In taking a history, I learned that he was a Lubovitch Jew and therefore more strictly observant than many American Jews, including myself. I still did not make too much of this. After all, a Jew is a Jew, right? I learned that family conflict was not the only reason Sam was in my office. He was also depressed. He explained that he was very much in love with his wife, thought she was beautiful and sexy, and wanted to have sex with her if not constantly, at least once or twice a week. Then came the surprise: The problem was not a difference in level of desire between them; rather, the impediment to the kind of sex life he wanted was a religious prohibition against sexual contact from five days before a woman's menstrual period until five days after the period. Sam also explained that this prohibition nixed all physical affection. I was aware of this prohibition and the importance of what Orthodox Jews refer to as laws of family purity, but I assumed that only sexual intercourse per se was prohibited. And so I suggested, naïvely as it turned out, that Sam and his wife could snuggle, hold hands, or otherwise be affectionate. The Clintonian solution had not occurred to me, and it was fortunate that it had not. I felt that I had committed a huge ethnocentric faux pas when Sam explained to me that touching of any kind was prohibited for the duration.

I learned a great deal from Sam about the importance of respecting cultural diversity. I especially learned not to assume that because I know something about a cultural group, I know it all. And I learned to ask questions. This was brought home to me when I was just beginning to work with Mary Jane, a 17-year-old African American girl. Mary Jane had struggled for years with dyslexia, and her parents had struggled for years with their school district. In one of our very early meetings, Mary Jane complained about her mother: "She always thinks that our district is biased against Blacks. It isn't. It's biased against special education kids." Mary Jane felt perfectly comfortable being Black in a mostly White school. She felt distinctly uncomfortable being a special education student in that same school. The salient diversity issue for her was not race, it was special education classification.

Language Differences

I am a native speaker of English. Some of my patients have been native speakers of Spanish, French, Dutch, and Hindi. They have all been bilingual, perhaps trilingual. I speak only one language, with the exception of a few halting phrases of high school French. From a linguistic perspective, I am the one who has a deficit. And yet, my polyglot patients routinely apologize to me about their "poor English." This seems to me a distortion of the reality of the situation. Their language abilities are far greater than mine. They are able to communicate in two languages at least, something I cannot do. I respond to this in several ways. The first is to explain that they have an ability I lack and one that I admire. The second is that I attempt to use the little bit of language skills that I do possess. So, if a Francophone patient offers to translate a note she has received from her husband that is written in French, I first offer to try to read it as is, in case there are nuances that will help me understand how the note sounded to her. In other words, I am willing to do a bit of work to overcome my lack of knowledge of her native tongue. I also ask questions, and often lots of them, about word meanings and usage. I allow myself to be the one who needs to learn because *I* am the one who needs to learn.

Who Decides Session Frequency?

The laissez-faire-to-authoritarian continuum in therapy is an interesting one. Where a therapist stands on the continuum probably depends as much on his or her personality as it does on his or her theoretical orientation. In general, the more authoritarian a stand the therapist takes, the more difficult it becomes for patients to hear their inner voice. If you insist that the anxious father of an anxious 8-year-old needs individual therapy, he may comply or he may rebel. In either case, he is responding to your edict and not to his own experience. Similarly, if you demand that a seriously depressed adolescent see you twice or three times a week, neither she nor her parents will have the opportunity to discover their feelings about having the additional support that more frequent therapy can provide.

On the other hand, the therapist cannot be laissez-faire with all patients. There are times when this is appropriate and reassuring. I recently was consulted by the parents of a 3-year-old who were concerned that he might be showing signs of obsessive-compulsive issues. It turned out that he was, albeit very mild ones. There were two aspects of this very brief (three sessions) treatment that the parents found very helpful and reassuring. One was our discussion of simple ways that they could help their child to enjoy change and experience it as playful, rather than as an upsetting deviation from the predictable. This child had become rigid about who got to take a bath first, he or his older sister. I suggested that his parents might play a game, such as asking each child to guess the color that Mom or Dad was thinking of to determine the order of baths. The second most helpful aspect of treatment was my reassurance that we could stop after the third visit and they could still call me whenever they wanted. It seems obvious to most therapists, but families are typically not at all sure that they can come back for more when it is needed. It is very reassuring to have the therapist give permission for this. When the patient is quite young, it is often helpful to remind parents that they may consult their child's pediatrician about a red ear and then, 6 months or more later, about another problem. Sometimes, after 8 or 10 or 15 successful visits, parents ask if further visits are needed. Mostly, the parents who ask this question have seen significant change in their child's behavior and they are asking "What more is there?" Usually I tell parents that I would not hesitate to tell them if I thought therapy was absolutely essential for their child. I also would not hesitate to tell them if I thought it was either clearly not necessary or a waste of time. I then tell them that their child is in the third category: He or she is reaping some benefit from therapy and is likely to do so in the future. However, one cannot identify any clear and present danger should they decide to discontinue treatment, and so the decision is up to them. Of course, even these choices can become complicated in practice. In the case of a little boy with obsessive-compulsive tendencies, it was important to stress that it would be far better for his parents to call sooner with what appeared to be a minor concern that to call later with a major one.

When children and adolescents have problems of greater severity, the question is often not "Is therapy necessary?" but "How much therapy is necessary?" Parents sometimes make this discussion easy by asking if one therapy session a week is sufficient for their depressed or self-injurious adolescent. But for every mother or father who asks if you think that twice-weekly therapy might help their daughter or son stay in school or out of the hospital, there is another whom you will have to convince of this. With some parents, all that is necessary is a simple statement that more frequent therapy would be helpful. Ask the adolescent first if he or she is interested in twice-weekly therapy. If the answer is yes, you will have more reason to recommend this to parents and more leverage as well. It is unusual for an adolescent to want *more* therapy, and that alone is an indication that it may be needed.

A problem often arises when therapist and adolescent see the value of more intensive therapy, but parents do not. Sometimes the cost is the problem, and one solution may be reducing one's fee as long as twice-weekly therapy is needed. When long-term psychiatric hospitalization was an option for adolescents (as opposed to crisis intervention, stabilization, and discharge), one could give families of very seriously depressed adolescents an option: very intensive therapy with constant parental supervision or psychiatric hospitalization. The option still exists in theory, but in practice the hospital (where stays are under a week) is best to ensure safety, not as a setting in which to receive intensive treatment. The option of month-long or longer inpatient psychiatric treatment no longer exists, with the exception of substance abuse treatment. We can no longer give parents of depressed but not suicidal adolescents the choice between inpatient treatment and intensive outpatient treatment. Rather, we have to provide the necessary information and let them decide. When you believe that you cannot effectively treat an adolescent unless you see him or her twice a week, say so. If you are willing to provide weekly treatment when parents do not concur with your recommendation for intensive therapy, say so. And if you are not willing to do this, say no.

An analogous but less anxiety-provoking situation occurs with school-age and younger children whose parents ask if treatment is possible on a once-per-month or every-other-week basis. The answer to this question depends a lot on the patient. An adolescent with mild Asperger's syndrome may be able to tolerate only monthly visits. As long as the child is not in and out of crisis, this can work. On the other hand, it is simply not possible to treat a selectively mute 5-year-old unless you see him or her weekly. Missing a week often means taking a large step backward. Missing a month may mean starting all over again. The same is true with treating encopresis. When parents ask about the possibility of every-other-week or once-per-month treatment for a condition that permits it, I point out the disadvantages and let parents decide. But when parents request infrequent treatment for a condition that clearly requires regular, if not intensive, treatment, we are obligated to point out that this will not work.

Because adolescents are so often seen individually, the issue of session frequency may emerge as a concern of parents, but one presented by the adolescent patient. Commonly, this involves concerns about cost. Your adolescent patient tells you that his parents are concerned about the expense of weekly therapy and are asking if once every other week might be sufficient. When I hear a concern of this sort expressed by a patient, not having heard anything about it from parents, I have a stock response. "Issues related to the cost of therapy, bills, and so on, are things I discuss with parents directly. The only question I have for you is, 'If cost were not an object, what sort of therapy schedule would you choose?' " The answers of the two adolescent patients to whom I most recently posed this question were these: "If it was free, I'd come every day" and "A lot, I love talking about stuff." I told both of these patients that given their response, I would let their parents know that weekly meetings were in order.

CHAPTER 8

Problems of Early Childhood

Truly wonderful, the mind of a child is.

—Jedi Master Yoda, *Episode II, Attack of the Clones, Star Wars*

In the little world in which children have their existence whosoever brings them up, there is nothing so finely perceived and so finely felt, as injustice. It may be only small injustice that the child can be exposed to; but the child is small, and its world is small, and its rocking-horse stands as many hands high . . .

—Charles Dickens, *Great Expectations*

Psychotherapy with very young children, under the age of 4 or 5, can be extraordinarily challenging and extraordinarily rewarding. There are few things that a child and family therapist can do that will have such a dramatic and profound effect on the life of both child and family as successful intervention that addresses a very young child's behavior problems.

Success in this area requires three sets of skills in addition to the general clinical skills you already have: familiarity with normal preschool development, understanding of behavior and the differential control of reinforcement, and the ability to connect emotionally with children as young as 3. This last item requires an intuitive understanding of the internal emotional life of your youngest patients and is an essential ingredient if your therapy is to be maximally effective.

Children of 3 or 4 brought to you by their parents because they are sometimes disruptive or have aggressive episodes require first of all a therapeutic relationship that is solid and real. In any child therapy, there will be times you will need to focus primarily on the parents as individuals and as a couple. But this aspect of working with your very youngest patients, though necessary, is not sufficient. A pediatrician may be able to successfully treat a child's inflamed ear without establishing much of a relationship with that child. But any pediatrician worth his or her salt will tell you that treating a more complicated physical problem such as abdominal pain, severe headaches, or diabetes requires a real doctor-patient relationship. This is true for all physical complaints, and even more true for emotional and behavioral complaints. Your ability to form a real connection with these young children determines the goals you can accomplish.

Behavioral techniques, which are easily enumerated, articulated, and learned, determine how quickly those goals can be reached. With some practice, techniques such as time-out and the careful and systematic use of rewards and punishments can readily be taught to parents, who will be implementing them at home. If you are able to form a relationship but lack specific skills, it is still possible to eventually produce change even in such areas as toileting and compliance, where the usefulness of behavioral techniques has been well documented. Treatment may take longer than it would otherwise, but it can still move in the right direction. The converse is not true, however. A therapist may have acquired a great deal of skill in behavior management, including great knowledge of empirically supported treatments, but if the ability to connect with children, and of course with their parents, is missing, many opportunities to be helpful will be lost.

Here I discuss some general techniques for connecting with these very young patients. Later in the chapter, I provide specific illustrations of how I do this. The most important general principle, learning to use your feelings to connect with children of 3 and 4, is not technical, but it is central to successful therapy. The therapist must understand the feeling world of these young children, not only intellectually, but emotionally as well. This may seem a daunting task, and it would be were it not for the one source of knowledge you already possess: You were once a child of 3 yourself. You experienced the same range of emotions as your young patients do. You may not have experienced them in the same situations or to the same degree, but you did experience them. And you still experience them in a modified way today.

The challenge, then, is how to access these emotional memories and how to use them therapeutically. Doing this, and combining this intuitive understanding with a focus on behavior, requires adopting a different mind-set from that to which you may be accustomed. Rather than an either/or approach, in which one either deals with the obvious undesirable behaviors or focuses on the far less obvious deeper emotional realities, this approach requires doing both.

For those practicing in outpatient settings, whether in a clinic or private practice, the most frequent reason parents of children under 5 seek treatment is for disruptive behavior. This chapter provides general guidelines and specific techniques for treating preschool boys and girls who exhibit disruptive behaviors, including aggression and tantrums. It also includes case material illustrating how these techniques can be used. Subsequent sections focus on other problems of early childhood that occur frequently, if not quite as frequently as disruptive behaviors: toileting problems and sleep problems. It also details treatment of a much less frequently encountered problem, but one with which every child therapist should be familiar: selective mutism.

Disruptive Behavior

Aggression among your youngest patients may be directed toward parents, siblings, peers, or (rarely) other adults. Before parents are willing to seek therapy, they have tried everything else they can think of. They have read parenting books and applied what they have learned. They have consulted with their child's pediatrician. They have sought advice from friends and relatives. When they arrive in your office, they are frustrated, and they are anxious. They are frustrated because nothing has worked, or more likely nothing has worked consistently. And they are anxious because of concern that their child will *always* be "out of control."

In general, treating aggression involves establishing therapeutic alliances with the parents and with the child, assessing the possible causes of the aggression, assessing the factors that precede and maintain the problem behaviors, and implementing a treatment package that incorporates the necessary parent training ingredients without coming across as a starched white coat.

The idea behind the integrated model is that by drawing on the insights, observations, and accumulated wisdom of the three component theories, one can accomplish more than by relying on any one of them alone. In treating aggressive children, the contextual perspective draws our attention to family history, to current family issues, to the need to consider each person's point of view, to the importance of having a wide-angle lens that takes in all the people who may be affected by what happens in therapy, and to the need to be willing to explicitly take the side of parent or child in some circumstances. The psychodynamic perspective draws our attention to the powerful, yet unspoken, emotions that family members are experiencing, to the way that both parents and children reveal their feelings nonverbally, to the huge importance of the therapeutic relationship, to issues of psychosexual and psychosocial development, and to the therapist's need to be aware of his or her own feelings and intuitions. The behavioral perspective draws our attention to the need for careful behavioral assessment and to the value of including parent management training (one of the treatments that has been the subject of controlled research and is frequently included in lists of empirically supported treatments) as one component of the treatment package.

As you read through the description of the first treatment case, you will notice that ingredients from the three component approaches are interwoven from the beginning of the first meeting. For the practitioner, this represents both good news and bad news. The bad news is that, for those beginning to use the integrated mode, this lack of a fixed step 1, step 2 structure can represent an additional challenge. Any treatment protocol that monolithically specifies something like "Always begin contextually, then introduce psychoanalytically derived elements, and then finally introduce the behavioral parent management package" is sure to be misleading and ultimately unworkable, because in its rigidity it will fail to accommodate individual differences. It will suit some treatment cases well, but others not as all. The good news is that the absence of a fixed order gives the therapist flexibility. Some cases may call for you to spend an entire first visit describing a behavioral plan in great detail.

Others may call on you to delve deeply into family history for 50 minutes. Still others may call on you to explore a parent's anxieties about his or her child's difficulties. Most often, treating a young child with externalizing behavior problems will call on you to visit all three sets of issues—psychodynamic, behavioral, and contextual—in the first session.

General Guidelines

Although you do have ultimate flexibility in structuring treatment, it is possible to offer some general guidelines. Before you do anything else, you must reassure these anxious and frustrated parents that you can help them. And before you can offer legitimate reassurance, you have to listen to them. Although checklists can be highly informative and efficient, I recommend that you begin simply by talking and listening, especially listening. If you still want the checklist information, you can easily send the forms home with parents after that all-important first interview.

As you begin the interview, remember that you are not just collecting data about when and where the aggressive behavior occurs. You are building a relationship. After all, it is unlikely that you will have technical guidance to offer that is radically different from what they have read in those parenting books. What you do have to offer that is radically different from what is contained in those books is technical guidance in the context of a therapeutic relationship. Begin with a developmental history, as discussed in Section One of this book and in Appendix A, and then ask about the presenting problem in detail. While you are asking these questions, though, keep your eye on the child. Notice his behavior. Notice how he reacts to what the adults in the room are saying. Notice how he looks at you. As his mother tells you of his latest outburst, does he sheepishly snuggle up to her? Does he hide his head? Does he do somersaults on the sofa? His parents tell you how affectionate he is with his baby brother, and you congratulate everybody. Does your patient then walk over to the baby and kiss him on the top of his head, and then look at you for approval?

Notice everything. And ask questions. Have parents noticed that their child is more often aggressive when he has not slept well the night before? Possibly they have noticed that he is more likely to be aggressive if he is hungry. Or perhaps his aggression emerges more often in certain circumstances that indicate attention-seeking is at the root of this particular problem. There are more questions to ask yourself and perhaps his parents as well. Is this aggression anger, or is it diffuse motor activity? If it is anger, to whom is it directed? Is there a reason for it? Do what you can to see the situation as the child does, or as a child might. This is another one of those treatment issues that can be moved along considerably if you can summon up an emotional memory of your own childhood. Getting a handle on the cause of a very young child's anger requires considerable empathy and intuition, and it requires willingness to go out on a limb. Of course, intuition must be tempered with judgment and experience. Not every intuition should be articulated.

CASE ILLUSTRATION
Mike

Stef, the mother of 4-year-old Mike, called me about 6 months ago at the suggestion of her pediatrician. When I returned the call, I learned that although Stef had been concerned about her son's behavior, it was her mother-in-law who had insisted that they seek professional help. I saw Mike, Stef, and her husband, Roger, about a week later. I began with a general question about the reason for their visit. I learned that they were concerned about Mike's sometimes disruptive behaviors. The next step was to ask some basic questions about developmental and medical history. Pregnancy, labor, and delivery were all unremarkable. Mike was in overall good health, except for seasonal allergies and intermittent mild asthma. He had been seen in an emergency room once, for a broken arm that resulted from a fall he took while playing. Stef and Roger told me that Mike had always been very active and that they had noticed him being aggressive to his peers by the time he was 18 months old. When he was 14 or 15 months old, he would head-bang and tantrum when frustrated. A local child psychologist they consulted when Mike was about 2½ had recommended that he get involved in karate. They followed this recommendation. Mike loved karate, but he continued to be aggressive.

The immediate precipitating event occurred when Mike's grandfather took Mike's arm to direct him away from traffic as they crossed a street together. Mike, apparently displeased by this unrequested assistance, spat at his grandfather, who became very upset, asked Stef and Roger to take Mike for psychological testing, and strongly suggested that he be medicated. He also reportedly said that he felt bad that Mike seemed to dislike him.

While relating this, Stef smiled and laughed charmingly. The incongruence between the story she was relating and her facial expression was striking. The psychodynamic component of the integrated model directs us to notice everything, especially nonverbal behavior. It also directs us to do what we can to help patients know what they are feeling and to feel what they are feeling. The contextual component of the integrated model directs us to consider how therapy may affect everybody in the family, parents as well as children. It also encourages us to be willing to take one person's side if a particular situation calls for it. With these as guiding principles, I responded in a way that reflects what I experienced in Stef's verbal and nonverbal communications. "All of this because he spat at him? I mean, I get it that he wouldn't like it, but it's kind of a reach from saying a child is behaving badly, which he was, to saying he ought to be medicated." Stef agreed verbally. Roger agreed nonverbally. I went on: "And what's this about Mike not liking him?

He sounds awfully sensitive." Stef and Roger told me that he was indeed extraordinarily sensitive. My response to that bit of information was something like this: "It sounds like this needs some help." When Stef and Roger agreed, I added, "We'll have to think about having him come in."

This discussion about Mike's grandfather was directly influenced by the contextual concept of multidirected partiality. Observing that he seemed to be overreacting reflected my willingness to support Stef's position about Mike's behaviors: that they called for attention but not as acutely as his grandfather felt they did. My suggestion that Mike's grandfather participate in therapy with his grandson represented another way to support Stef and Roger's position that Mike's grandfather might be overreacting. It did more than this, though. It also was a way to be partial to Mike's grandfather, to offer him an opportunity to give voice to his concerns at the very least, and perhaps to gain something for himself. Although it may be obvious, intervening in such a way that all three generations were supported was not my way of unbalancing the family system. I've never been completely convinced that phrases like "unbalancing the family system" have any real meaning anyway.

Having heard about Mike's behavior in more detail, I was able to offer a general description of how they might manage his behavior differently and more effectively. I wanted them to know that they would not be alone in this, so I made it clear that I saw this endeavor as a team effort: "We need to come up with some clear guidelines for Mike and some way to show him what is okay and what isn't." The "we" in this statement is not mere style. Parents of children with challenging behaviors need to know that they are not alone, that you are willing to be part of the solution, not a distant technical advisor. I wanted to reassure them and to let them know that we would have to get specific about identifying some target behaviors.

I returned to the question of just what Mike was doing that concerned his parents and his grandfather. I asked Stef and Roger to give me some more specific information about Mike's aggressive behavior. "Is he ever aggressive toward you, or his baby sister?" Yes, he had been. Stef and Roger were particularly concerned that Mike sometimes "hugged" his little sister much too hard. In talking about this in more detail, I learned that Stef and Roger had a good general idea of what to do about this. When they saw Mike being aggressive with his sister, they expressed their disapproval and took him to his room in what they thought of as a time-out procedure. They did the same thing when he had a temper tantrum. They wanted to exert some control over his behavior, but they had not mastered the technology. They thought of Mike's room as a place for time-out, but Mike did not. Why would he, when his room was full of toys? Neither had they been sufficiently vigilant, structured, or consistent in the way they used reinforcers.

The next 20 minutes of this first office visit drew heavily on well-established (and empirically supported) ways of teaching parents to use behavioral techniques for managing disruptive children. I explained that we would be working on techniques to increase their success in managing Mike's behavior and asked if a short demonstration might be helpful. I then asked Mike if he would help me, using some of the toy dinosaurs he had brought with him. Mike was interested, so we did a demo for his parents using the toy dinosaurs. Mike identified one of the dinosaurs as "bad" and several other dinosaurs as "good." Mike and I explained the difference between good behavior and bad behavior to the dinosaurs. When the bad dinosaur broke a rule, Mike put him in time-out. After the demonstration, I asked Mike how the bad dinosaur was feeling. Mike responded that the dinosaur was feeling sorry and that he wouldn't do it again. Of course, this was only play, and nobody expected that this little bit of role-play would result in the end of Mike's aggression. It did help him understand that there would be a connection between behavior and consequences, though. It also served to teach his parents that he understood the difference between desirable behavior and undesirable behavior.

After the demonstration with Mike's dinosaurs, I talked with Stef and Roger about new ways to manage Mike's behavior and new ways to help him learn the difference between acceptable and unacceptable behaviors. I began by explaining that Mike was like a very energetic puppy who had not yet learned what is really expected of him, and that he would do better if they could make their preferences as clear as possible. I find that many people like analogies, and so I provided several to illustrate this point. The first analogy took advantage of my knowledge that they had a dog and that they had met Shira, my friendly, very enthusiastic, and rambunctious Portuguese water dog. I explained that Mike was a bit like Shira: outgoing, enthusiastic, engaging, extremely energetic, and in need of lots of attention and very crisp and clear rules. Both need discipline, I explained, not to squelch their enthusiasm, but to help them channel it in positive directions. I then told Stef and Roger about my conversation with a friend who directs television commercials. I told them that my friend explained that his job was to say yes or no. "Yes," that shot is exactly what I had in mind. "No," that shot is too close up, or not sufficiently close up, too dark, or not dark enough. "That's what Mike needs," I said, "yes or no. Yes, that's great behavior or no, that is unacceptable behavior." I explained how the shades of gray are confusing to young children and told Stef and Roger about research suggesting that young children become confused when verbal and nonverbal channels of communication are incongruent, as when a parent says "No" while smiling. My recommendation was that Roger and Stef be very clear about which behaviors they found unacceptable and that they leave as few items in the gray category as possible.

I had some specific recommendations about time-out. Instead of sending Mike to his room, where he could play with toys or somersault on his bed, I recommended that they establish a time-out spot in a corner near the kitchen or family room. I also explained that if time-out is to be effective, it must be administered calmly and dispassionately. I suggested that they try to convey the same emotional tone that might accompany picking up the morning newspaper from the front step: neutrality to boredom. I showed them how to guide their son to the previously designated time-out spot in a way that would not be inadvertently enjoyable or exciting for him. I stressed that it was important that they be emotionally very low-key, that they say only "no hitting" or "no kicking" as they took him to the time-out spot, and that they not give in to the urge to lecture him.

The appointment was concluded and a time for the following week agreed on. Appointments over the next several weeks focused on helping Stef and Roger increase their comfort and skill in managing Mike's behavior. Whenever Roger or Stef mentioned Mike's grandfather, I reiterated that I would welcome his participation in our sessions as soon as he was willing and they were comfortable. About 2 months into treatment, Roger and Stef told me that Joe, Mike's grandfather, had expressed his interest in joining us. I told Roger and Stef that I was pleased about this. Sensing their anxiety about the meeting, I reassured them that in all likelihood nothing very dramatic would happen in the meeting.

Meeting with Roger, Stef, Mike, and his grandfather called for application of contextually based techniques and concepts. It also called for paying attention to nonverbal communication and transference issues. Beginning with the most obvious, I kept the principle of multidirected partiality in mind as this interview began. I wanted to support Roger and Stef, who had made it clear, both verbally and nonverbally, that they were anxious about having this meeting. They had made frequent references to Joe's sensitivity. Stef had also said that she sometimes worried about Joe's opinion of her parenting.

I began by asking Joe how he saw things with Mike. To my surprise, given what I had been told, he was generally positive about changes he had seen in Mike's behavior. He also pointed out some problems, including an incident in which Mike reacted aggressively after being teased by his uncle, Stef's brother. I agreed with Joe that Mike shouldn't be aggressive. The principle of multidirected partiality served as a reminder to see what I could find out about Mike's side of this story. I asked what Mike's uncle had done to provoke Mike's outburst and was glad that I did. Uncle Larry had lifted Mike up in the air by his feet and held his head in a stream of water from a sprinkler. My reaction to this was quick: "Uncle Larry is out of control, too!" I said this gently and with a smile, but all the adults present got the point. A long discussion ensued about what constitutes fun and games, what is teasing, and what is over the line. Stef was good-humored about it, but she had become so accustomed to Larry's impulsive style that it was a while before it registered with her that he had actually provoked Mike, whether he meant to or not. She agreed to talk to her brother about this.

We moved to the more delicate subject of Joe's belief that his grandson disliked him because Mike never approached him spontaneously as he did his parents. Observing Mike's interactions with his parents and with me left me with the impression that he was most comfortable when approached playfully, while still letting him have some choice in the matter. The unfortunate episode with his uncle was characterized by his uncle's grabbing him without warning. On the other side, his grandfather tended to be so tentative that Mike became anxious. I asked Joe if he was ever playful with Mike, at the same time placing my hand on Mike's shoulder and patting him gently. As Mike giggled, I asked Joe. "Do you ever do this?" When he said that he wasn't sure how to be playful, I said something like, "We'll have to work on that." The nonverbal part of this interaction was more important than the verbal. Were it not for the very positive nonverbal signals I received from Stef and Roger, I would never have so much as touched Mike. Were it not for the nonverbal communication from Joe that signaled his comfort with my talking with him about his relationship with his grandson, I would not have made so bold a statement as "We'll have to work on that." Were it not for the happy coincidence that Joe and I were about the same age, I would not have been so quick to make this comment.

I felt that I had made a good connection with Joe but was not positive until the next week. Roger and Stef came to the office with Mike, but without Joe. My intuition was to handle this playfully, much as I had advised Joe regarding Mike. I also had quite a bit of clinical data, much of it nonverbal, to bolster my inclination to be playful. Stef and Roger were comfortable with Joe's involvement the previous week. They were comfortable overall with therapy. And, most important, they were playful people themselves. So, rather than initiating a serious discussion about why Joe was not there and how they felt about this, I simply said, "Where's Grandpa?" When Roger told me that he had a work conflict, I said, "We need him, I'm going to call him up." I then added, "As long as you don't mind." Neither Stef nor Roger minded, so I called Joe at work. Staying with the playful approach, I told Joe that we needed him with us. His response confirmed that he wanted to be involved and was feeling comfortable with therapy: "Maybe I should come in by myself."

Joe did come in by himself the next week, and as we began to talk about the reason for what Stef saw as his "overconcern," the answer became apparent. Joe was able to give me a much more complete family history than Roger had, including the existence of several close relatives with obsessive-compulsive disorder and several more with bipolar disorder. Joe thought that he saw signs of serious disturbance in his grandson's behavior and was worried that Stef and Roger were glossing over real present problems and real potential problems as well.

This kind of anxiety—that a child may be carrying the germ of a disorder that other family members have had—occurs frequently when that disorder is serious and had serious consequences for the family. The kinds of disorders that cause the most concerns are those for which no adequate treatment existed when that family member was diagnosed, or ones for which no truly adequate treatment exists now: bipolar disorder, severe depression, schizophrenia. So Joe's anxiety was not unusual. What was unusual was his response to this anxiety. Many parents and grandparents with this kind of anxiety are conflicted: They want their child to receive treatment to help with present issues and hopefully to reduce future problems. But they also want to make the whole issue go away: Talking about it makes them even more anxious. Because Joe's anxiety was focused on the possibility that Mike might not receive adequate treatment, I was able to discuss that issue directly with him without concern that doing so would exacerbate his anxiety and reduce the odds of his continuing. Based on the history Joe provided, it did seem that Mike might be at risk for more difficulties down the road. I explained that we could not know for sure and that the best course was to help Mike now and to continue to monitor him. I also explained that helping him manage his feelings now would help him whether or not he developed a more serious mood disorder in the future. I encouraged Joe to continue sharing his observations and concerns with Stef, with Roger, and with me.

As I write this, Mike is not quite 5 years old. He is much less disruptive, although there are times when he is aggressive toward other children. All three elements of treatment (behavioral, psychodynamic, contextual) continue to be important in helping him and his family.

This case illustrates how the integrated model works by drawing on three streams of clinical thinking and three sets of interventions. The idea of inviting Mike's grandfather, the repeated suggestions to Roger and Stef about the possibility, and treating Joe as a valuable source of information and help in the therapeutic process came straight from contextual therapy. The careful attention paid to nonverbal communication, to my intuitions about this family as a whole and its individual members came from psychoanalytic practice. The detailed discussion of techniques to manage Mike's behavior came from social learning theory and the literature on parent management training.

From a behavioral perspective, children are aggressive for one of four reasons: (1) to gain access to something they want, (2) to avoid an unpleasant task or activity, (3) for attention, and, more rarely, (4) simply because they enjoy being aggressive. Antecedents are also important in understanding aggression, yet they are frequently overlooked. I often advise parents of preschool and even school-age children to remember how they thought about their child's fussiness when he was a baby: "You probably first asked yourself if he was tired, wet, cold, hungry, or sick." I then recommend that they consider these factors when their child seems to become difficult or aggressive "with no reason."

From a contextual perspective, young children may be aggressive in response to an unfair event or series of events. Mike's aggressive outburst after his uncle turned him upside down is one example of this. Children also become aggressive in response to being harmed by events outside of their control or influence: Traumatic injuries, developmental disabilities, life-threatening chronic illnesses, and parental separation and divorce are but a few examples.

Aggression toward Parents

Any therapist who sees very young children is sure to encounter children's aggression toward their parents from time to time. I've seen a number of little boys who on occasion slap or pinch their mothers. Most often, the line between playful affection and aggression is blurry, and that is typically the root of the problem. In the cases I've seen, the mothers are not sure that their child's behavior is over the line. They don't like it, but they have not yet identified it as unacceptable, even to themselves. Parents who are psychologists and pediatricians can have as much trouble with this as anyone. The woman whose child is aggressive toward her does not *think* that there is any conflict between being a loving mother and a firm disciplinarian; often, though, she *feels* that there is a conflict between being a loving mother and a firm disciplinarian. Her child is undoubtedly cute, perhaps adorable, most of the time. She needs to know that you see that side of him before she can hear anything from you about his aggression. Unless her child has developmental delays, she also needs your reassurance that he is developmentally intact, reassurance you can offer only after taking a thorough history. If her child has delays, she equally needs reassurance that he is meeting expectations given those delays.

After establishing rapport, the next step is to give voice to your empathic response to observing a child engage in an unprovoked act of aggression toward his mother. Ask her, "Did he just hit you? Is that something he does?" Let her know that you are shocked. Let her son know that you are shocked. Connect with her. Talk with her about the other issues that are impinging on her relationship with her son. This pattern of aggression occurs frequently in single-parent households. Whether she is a single parent or not, find out about the extent to which the child's father is involved in his life and whether the father's influence is overall positive or negative. Find out about her life, especially her emotional life. Clarify with her that she wants the slapping and pinching to stop. Ask if she is comfortable giving the child a consequence such as time-out if he does this again. If she is, and she will be, teach her how to use time-out, and make sure that her son is there to hear this. Even better, ask him to help you show his mommy how it works.

Then talk directly to the small boy in your office. You have to rely on your intuition about whether or not to talk with this 4- or 5-year-old alone or in his mother's presence. In either event, look the boy in the eye and talk to him about his behavior and its implications without mincing words. The last time I had a "man-to-man" discussion of this sort with a preschooler it went something like this:

P.G.: Benji, I wanted to talk with you for a couple of minutes. Is that okay with you?

Benji: Okay.

P.G.: How are you feeling today?

Benji: Good.

P.G.: That's good. Benji, I wanted to ask you, is your mommy nice to you?

Benji: Uh huh.

P.G.: And do you love your mommy?

Benji: Uh huh.

P.G.: And your mommy loves you.

Benji: (nods).

P.G.: Is it nice to hit people you love and who love you?

Benji: No.

P.G.: You're right. It's not nice. So you can't do that anymore. Right?

Benji: (nods).

P.G.: So that's why your mommy is going to use the time-out that we practiced, to help you remember that you can't hit people, especially your mom. Do you understand?

Benji: Yes.

P.G.: Okay, let's go back now.

To some this may sound too much like Mister Rogers for comfort, but Mister Rogers was a man who understood young children very well. Although Benji was only 4, this was not play therapy. It was, rather, a focused and serious conversation, and one that apparently had a positive effect, along with the rest of the session. At follow-up 1 week later, Benji's mother reported a dramatic change in his behavior and no aggressive incidents of any kind. We agreed that she could call as needed in the future.

———————— CASE ILLUSTRATION ————————
Amanda

It does not happen often, but once in a while you are asked to treat a child for a problem she doesn't have. This sort of thing always serves as a reminder of the importance of doing one's own assessment, regardless of the referral issue and referral source. Several years ago, parents who had heard me speak about sibling issues asked me to see Amanda, their 4-year-old daughter. The director of Amanda's preschool had expressed increasing concern about what she described as Amanda's aggression toward her peers. Amanda's parents had confidence in the preschool, took these concerns to heart, and immediately called me.

Within 10 minutes of meeting Amanda and her parents, I wondered if I had correctly understood the referral. Her parents were very gentle and soft-spoken people. Amanda was a tiny, sweet, and quiet, almost shy child. If she manifested anything out of the ordinary, it was anxiety, not aggression. I listened as Amanda's parents relayed what the preschool director had told them about Amanda pushing and jostling other children. I believed the stories, as far as they went. All my intuitions went in the other direction, however. It was hard to imagine this child being aggressive in the same way that I was used to seeing aggression.

So I began to talk to Amanda about school, and I learned a lot. It turned out that other children would sometimes say things to her that she took as intentionally hurtful. Interestingly, she actually was sometimes aggressive: She acknowledged becoming upset by these affronts and pushing the child who had hurt her feelings. She was aggressive if one stuck to a very rigid definition of that word. But under the surface, she was anxious and highly sensitive. So, rather than develop the sort of management program that would have been called for if her aggression were of the sort one sees in generally disruptive children, we focused instead on her feelings and on helping her search for alternative ways of dealing with those feelings.

At my request, Amanda had brought several small toys with her to the office. My standard suggestion is that these be toys that the child has imbued with personality, and they were. The four plush toys had names and distinct personalities. Amanda and I used the animals to enact several scenes that paralleled her difficulties with peers at preschool. After going through several enactments with her animals, we began to problem-solve to come up with solutions that might work. All the while, we talked about the animals, not about Amanda. Rather than ask Amanda about preschool, I asked if Bunny's feelings were ever hurt by Cinnamon. Rather than asking directly about what she could do differently, I asked what Bunny could do differently. Finally, we came up with a possible solution: Bunny might ask Cinnamon if he meant to be mean and to hurt Bunny's feelings. Amanda played this out with the animals, and it seemed to work fairly well.

Now came the real test. Might this strategy, I asked, work for Amanda at school? If someone in her class were to say something that hurt Amanda's feelings, could she ask that child if he meant to hurt her or if he was being playful? No, she couldn't do that, Amanda explained: It would be "too scary." I wondered aloud if there was someone at school who could help with this scary situation, perhaps a teacher. After some more discussion, Amanda and I, with help from her parents, developed a plan. If another child said something that hurt Amanda's feelings, Amanda would walk to the nearest teacher and ask her help in talking with the other child. An essential part of this plan was that Amanda's parents would prepare the teacher, which they did. The teacher was very pleased that Amanda's parents were taking the problem seriously and equally pleased to help with the plan.

Not many days after the meeting in which this plan was hatched in the office, it had its trial. A little boy said something that bothered Amanda. She asked her teacher to help her talk to the boy. The teacher did talk to him and learned that he did not want to hurt Amanda's feelings. And the teacher was thrilled that Amanda was not aggressive. We met several more times to solidify the changes, but there were no more aggressive incidents of any kind.

CASE ILLUSTRATION
Katherine

Katherine was the youngest of three daughters. Her parents, Tom and Rachel, asked for help managing 4½-year-old Katherine's "meltdowns." Tom told me that, with what appeared to be no reason or a trivial reason (e.g., having the wrong barrette in her hair), Katherine would clench her fists, become very upset, and dissolve into tears. He explained that these meltdowns occurred every day. Noting my dog's bowl and toy in the office, Tom and Rachel told me that Katherine was afraid of dogs. Katherine heard this and asked about my dog. Responding to her question, I described Shira as a very big, very black, and very furry dog. Katherine said she wanted to see her. After obtaining her parents' permission for this, I agreed to bring Shira to Katherine's next appointment.

A week later, Katherine, accompanied by Tom and Rachel, came to see Shira and me. After a few moments, Katherine began to pet Shira. By the end of the hour, they were fast friends. Katherine did not want to leave. We had not directly addressed the meltdowns, but Katherine was definitely over any fear of dogs.

The next meeting was adults-only, at Tom and Rachel's request. At that time, they told me something they had not wanted to say in front of Katherine: that her tantrums sometimes included lashing out with her fists. They were also more open about their anxiety that something was "really wrong" with Katherine. I reassured them that nothing awful was wrong with their little girl and made four recommendations to use regularly for behavior management: (1) provide reassurance when she is anxious, (2) establish a family rule of zero tolerance for physical aggression, (3) use time-out when this rule is broken, and (4) enthusiastically reinforce Katherine in a specific way.

The specific technique I suggested is reinforcement flooding, an extension of the popular advice to parents to "catch them being good" into the territory of "catch them being notbad." This management strategy has two goals: increasing desirable behavior and eliminating any need the child may have to seek attention by acting up. The technique is simplicity itself. Parents are instructed to identify 50 things about their child each day that they can positively acknowledge. Parents are usually nonplussed by this recommendation, so I provide multiple age-appropriate examples: "I noticed you were watching television with your sister and you didn't fight about who got to sit on the sofa first. That was so great that your little brother walked by and you didn't trip him." On observing a preschooler coloring: "That is soooo blue!" The idea is to show parents that the 50 positive remarks need not be, in fact should not be, effusive praise. Rather than thinking of the statements as praise, parents should think of them as "I notice you" statements. That is why remarking on the blueness of a child's coloring is more than sufficient. There is no need to compare the child to Picasso, Cezanne, or Chagall. Remind parents that they need not write down their 50 statements. Parents who do this quickly exhaust themselves.

Help parents anticipate children's reactions to this change in parental demeanor. If children say, "You're just doing this so I'll be better/nicer," parents should agree. If children say, "You're just doing this because (therapist's name goes here) told you to," parents should also agree. Rachel and Tom agreed to give these four recommendations a try and to return the following week with Katherine.

The previous meeting with Rachel and Tom focused on management techniques. The next meeting with Katherine and her parents focused on emotion and on helping Katherine become aware of her feelings so that she might express herself in ways that her parents could respond to. At Katherine's request, Shira was present for this visit. Katherine tried to interest Shira in retrieving a ball, and Shira's lack of response to this invitation provided an opportunity to help Katherine put disappointment and sadness into words. The next topic provided another opportunity for me (with Rachel's help) to tell Katherine that feelings are okay. I asked Katherine about her teachers. She replied that they were nice except for Miss Hodgton, her piano teacher. I could see that Rachel was feeling more relaxed than she had initially been—Katherine's getting over her fear of dogs helped a lot—and so I felt that I could safely be playful with the subject of Miss Hodgton, and even to ham it up a bit. "Oh, Miss Hodgton, she is so yucky," I began. Katherine giggled. Emboldened, I continued, "Isn't she horrible?" Of course, I had no axe to grind with Miss Hodgton, but I did want to help Katherine go a bit deeper into her displeasure with her. Better anger about Miss Hodgton than temper tantrums directed at no one in particular and affecting everyone.

Rachel brought all three girls to the next visit and announced that it had been a very good week. The session was spent talking with the girls about things they were involved in, including adopting a puppy. Rachel said that she and Tom would like to talk about extended family concerns the following week. During that visit, I consciously thought about multidirected partiality for the first time in working with this case. Tom and Rachel had some disagreements with their parents regarding parenting. Their parents had medical problems. We talked about all of this and came to the conclusion that it was possible to be respectful to and supportive of their parents while still staying in control of their parenting decisions. This discussion heightened Rachel's awareness of her own anxieties and her inner conflict about being in control. I saw Rachel individually the next week with the plan of focusing on this ambivalence. She began the session by saying that the previous week had gone very well and concluded by saying, "I am in charge." The appointment two weeks later was scheduled as a follow-up visit in case new problems emerged. Because everything was going well, no more appointments were scheduled.

Eighteen months later, I was walking through a parking lot when my path crossed that of Rachel and her three daughters. They all looked happy. Rachel said that things had been great, that it was wonderful to "have my daughter back," and that they had adopted that puppy.

Toileting Issues

This section focuses on uncomplicated toilet training. The treatment of encopresis is discussed in Chapter 9.

When parents ask for your help with toilet training, they have already talked with their pediatrician and read at least one how-to book and have exhausted these resources, and likely themselves as well. Toileting issues often arise as a "by the way" question, inevitably 5 minutes before a therapy session ends. Do not try to address the issue in those 5 minutes. Let parents know that you can help them and schedule another appointment for the purpose.

As you begin the visit scheduled for dealing with the toileting issue, set a comfortable tone with parents. Let them know that you will be asking them to get quite descriptive and specific about the toileting issue, that it is necessary, and that you are totally comfortable with it. Then start asking questions. Will their son urinate in the toilet? Parents rarely have problems with toilet training their daughters, with the exception of girls who have developmental delays. The techniques that work for typical boys are equally effective when used with girls with delays. Has he ever had a bowel movement in the toilet? Does he have constipation? Establish that your patient is not constipated and has never had a bowel movement in the toilet. Explain to his parents that you will be beginning a process that will work, but that will require their focused attention. Ask if this is the right time for them to do this. Some parents may say that they are too overwhelmed by other issues. Once you and the parents have established that this is the right time, the process is straightforward.

The key to successful toilet training lies in helping parents to adopt an appropriately patient and consistence approach. I begin by going through the following toilet-training protocol: The idea is to teach the child that using the toilet for bowel movements will result in reinforcement and that having accidents will not be reinforcing. In other words, the goal is to increase the child's expectancy that good things (e.g., praise, physical rewards) will be available contingent on appropriate use of the toilet. Punishment, whether verbal or physical, tends to lead to physiologic responses that are incompatible with successful toilet training and so is not part of this approach. Rather, the goal is to be neutral and emotionless when accidents occur and to contrast this with joyous celebration when the child uses the toilet as parents hope he will.

Ask parents to take their child to the bathroom approximately 20 minutes after each meal, but not to pressure him to "produce." Be sure they do praise him for sitting. It is important for parents to praise him and reward him for any bowel movement, however small. Parents should take him to the bathroom if they believe, based on his behavior, that the time is right.

Having gone through the mechanical aspect of toilet training, turn to the interpersonal side. Emphasize that although they may be frustrated that the process is taking so long, they must exude patience, not anger. If they can follow these instructions and guidance, the odds are that when you next see them, they and their child will have reached their goal.

Sleep Problems

A direct referral for help with the next set of issues of early childhood is unusual. Inevitably, parents have consulted their child's pediatrician first. As a next step, the pediatrician has referred them directly to you or has made a more general recommendation that they consult a child psychologist. This is both good and bad. The vote of confidence the pediatrician has given you is helpful. The frustration and anxiety that parents have experienced when the first attempts at resolving the problem failed is not. So, often, the very first order of business is reassuring parents that there are alternatives and that by working together, you will find a way.

Interventions for young children who repeatedly get out of bed and have trouble settling down are discussed here.

Bedtime Issues

Much more common than the child who sleepwalks or has night terrors is the child who will not stay in bed, instead wandering repeatedly into the master bedroom. The approach that I advocate for this problem combines elements of environmental manipulation and patient limit setting. Sleepwalking and night terrors are discussed in Chapter 9.

——————— CASE ILLUSTRATION ———————
Kyle

Four-year-old Kyle did not like to sleep alone. If he wasn't allowed to climb into his parents' bed, he managed to convince one of them, usually his dad, to keep him company in his bed. His parents were not happy with this arrangement but had resigned themselves to it. They had developed a routine that at first seemed like an example of what my pediatrician colleagues call "good sleep hygiene." After dinner, Kyle had some playtime, a bath, and then several books read to him before lights out. Then the fun began, with many last-minute requests, questions, and needs. By the time his mom and dad got him to bed, it was way past Kyle's bedtime. An unfortunate side effect of this was that Kyle, chronically sleep-deprived, was often irritable and sometimes hyperactive in the morning, especially following a particularly late night.

Kyle's parents and I discussed all of this in detail, and I learned several key bits of information. First, Kyle often collapsed around 4 o'clock to nap for an hour and a half. Second, the after-dinner play often consisted of exciting video games. We decided that the after-dinner video gaming was probably too exciting in the evening. We also agreed that they would try to drastically limit Kyle's napping in the afternoon. This took about 2 weeks to institute, but when all the changes were in place, Kyle and his parents were sleeping better. Kyle's parents also reported an improvement in his behavior. The change we could have made, but that turned out not to be necessary, would have been to change their responses to Kyle's habit of leaving his bed once in it. Had this pattern continued, they would have been well advised to simply return him to his bed each time he left: no explanation, no song and dance, just back to bed.

Play and Playfulness

The tools that every child therapist carries around with him or her are of course useful. You will want to encourage the child to color or draw, to play with puppets or small animal figures, to explore your office. As I noted earlier, there is logic to the freedom of play when one is treating an inhibited child. The way you interpret the child's play is important. Focus on emotion and movement. Remember that your goal is not to analyze children's free associations but to help them express themselves, to help them free themselves. Be more like Anna Freud than Melanie Klein. Do whatever you can to encourage children to loosen up and avoid anything that will undo the loosening up. If a child sits in your desk chair and starts to swivel about, go ahead and remark that she is the doctor now, but do it playfully. To act playful, you must, of course, feel playful. And to feel playful, you have to be comfortable with that aspect of your personality.

Selective Mutism

Children with selective mutism have normal language abilities but choose not to speak in some situations, most typically restricting speaking to family members. Some children with selective mutism do speak to other children outside of the home, but only when no adults other than their parents are present. They are quite literally selectively mute.

Conceptually, this problem can be understood as having multiple components. Children with selective mutism are anxious. They have often inadvertently been reinforced for not speaking in public; they may have gained a small element of control by choosing when and with whom to speak; they may be withholding their speech in a way analogous to how some children withhold stool. The integrated model approaches this case from multiple directions concurrently. The therapeutic relationship is as important here as it is in the treatment of any disorder. One must address the anxiety these children experience, and because the children themselves are not able to provide verbal information about the sources of those anxieties, one must rely on nonverbal information and on one's emotional response to the child. It is also important to address parents' anxieties. A social learning perspective is also crucial, especially awareness of children's expectancies regarding possible consequences of speaking to nonfamily members and in public.

Family history can be particularly illuminating and often includes at least one parent who was either slow to speak or very shy as a child. It is also typical for at least one parent to have significant anxiety. Equally important is the child's developmental history, especially the history of language acquisition. As you begin treatment, be sure to learn about parents' expectations regarding treatment. I have had calls from distraught parents who, after explaining that they have been concerned about their child's refusal to speak in public for 2 years, express dismay that weekly sessions are standard and that treatment may take 6 months, a year, or more. With very few exceptions, there is no shortcut to the treatment of selective mutism.

The consensus of experts is that selective mutism is best thought of as an anxiety disorder. There are exceptions, such as children who, for a period of time, refuse to speak to selected adults as a way of asserting themselves or as a way of being oppositional. These children are typically oppositional in other ways as well. The therapist must rely on his or her clinical intuition to distinguish between these two situations: the child who is *fearful* of speaking and the child who *will not* speak because he or she is angry. The refusal to speak in an angry child is best treated as one would treat refusal to perform other expected activities, such as getting ready for bed, brushing teeth, or sitting at the dinner table. Here I describe the way that anxiety-based selective mutism in a preschool-age child is treated using the integrated model. Chapter 9 contains a case illustrating the treatment of selective mutism in a school-age child.

Successful treatment of selective mutism requires the active participation of parents. It also requires the active participation of the child. In this way, it differs from treatment of some disruptive behavior problems that may be accomplished by meeting with parents only after the first several sessions. In treating a child's disruptive behavior, the family is your patient. In treating selective mutism, the child is your patient, and the parents are your cotherapists.

CASE ILLUSTRATION
Jay

When 4-year-old Jay first came to my office, he was absolutely silent. He did communicate, albeit nonverbally, from the beginning: He made eye contact and he smiled once or twice. After several visits, he began to pretend to be an animal, to climb on the furniture, and from time to time to growl like a dog, squawk like a monkey, and roar like a lion. A bright child, Jay was completely free of any form of developmental disability and without the slightest indication of pervasive developmental disorder of any kind. Neither was there any indication of hyperactivity. Even when climbing on the furniture, he was remarkably well-behaved and responsive to his mother's requests to be careful, to avoid a particular piece of furniture, to carefully remove his shoes before getting on the sofa. When he began to do this, I remarked to his mother that he was no longer selectively mute, that he was only selective for intelligible speech.

As he climbed on the furniture and pretended that he was an animal, he began to be much more active and freer in the office, making hiding places in the corners and swiveling the desk chair. I was intentionally playful in my interpretations, joking about how noisy the animals were and being startled when he hid behind my chair and pushed it a bit. This was not the right time to set a limit on his behavior. Instead, it was the right time to get into the game. After several visits during which Jay pretended to be an animal, Jay's animals began to grow progressively more aggressive. The "animals" became nosier and angrier, and Jay began to be far less responsive to his mother's requests. This was not at all like him, she told me, adding that he had previously been a poster child for compliance. Fortunately for me and the progress of therapy, Jay's mother took his increased aggression and defiance as a sign that he was becoming freer to express himself. Rather than expressing displeasure with him or with therapy, she applauded his growth.

Jay and his family took a trip to visit relatives, and I did not see them for a week. Upon their return, Jay was even more boisterous than before. His parents told me that he had been far less shy than previously and that he had spoken to his grandparents for the first time. Freedom to express himself in therapy had begun to generalize to other settings. In therapy, he had begun to feel free enough to experience and show the aggression typical of a 2- to 3-year-old, a developmental phase he had passed through but not yet experienced. In that first meeting after his trip to his relatives, his reexperiencing of an earlier time became clearer. Mixed in with Jay's animal noises were words that he blurted out repeatedly and angrily: "Caca! Caca!" Once again, I credit his mother, who identified what he was saying, laughed a bit, and repeated to him what she had heard. She accepted his need to be younger so that he might grow. Her playfulness helped him experience and grow. You can't treat an uptight kid if you are uptight yourself: You must be totally comfortable inside yourself; if you are not, do not attempt play in therapy until you are comfortable.

The next phase of treatment with Jay began when he started to construct hiding places in the office. After several attempts, he managed to create a kind of tent by stretching a small blanket from the chair to the adjacent sofa and anchoring them in place with books. From his new hiding place, animal sounds quickly began to emerge: growls, squeals, and squawks. Staying with the playful attitude, I began to speak to anyone who might be listening about the "animal."

P. G.: Animal, are you there?

Jay: (animal noises).

P. G.: Good. Animal, can you make a "buh" sound?

Jay : Buh.

P. G.: Great. Animal, can you make a "puh" sound?

Jay : Puh.

This continued through the consonants and then the vowel sounds, one at a time. Jay was gradually allowing himself to use language in the guise of his animal persona.

By allowing himself to pretend that it was his "animal," not himself, speaking, Jay freed himself to overcome this developmental hurdle. Playfulness, but not play therapy, was the essential element here. Equally essential was his mother's very active participation in therapy, her encouragement of Jay's emerging sense of self, and her reassurance that she could tolerate his anger and verbal aggression. Therapy with older children and adolescents also benefits from a therapist's willingness to be playful, and from her capacity to be playful, as the next two chapters illustrate.

CHAPTER 9

Problems of School-Age Children

Pretty much all the honest truthtelling there is in the world is done by children.

—Oliver Wendell Holmes

The distinction between problems of preschool children and those of school-age children is admittedly artificial. The principles that were detailed at the beginning of the previous chapter apply equally to working with school-age children, and some of the problems overlap as well. Selective mutism is seen in both school-age and preschool children, and a case illustrating this is included here. The treatment of encopresis, which is included in this chapter, could have easily been included in Chapter 8. School-age children are sometimes disruptive in ways similar to preschoolers. I chose to assign the problem of keeping a young child in bed to Chapter 8 and the problem of sleepwalking to this chapter, but the order could easily have been reversed.

Sleep Problems

Sleepwalking and night terrors are developmental issues. Children with these sleep disturbances are not treated as having disorders per se, but they worry parents, and so it is a good idea to be familiar enough with them so that you can offer information and reassurance.

Both night terrors and sleepwalking occur when a child is partially awake. Parents recognize that children who sleepwalk are, in fact, asleep. They often do not recognize that children experiencing night terrors also are asleep. This results from equating night terrors with nightmares. Nightmares differ from night terrors in several ways. Night terrors occur within the first several hours after a child falls asleep; nightmares are more likely to occur toward the middle of the night or later. Children wake up after nightmares and are able to tell parents what frightened them. Children who experience night terrors do not wake up; although they may move about, talk loudly, or scream and cry in fright, they are still asleep. Parents often say things like "It was as if he was looking through me." Parents are often upset by this, believing that their children are frightened of *them*. For this reason, it is important to explain that their child is actually dreaming and is still asleep. Parents who mistake a night terror for a nightmare will try to wake their child up to "snap out of it." This will not work. Instead, parents should observe their children to be sure that they do not accidentally injure themselves.

Night terrors are usually fairly brief, and children will eventually lie down and resume sleeping quietly. Sleepwalking occurs relatively earlier in the night. Waking a sleepwalking child can be quite difficult, and there is no need to do so. Instead, parents should be advised to watch their sleepwalking children to make sure they do not fall or hurt themselves in some other way. It may be possible for parents to guide the child back to bed without waking him or her up. When children sleepwalk habitually, parents should take steps to sleepwalk-proof their home, including installing appropriate locks on outside doors.

Encopresis

When children past the age of toilet training have persistent problems with soiling, their parents almost always consult their child's pediatrician or family doctor first. Although this problem can, and does, occur in preschoolers as well as school-age children, many parents take a wait-and-see attitude until just before the child enters school.

This section could as easily have been included in the previous chapter: The treatment is the same whether the child is 4 or 7. General pediatricians typically refer children with encopresis to child and family therapists when the standard protocol does not work, or when parents are resistant to one or more aspects of the standard protocol.

Although it is possible for a child to have encopresis without constipation due to Hirschsprung disease, this is extremely rare. Far more common is encopresis with constipation, or more accurately, encopresis due to constipation. When a child is chronically constipated, the child can develop megacolon, a condition in which the colon begins to stretch and to lose elasticity. Megacolon can also lead to decreased sensitivity in the colon, so that children with this condition receive a weaker signal when it is time to move their bowels. The colon becomes full of hard, dried-out fecal material. Sometimes this is so extreme that a child appears to have a pot belly. Encopresis occurs when liquid stool flows around the mass of hard stool and leaks out of the rectum.

Because the cause of the encopresis is constipation, the first step in treating encopresis is to treat the constipation. Backing up one more step, the most frequent cause of constipation is that the child has had one or more very painful bowel movements and has begun to intentionally hold his (over 75 percent of all encopretic children are boys) stool in to avoid having another painful bowel movement. This withholding of stool becomes habitual. The more the child holds stool in, the larger and more painful the eventual bowel movement will be.

When encopresis with constipation occurs in an otherwise healthy child of 10 or older, serious consideration must be given to the possibility that the child has been sexually traumatized. The best way to discover this is through the same sort of clinical interview you would conduct with any other child of this age who was referred to you. Because such a significant part of the treatment of encopresis is behavioral and medical, it is tempting to forgo your usual clinical interview. Don't. When I was on the behavioral pediatrics team at the Children's Hospital of Philadelphia, we were scheduled to see a 12-year-old boy with severe constipation and encopresis. As we discussed the referral prior to seeing the boy, I mentioned to my medical colleagues that the clinical lore of psychodynamically oriented treatment would suggest that this boy may have been sexually abused and was unconsciously attempting to protect himself against this in the future. Although I had been the one to introduce this possibility, I was not much more comfortable with it than were the pediatricians, so when they suggested that we focus on his colon and not on his psyche, I was happy to oblige. By the end of this boy's interview and exam, however, we learned that he had been repeatedly raped at knifepoint by a relative. Had the right questions not been asked, it is doubtful that he would have revealed the traumas he had experienced.

The Physical Medicine Side of Encopresis Treatment

The treatment of encopresis with constipation has both psychological and physical medicine components. Although general pediatricians can provide this treatment, their schedules are often so packed that they cannot spend the several hours with the family that are often required. Developmental-behavioral pediatricians have even more specialized training and experience in treating encopresis. However, because developmental-behavioral pediatricians are few in number and mostly hospital-based, the chance of a family's seeing one of these specialists is limited. Many cases of encopresis are treated by a general pediatrician monitoring the physical aspect of treatment in concert with a child psychologist or child and family therapist addressing the psychological aspects.

Some of these patients will come to you from a pediatrician who has already made a diagnosis of encopresis with constipation and requests your help in implementing treatment. Others will arrive in your office for some other reason, and you will be the first professional to hear that the child is "having accidents." Your standard diagnostic interview will need some additions when you see a child whom parents describe in this way but who has not been thoroughly worked up medically. As with most subjects that are not discussed in "polite company," the more frank and straightforward you are, the easier it will be for parents. Ask what they mean by accidents. Do they happen every day? Do they find streaks in their child's underwear? Or do they find clumps of stool in his underwear? Is the stool formed or runny? Keep asking questions until you are certain that you know all the messy details. It's a bit like asking someone about their Rorschach responses: You need to inquire until you are sure that you can "score" the response. I once was interviewing a woman on the subject of her son's soiling and received her reassurance that he was not constipated, only to later learn that he had been constipated for many months but now had totally liquid stool due to taking too high a dose of stool softener.

Although the details vary, treatment of encopresis usually involves a bowel clean-out procedure followed by a period of bowel retraining. The clean-out procedure usually begins with one or more enemas to remove the hardened stool that is blocking the colon, followed by introduction of high-fiber foods, increased fluids, exercise (especially sit-ups), and the use of stool softeners such as mineral oil. Although neither the enemas nor the stool softeners require prescriptions, it is best to leave the decision about dosage and type to the child's pediatrician. In cases of extreme constipation, the child's pediatrician may use stronger, prescription-only agents or, in truly extreme cases, hospitalize the child for bowel clean-out.

Once any necessary clean-out has been accomplished, the physical side of treatment focuses on ensuring that the child does not become constipated again while the colon regains its normal shape and function. This means that parents have to be religious about administering whatever stool softener or laxative the child's pediatrician has recommended. It also means that they have to be very patient because there will be occasional accidents as the bowel recovers and the child gradually gets over the anxiety that has become associated with painful bowel movements. This is different from what happens when one sees children who have not yet been toilet trained but who have no history of constipation. Once these children begin to have bowel movements in the toilet rather than in a diaper, they rarely go backward, except for a very rare accident when they are ill or don't make it to the bathroom on time. Children with histories of constipation, on the other hand, are apt to fall back into it at any time if their new regimen of high-fiber foods, fluids, and stool softeners is not consistently maintained.

The Psychological Side of Encopresis Treatment

The preceding section is all by way of background for what happens in your office. If everything goes according to plan, if parents and child are totally cooperative with the pediatrician's recommendations, a psychologist will never see the child. We see the other children and their parents. We see the children who refuse to take their mineral oil. We see the parents who can't bring themselves to give their child an enema. And we see the parents who stop giving their child his laxative or stool softener as soon as the child has one formed stool and is accident-free for 2 or 3 days.

So, as if by definition, we therapists see only the difficult cases. As you begin treatment of these challenging cases, you will not go wrong if you remember these three principles: reassurance, reassurance, reassurance. Parents, and this almost always means mothers, of encopretic children need reassurance that you can help them. They need reassurance that this is not a symptom of some awful underlying pathology. They need reassurance that their child's encopresis is not conclusive proof that they are bad parents. They need to know you are with them. Once that is established, therapy involves reiterating what the pediatrician has said, explaining what causes encopresis, and offering support in staying with the plan.

The preceding discussion of the psychological side of encopresis treatment assumes that the toileting problem developed and is being maintained by factors such as a history of painful bowel movements, insufficient fiber in the diet, and significant constipation. And many, perhaps most cases of encopresis do involve these issues. Others are not so simple. These are the cases in which soiling is largely, or even totally the result of emotional factors. Seven-year-old Josh was temperamentally very sensitive. He was small for his age and had been slow to speak. In many ways, he appeared to be a year or 18 months younger than his chronological age, an impression reinforced by his shyness. He was a child who would have done well in a gentle, quiet family relatively free of conflict. But he was not fortunate enough to be born into such a family. His parent's relationship was highly conflicted. His father was more than a bit cool, and his mother could easily overwhelm him with her emotional intensity. As a result, his gut was almost constantly in uproar: sometimes refusing to move, and sometimes forcing him to run to the bathroom, and sometimes getting there too late. His treatment was multipronged: behaviorally oriented treatment of the encopresis, therapy to address his anxiety, and work with his parents to increase their understanding of his sensitivity.

Five-year-old Andrew's family was unhappy in a different way. His mother had cancer as a young woman, and while she and her husband hoped that her treatment had resulted in a cure, knew that it could recur anytime. It was one of the elephants in the home of which no one spoke. The other elephant was his father's history of alcoholism. Although it would have been convenient to lay blame for his drinking on anxiety about his wife's health, they both knew that this was self-deception in the extreme. He had attended enough AA meetings to know that drinking was the problem, not the result of a problem. When he had a month-long period of sobriety, the standard encopresis treatment package, as described in previous sections, was well on its way to resolving the problem. When he started to drink again, Andrew's accidents returned with vengence. He had to get his drinking under control in order for him to help Andrew get his bowels under control.

Anxieties, Fears, and Phobias

Anxieties among school-age children typically manifest in one of three ways: anxieties about going to school (school avoidance), specific phobias, and somaticizing problems such as stomachache and headache.

────────────── **CASE ILLUSTRATION** ──────────────
Greg

Louise and Steve were concerned about the extent to which 11-year-old Greg's fear of thunderstorms (astraphobia) was affecting his life and theirs. Greg refused to go out of the house if it was raining (a thunderstorm might be on the way), if the sky was dark and ominous-looking (a thunderstorm might be on the way), or if the Weather Channel announcer said that there was a chance of a thunderstorm (a thunderstorm was definitely on the way). One result of Greg's phobia was that many family trips were canceled or postponed. Another was that he had begun to miss a lot of school.

There were two factors largely responsible for Greg's fears. The first, and most obvious, was that a cousin in another state had been on the telephone during a thunderstorm, lightning had struck a nearby phone line, and he had received a frightening shock. The second factor was that Greg, a very bright boy and a boy with considerable intellectual curiosity, had done far too much research into all the possible horrible things that can happen if one is struck by lightning and the randomness of such events.

Steve and Louise had very patiently addressed Greg's fears and talked with him about the difference between taking reasonable precautions (e.g., not standing in the middle of a golf course holding a metal umbrella during a thunderstorm) and unreasonable precautions (e.g., refusing to go to school when the Weather Channel said there was a 10 percent chance of rain sometime during the day). These explanations got them nowhere. They had tried forcing Greg to go to school. Sometimes he went, and sometimes he didn't, but the whole family was upset whichever occurred. That was when they started looking for another approach.

The treatment approach for Greg included work with his family and with him individually. Because Greg was both frustrated by his phobia and embarrassed by it, it took quite some time for therapy to actually get going. After six meetings, Greg dropped out, saying that seeing a psychologist made him feel that there was something wrong with him, and so he would no longer participate. Much to his parents' credit, they continued to meet with me weekly, focusing both on Greg's fears and on a career-related dilemma that had recently confronted Steve. This transition exemplifies the approach this model takes to working with parents in the context of a child treatment case, as discussed in Chapter 6.

Eventually, Greg returned, saying that he wanted help in overcoming his fear of storms. He had made it clear that talking about the actual probabilities of lightning striking the spot where he was sitting or standing was not going to help him. So we took a deeper look at the emotional aspect of his fears. Here is how he explained the school avoidance that had developed secondary to his phobia: "If it starts to get really dark and rainy when I'm in school, I'll start to worry about thunder and lightning. I might start to cry. Kids will notice. I'll be really embarrassed." It was crucial at this point that all the adults present "got it." Nobody told him he shouldn't feel that way. To the contrary, his feelings were solidly validated.

Greg needed to know that there was something concrete he could do if he started to worry about a storm. My offer to teach him to control his pulse, blood pressure, and skin temperature appealed to his scientific side and to his desire for control. We began with diaphragmatic breathing, later adding the use of a simple biofeedback device (e.g., a Walkman), and finally making him a tape that included imagery we had decided on together and that he could listen to on his Walkman if he was beginning to get worked up about a possible storm. (A protocol for all of this is included in Appendix C.) The combination of these elements was successful. School attendance was no longer an issue. Later that fall, he and his entire class ran into a huge thunderstorm while returning from a field trip. He had his tape with him but did not need to listen to it. Knowing it was there was sufficient.

School Pressures

Elementary and middle school students experience extraordinary pressure to excel—not just to succeed, but to excel. Fourth- and 5th-grade teachers talk about preparing for high school; middle school teachers talk about college admissions. Even academically gifted high school students worry about how their school grades will affect their chances of admission to a prestigious law, business, medical, or veterinary school. And most of this is without parental pressure.

Some students try to deal with this pressure by pretending not to be interested in their grades. Others try self-medication with alcohol or marijuana. The healthiest of them tolerate the anxiety and end up in our offices, totally stressed out. Some of these stressed-out adolescents have been pushing themselves since elementary school. They do not know how to relax. They worry that only two possibilities lie ahead: the Ivy League or its equivalent and success, or "somewhere else" and failure. They are pure Aristotelians: Life is A or not A. One of the goals of therapy should be to help them see other possibilities.

The second group of anxious preadolescents and adolescents are those who are not yet ready to deal directly with their anxieties, instead experiencing them physically. In my practice, this has tended to mean gastrointestinal involvement of one kind or another. Some patients have diagnosed conditions (e.g., Crohn's disease, colitis). Others have what medical people refer to as "abdominal pain of unknown origin." They have had all the appropriate tests, and nothing appears to be physically wrong. After pediatric gastroenterologists rule out the diseases and conditions they are trained to treat, a therapist's office is often the next step. One gastroenterologist summed it up: "There's a direct connection from the gut to the brain." Gastroenterologists treat the gut side of this connection, and we treat the rest.

Treating this sort of physical manifestation of stress means helping the patient become aware of the stress and anxiety so that he or she can join the first group of patients, those who know that they are anxious. For these children, you may wish to be more self-disclosing than usual. We have all been through middle school, high school, and the college application process. The memories are typically sharp enough to be useful and have been subjected to enough analysis to no longer be areas of acute vulnerability. Self-disclosure can also help further the patients' process of discovering what the anxiety is about. Relaxation training of the sort that helped Greg is often helpful to these children, too.

—————————— CASE ILLUSTRATION ——————————
Doug

Treatment of school-age children with focused anxieties can sometimes be very brief indeed. If we can help children put their worry into words, parents are eager to do what they can to alleviate it.

Doug's father called on a Friday afternoon to ask if I could help his son overcome an acute fear of going to school. I had an opening early the next Monday morning and invited him to bring Doug in. My goal was to see if we could get Doug to school that day, thinking that we could handle other issues later. After quickly taking a history, I learned that pregnancy, labor, and delivery had been unremarkable; and that Doug had hit all his developmental milestones, had never been in the hospital, took no medications, and was in good overall health, as were his siblings and parents. I also learned that there had been no obvious acute stressors. I then talked with Doug and within 15 minutes learned that he was afraid he would not hear the announcement over the school public address system dismissing children whose parents were picking them up and that his mother or father would not see him and so would leave without him. His father responded, as I was certain he would, by reassuring Doug that he or Doug's mother would wait and that they would not leave without him, no matter if he was dismissed early or late. Having reached that conclusion after about 35 minutes, I asked Doug if he was ready to go to school. He was. His father and he left with the understanding that they would call if there were any further issues, which there were not.

——————— **CASE ILLUSTRATION** ———————
Suzy

Suzy was about 8 years old when her parents brought her to me. She had not spoken in school since preschool, and the very small and nurturing school she attended had made accommodations for her. Her parents and her school believed that she would "grow out of it." She had not. Family history revealed that her mother and several other relatives had been extremely shy as children. Suzy's parents told me that Suzy spoke freely at home, with a few close relatives, and with other children as long as no adults were present.

It was easy to understand how Suzy's teachers could so readily accommodate her absence of speech. A pretty child, she smiled and connected very well nonverbally. It would be easy for any adult to believe that she was simply shy and would begin to speak in public if the adults around her were sufficiently supportive and patient. The problem was that the adults around her (especially her parents) were extraordinarily patient and supportive, and yet she had not begun to speak in public. Clearly, something else was called for.

After completing the initial interview, I talked with Suzy's parents about selective mutism and how we would treat it by trying to learn more about what made Suzy anxious and by arranging situations where she could gradually become more comfortable having people hear her voice. I emphasized that this would be a joint effort, that I needed their help and involvement for treatment to be successful.

Medication was helpful in this case, but the most crucial ingredient was the active participation of Suzy's parents. The turning point in treatment came when Suzy, at the encouragement of her parents, brought a board game from home. The game was one involving the usual roll of the dice and spin of the spinner, followed by one player reading a question from a randomly selected card. Suzy's parents encouraged, cajoled, and gently pushed Suzy to begin to read from the card when it was her turn. After she had been doing that for several weeks, they similarly encouraged, cajoled, and gently pushed her to begin to answer questions when it was her turn. She did so, at first with one-letter responses only, taking advantage of the multiple choice (A, B, C, D) format of possible responses. Gradually, she uttered one word and ultimately full-sentence responses.

I am not suggesting that my only role was to sit back and watch. Rather, I am suggesting that perhaps my most important contribution was in supporting Suzy's parents as they helped her break free of her fear of speaking.

Children with Social Understanding Deficits

Social understanding problems can be part of the picture for children with autism, Asperger's syndrome, nonverbal learning disabilities, or pervasive developmental disorders (PDD) not otherwise specified. They can also be a problem for children who do not clearly fit any of these diagnostic categories. In an outpatient private practice, one is more likely to see children at the margins than one is to see children who are clearly Autistic. The same child may be diagnosed with mild Asperger's syndrome by one clinician, with attention-deficit disorder with social skill deficits by another, and with a nonverbal learning disability by a third. When a young person has reached adolescence without receiving treatment, the stresses of that time of life may precipitate a crisis. Some of the behavioral aspects of that crisis can lead to diagnostic errors. An adolescent boy with undiagnosed Asperger's became overwhelmed by anxiety when he was subjected to daily taunting and bullying at school. When he exploded in school and threatened to kill the bully, the consulting psychiatrist told parents that their son was schizophrenic. There was no doubt that this boy had acted "crazy." The mistake was in assuming that crazy behavior always has the same cause. This boy had reacted to what was unbearable stress. Another child might have reported the bullying to teachers and parents long ago. My patient, however, did not understand the situation well enough. Neither did he have an understanding of how to ask for help.

Therapy for children and adolescents with social understanding problems proceeds at a different pace from the treatment of many other patients. Children and adolescents have to learn to compensate for their difficulty in understanding social realities. Pediatric medicine provides useful analogies. Treatment for these children is analogous to treatment of chronic illnesses. Pediatricians who treat chronically ill children form lasting relationships with their patients and their patients' parents. They help both child and family manage symptoms. They follow the child for many years. The use of the word "follow" can be illuminating: It implies careful watching, and it implies that intervention is tailored to the patient's need at the time. So, too, do we follow patients with social understanding issues. There may be times in a child's life when weekly therapy sessions are needed, such as during early adolescence. At other times, a patient may be responsibly followed at intervals of 4 to 6 weeks. I always encourage parents to call if problems present during the intervening weeks, reminding them that it is far easier to intervene when problems are smaller.

The rationale for this pattern of treatment, every 4 to 6 weeks for as long as 6 or 8 years, rather than weekly for 6 months or a year, is straightforward. The condition being treated is not an illness to be cured. It is an intrinsic part of the child's or adolescent's life and self. The child who has problems making friends in 3rd grade is the same child who mistakes friendly teasing for bullying in 5th grade. He is the same child who gets set up to be embarrassed in 8th grade. And he is the same adolescent who is unsure about how to react to a girl who smiles at him in class in 10th grade. This life is all of a piece; this challenge is present throughout. Helping him and his family means being present and *with* him as he faces various development challenges. It means doing some basic social skills training. It means helping his parents work with his school. It means being as real with him as he can tolerate you being. And it means being willing to problem-solve with him. An adolescent with social understanding issues does not need a passive interpreter. He or she needs a guide, a friend, a mentor.

Talking with Parents about Diagnosis

Children with social understanding issues need parents who understand what these children are dealing with and how to help them manage their feelings. When a child appears to have some Asperger-like features but does not meet the diagnostic criteria for Asperger's syndrome, it is never completely clear how best to respond to parents' questions about why he or she has persistent difficulties.

My rule of thumb has become "When in doubt, say so." I open such discussions by sharing my belief that the diagnosis of Asperger's syndrome has been oversold. It can be useful, but it is far less precise than many believe and it has far less explanatory value than it appears to have. I continue by reviewing what I and the parents know about their child: that he is bright, that he wants to do well, that he has difficulties with interpersonal situations, and that he can get hung up on one idea or activity in an obsessive way. I explain that we can be most helpful by focusing on their child's strengths and specific problems rather than becoming obsessive ourselves about whether he meets diagnostic criteria for syndrome X or Y. With all of this as background, we are then able to talk about social understanding issues as being associated with social anxiety, with Asperger's syndrome, with nonverbal learning disabilities, and, in the more severe cases, with other forms of PDD. When the child in my office is on the very mild end of this continuum, we talk about how his problems are similar to those that people with Asperger's have but are much milder.

Biofeedback in Relaxation Training

Biofeedback procedures have been used in the treatment of a number of problems of childhood and adolescence. The more established uses involve the treatment of pain (especially headache pain) and anxiety. Some practitioners have begun to expand this to include treatment for attentional issues as well. A basic point regarding biofeedback is that it is not really a treatment, just as a cholesterol reading is not a treatment for hypercholesteremia and a blood pressure cuff reading is not a treatment for hypertension. Biofeedback devices are measurement devices that have the advantage of providing instantaneous feedback to both patient and practitioner. The name says it all: Biofeedback devices provide feedback about biological (i.e., physiological) processes. These data can be used singly or in combination to help patients learn to control and manipulate physiological processes that are usually not under conscious control. As such, they can be useful as long as one basic principle is headlined.

That principle is that the use of a biofeedback device should be meaningfully integrated into therapy; it should be delivered in the context of a therapeutic relationship. Attaching wires to a patient's hands, chest, or scalp can provide interesting physiological information, but it is not by itself therapy. On the other hand, it can be a very useful adjunct in treating anxiety-related conditions. I use a very simple and inexpensive biofeedback device to facilitate patients' learning relaxation techniques. After talking with patients about relaxation, I explain that when people have been anxious for a long time, they may not know what it feels like to relax and that it can be helpful to have some feedback in the early stages of this process of learning to relax. This is followed by an explanation of biofeedback and introduction of the device, a small indoor-outdoor thermometer. I briefly explain how capillary vasodilation occurs during relaxation and how this results in increased peripheral skin temperature, reflected in elevated thermometer readings.

Collaboration and Advocacy

Providing treatment for children and adolescents means that you will be communicating with and, ideally collaborating with teachers and guidance counselors and perhaps principals, reading specialists, and others. In the best of all possible worlds, there will be open communication, shared goals, and mutual respect. Sometimes these three features flow together like three rivers running into a great bay, and the results can be very grat-ifying.

I saw my first selectively mute child, a 4-year-old boy, in the beginning of the spring of 1984. When he entered kinder-garten the following fall, he was just barely beginning to speak. I observed him in his classroom. His kindergarten teacher and I met and we developed a plan: I would continue to see him with his family for therapy; she would clearly communicate the expectation that he speak in class, would ignore him when he did not, and would reinforce the heck out of him when he did. By late spring that year, he was just like any other kinder-gartner, and treatment was concluded. Five years ago, his mother called me. She asked if I remembered her family—How could I forget?—and told me that my former patient was in his sophomore year of college and doing very well. This kind of collaboration works well for everyone involved: teacher, thera-pist, child, and parents. Much as I wish that I could claim credit for it, much of the success of this collaboration goes to the kindergarten teacher. She was experienced, unflappable, sure of her expertise, and still open to suggestions. Most im-portant, she was not anxious about my patient's selective mutism. Unfortunately, we therapists do not get to choose our patients' teachers, and not all possess this happy confluence of personality traits.

A proactive therapist can increase the odds of a happy col-laboration by being respectful of teachers' expertise and ex-perience, by asking for their help, and by getting out of the office to meet with them. Of course, one cannot meet every child's teachers, and one need not do so. But when treating conditions that demand collaboration (e.g., selective mutism, disruptive class behavior), a face-to-face meeting is worth the effort. The classroom teacher has developed implicit norms about classroom behavior, just as you have developed implicit norms about how children of different ages act in your office. A classroom visit gives you an opportunity to see your patients in their natural setting. It also shows the teacher that you are interested in knowing what happens in school and in learning from those who work with children in their classrooms. All of this is far better done before there is a major problem, rather than after.

As a standard part of my intake procedure, I request names and contact information for children's teachers and permission to place a brief phone call to inform the teachers of my involvement. On occasion, parents prefer that teachers not be informed that they have talked to a psychologist, but this is a relatively rare exception. Most parents appreciate knowing that their child's teacher and therapist are communicating.

Teachers and school administrators, principals and assistant principals, spend their days with children and so have many opportunities to observe children interacting in this important natural setting. Their observations of classroom, hallway, and recess behavior have great value. However, teachers and principals are not able to focus at length on individual children, as their responsibility is to ensure that the school as a whole runs smoothly. By necessity, this means that educators will be tuned in to behaviors that affect learning and that may reflect learning difficulties. These include off-task behavior, obvious indications of inattention, aggression, and other disruptive behavior, refusal to speak, and isolating from one's peer group. Some teachers may be especially psychologically minded or particularly intuitive and so may be aware of what children are experiencing beneath the surface, but it is not reasonable to expect all teachers to be able to do this. Educators are not therapists. They are not trained to recognize a child's anxiety when that anxiety is not interfering with classroom performance in obvious ways.

Recognizing the overlap in what child therapists and educators do, as well as the differences between what the two professions do, facilitates good communication. Approach educators in a collegial way, a way that actively searches for common understanding and shares problem solving. Look for someone with whom you can form an alliance. That person may be a principal, a classroom teacher, or a guidance counselor. Begin by sharing your observations, then ask that person's opinions as to what can be done. The solution that seems obvious to you may not be mentioned. The solution that is presented may not be what you would have thought of or even what you had hoped for.

Last September I saw Allison, a 1st-grader, in consultation as a result of anxiety that had become so severe that she was vomiting every morning before school. Allison described her school bus, which carried children from 1st through 6th grade, as being noisy and "scary." She needed some extra support in the morning, and I hoped for some flexibility on the part of school personnel in altering their policy of discouraging parents from being present in the school building. The obvious plan would have been to have her mother drive her in the morning and to walk her to class. This support could have been gradually removed over a period of a week or so. This environmental therapy could have been combined with several office-based sessions focused on helping Allison feel more confident about riding the bus and the transition to 1st grade. Allison's principal saw the situation differently. He did not know that Allison was vomiting in the morning; he knew only that Allison's mother had told him of Allison's anxiety about riding the bus, that Allison behaved well in the classroom, and that he was not comfortable having parents in his school on a daily basis. His recommendation to Allison's mother was straightforward: Put her on the bus.

This difference in perspective is typical and reflects the differences between the culture of the school system and the culture of therapy. Working effectively with schools means learning about and appreciating that culture. The difference between my warmer and fuzzier approach to Allison's fearfulness and her principal's no-nonsense recommendation only meant that relatively more work would have to be done in the therapy office. It did not stop Allison from receiving appropriate educational services.

Unfortunately, there are instances in which a difference of opinion, or a cultural divide, does affect a child's learning directly. Some schools, and school districts, are happy to make accommodations and, if needed, special education services. Others are more reluctant to do so. When a collegial approach reaches a stalemate, parents sometimes choose to obtain the services of a professional educational advocate.

Advising Parents on School Selection

One of the major differences between treating a child in a public school and one attending a private school involves the degree to which both teacher and school experience ownership of the child and his or her educational program.

Parents who are weighing alternatives for their children's education often ask therapists' advice about making this decision. In my practice, this occurs most often when children have special needs and are about to enter school. The first question parents often have concerns the choice between public and private or parochial school. In general, the smaller class size of a private school can be a significant advantage for a child who tends to get lost in the crowd. Some children with mild learning issues do well in schools with a curriculum tailored to their needs.

There are several distinctly different types of private schools. Standard independent college preparatory schools (prep schools) have been around for many decades; some have been in operation for more than 150 years. These, often elite, schools offer small classrooms, individualized attention, and a demanding curriculum. In recent years, they have begun to offer academic supports such as untimed testing and tutoring in selected subjects. They do not exclude, as they once did, applicants with attention and concentration issues or those taking medication for mood issues. These traditional prep schools include those with an extraordinarily demanding curriculum suitable for gifted students and those appropriate for students of average ability. They are not, however, schools for those with learning disabilities or behavioral problems. Promotional materials for schools in the latter category typically state that they seek average-ability students, but this need not dissuade parents of children with low-average abilities from applying.

Some schools are geared to the needs of children and adolescents with mild to moderate learning issues. Their promotional materials typically refer to helping children identify and utilize their strengths, identify their personal learning style, and, of course, prepare for college. Faculty at these schools include some special education teachers and reading specialists. Schools in this category often have specific intensive programs designed to turn nonreaders into readers, and they often succeed. Although these schools will accept children with a diagnosis of attention-deficit/hyperactivity disorder, they are not equipped to manage disruptive children. Neither are they able to manage or treat children with such problems as selective mutism or obsessive-compulsive disorder.

Parents often assume that more expensive means better, but this is not always true. Many public schools do an excellent job of addressing children's learning issues. In addition, there is the very considerable advantage that the public school often has a greater investment in the child, a sense of ownership. Sometimes, a child presents issues or needs that are beyond those that his or her private school is prepared to address. Parents, who considered carefully before selecting that school, are often distressed to hear the school's recommendation that they consider the possibility of a different educational placement for the following year. Parents are more distressed when, in place of such a recommendation, they are told that their child must be withdrawn from the school immediately. This happens most often when the particular child presents issues at the edge of that school's comfort zone. A school that prides itself of being nurturing and helping children gain self-confidence may not feel that it is able to go as far as helping a selectively mute child overcome her anxieties about speaking in public. The fact that they may be underestimating what they can do, that they might be able to do a great job of helping that child, alters nothing. If having the child in one of their classrooms will make administrators and teachers anxious, they will not be able to help. Another private school may be unwilling to take a chance on a child who had some behavioral outbursts in the past, despite the absence of such outbursts for a year or longer. It is not at all uncommon for private and parochial schools to ask parents to remove children from preschool or kindergarten who are experiencing toileting problems of the sort I have presented here.

It is because the public schools do not have the option of asking parents to find another school that they have that strong sense of ownership. The feeling is: "This child is ours to educate, and we need to find a way to do that as effectively as possible." It is of course the law as well, but at better public schools, the commitment to finding a way to educate every child goes well beyond the legal mandate. Some children, such as those with mental retardation and autism, have needs that truly go beyond those that can be addressed in a regular public school classroom. For these children, too, the best programs are often those either run directly by the public school system or specialized private programs largely funded by school districts, either directly or indirectly.

CHAPTER 10

Problems of Adolescence

A violet in the youth of primy nature,
Forward, nor permanent, sweet, not lasting,
The perfume and suppliance of a minute.
> —William Shakespeare, *Hamlet*, Act 1, Scene 3

When treating adolescents, we must be ready to be at once the voice of adult experience and wisdom as well as the voice of someone who is willing to completely suspend judgment. This is not always an easy or happy combination, but it is necessary. Younger children are happy to relate to us as quasi-parents, sometimes quasi-grandparents. Adolescents are always conflicted about their relationships with their parents. The healthier among them recognize their need for limits and guidance, but they do not want it to come from their mother or father. For a therapist, assuming a traditionally parental stance at the beginning can drastically interfere with the developing therapeutic relationship. Every adolescent feels the need for an advocate. No adolescent feels the need for a judge. A therapist who tries to be a peer, on the other hand, is quickly labeled a phony. And a therapist who never disapproves of anything is irresponsible. The solution is to keep it real.

I had seen Sally for about 6 months when she was 10 years old. Five years later, her mother called to say that Sally had asked her to make an appointment. On the appointed day, Sally walked into the office dressed all in black, with chains on her neck, wrists, and waist, black makeup under her eyes and on her cheeks, and a small chain looped across the right side of her face from her pierced ear to a ring in her nose. We said hello and then talked about the issues that were on her mind. Seeing her concerns as far more important than how she was dressed, I made no mention of her "costume" at all. At her next visit, Sally expressed dismay: "That was really weird last week. You talked to me like I was a real person." I answered as any therapist would have: "You *are* a real person." Only after this exchange did Sally acknowledge that she had dressed as she had as a "test" to see if I would indeed treat her as a real person.

It has been said many times that adolescence is equal parts childhood and adulthood and that adolescents themselves fluctuate between the two developmental positions. Therapy with patients between 13 and 19 reflects this. In some ways, treating a depressed or anxious adolescent is similar to treating a depressed or anxious adult. Unlike younger children, but like adults, adolescents must buy in to the idea of therapy for it to work for them. Like adults, the best adolescent therapy candidates are those who seek it out, or at least request it, themselves. And like adults, the more psychologically minded adolescents gain the most from therapy. But patients between 13 and 19 are also like younger children in some ways. They often need to know in a more explicit and concrete way than do adults that we are on their side. This can mean several things: keeping their confidences, even when we know that parents would be disapproving and perhaps shocked if they knew what we come to know; helping them fully experience their anger toward parents and teachers, even when we know that parents and teachers would be disapproving, if not shocked, by these revelations. It also means being willing to be directly helpful and useful and not standing on ceremony. I have helped high school students decide what to write about for college application essays; explained the relationship among temperature, volume, and pressure of gases; and looked up many words in the dictionary. I have also helped adolescent patients anticipate and plan difficult conversations with boyfriends and girlfriends, figure out how to get what they want from parents, and how to confess to having misled parents, too.

Privacy Issues in Therapy with Adolescents

Because adolescents are minors, parents have the right to insist that all information be shared with them. So therapists cannot automatically promise that we will not share information with parents; this has to be discussed. I routinely discuss this in a first meeting with the adolescent and at least one, and preferably both, parents: "I prefer to treat all the discussions I'll be having with Joey/Samantha as private, unless, of course, I believe there is a risk of Joey/Samantha or someone else being hurt. Is that okay with you?" I have never had a parent say that it was not okay. I continue, "I can't make the same promise to you, though. If you come in or call and tell me about something that happened over the weekend, I will probably talk to Joey/Samantha about it. Of course, if we talk about your personal concerns, that will be private." I do not require patients or parents to sign a form attesting to this, as I do not want to begin my relationship with the family on a legalistic note. Rather, I write a brief chart note about the discussion.

Once in a while, an adolescent will preface a remark with a statement such as "I know you can't ever tell anybody anything I tell you here." The first time this happens, I explain that parents have a right to demand that I tell them everything (although, frankly, this has never happened), that I am obligated to repeat suspected child abuse, that I must take steps if I believe a patient may harm himself or herself or someone else, and that a court may, under certain circumstances, compel my testimony. My adolescent patients listen to this litany of caveats and then continue with what they were going to say. I have two reasons for going through this exercise: I want patients to be clear on the ground rules, and I want them to know that I take their privacy seriously.

Privacy issues become much more complex when one sees adolescents and parents jointly. I often use such sessions, or parts of sessions, to give adolescents an opportunity to tell their parents something difficult after having tried it out on me first. The process often goes like this: The adolescent tells me something, adding that he or she thought about talking with a parent about it but couldn't. We talk; then I ask the adolescent if he or she would like to share this concern with the parents now. The answer is yes about half of the time for 13-year-olds, decreasing with the adolescent's age until it reaches its nadir at 16 or 17.

Why Include Parents in the Treatment of Adolescents

The issue of when, whether, and how to involve parents in therapy with their adolescent children is a fluid one. I encourage parents to be present for an adolescent's first appointment. Subsequent to that first appointment, I give considerable weight to the adolescent's preferences, and those preferences vary considerably. Sixteen-year-old C.J.'s reaction to the possibility of a family session was that it sounded "weird," and was something without which he could do nicely. Seventeen-year-old Jay asked me not to meet with his parents and not to share any unnecessary information. He did agree that I would call to let them know that he had been in to see me and that he was not at imminent risk of hurting himself, and that I would inform them immediately if I ever had concerns about his safety. Sixteen-year-old Ely welcomed his parents' participation in therapy sessions: "They know me best and help me keep things in perspective."

The most complex situations arise when one is regularly meeting with adolescents and equally regularly, but separately, meeting with their parents. When the adolescent patient is doing well, and the parents' therapy focuses on individual or marital issues, rather than on parenting, the complexity is manageable and allows adhering to the standard contract regarding privacy. But, when the adolescent's emotional and or behavioral issues are spiking, and his or her parents are coming to see you specifically out of concern about their child's welfare, some modification to that contract may be called for. I rigidly adhere to my promise to the adolescents to treat information they share with me as private, including information about sexual behavior and drug and alcohol use, as long as these behaviors do not place the adolescent at imminent risk. There are limits, however. If, however, one of my depressed adolescent patients who experiences occasional suicidal ideation were to tell me that he was planning to ingest one of the various "designer drugs," I would inform his parents and tell him that I was doing so.

Even while honoring a commitment to privacy, there are ways to share observations with parents. One way that I do this is by sharing some of the things I have said to the adolescent, rather than things he or she has said to me.

Being a Reliable Parent without Being Parental

Fifteen-year-old Sherri informed me that she planned to smoke marijuana with a friend on the weekend and that there was nothing anyone could do or say to dissuade her. I was sure that this was true, but I was also convinced that this was in part a test: Would I be a reliable "parent?" Blaming, moralizing, or judging were not options. I chose instead to be an advocate and a provider of information. I explained that pot smoking would interfere with the antidepressant medication she had started 2 months earlier, which seemed to be helping. We talked about the central nervous system depressing aspects of marijuana use. I asked her what would happen if her parents found out and how she would feel about that. I told her a cautionary tale about a young patient of mine who was arrested because he was in the wrong place (handing money to a drug dealer) at the wrong time (when police had the dealer under surveillance). I expressed my concern about the possible adverse reactions of smoking tainted or chemically treated marijuana. I made sure she had my cell phone number in the event that she needed to talk.

Underachievement and Low Motivation

All too many parents labor under the erroneous belief that it is possible for children to be totally unmotivated and that this "lack of motivation" can be directly responsible for less than stellar grades. This belief is erroneous because their children are always motivated, but they may be motivated to achieve different goals from those their parents deem to be important. Rather than valuing high grades, for example, an adolescent may value showing his parents and authority figures that he can't be "pushed around." Another adolescent may place greater value on creativity than on high grades. A third may be more motivated to be popular. And a fourth may be motivated by creating an opportunity to demonstrate that she can do enough work in the last 4 weeks of a term, having done nothing whatsoever until then, to earn a B plus. Having observed the ways adolescents, and younger children, too, can be motivated, it is equally difficult to accept the notion that they are lazy. They are not lazy. Rather, they have different goals. The reinforcers for which they strive, and the values attached to those reinforcers, differ from what parents and teachers expect them to be.

During the late fall and early spring, parents call therapists for someone who can "motivate" their son or daughter to work harder and thus earn better grades. Such referrals are fraught with traps for the unwary. Parents have been blaming their children for not working hard enough or for not carrying out their responsibilities. If these parents believe that you are offering a means to change this pattern by the end of term, and it does not happen, they will be similarly upset with you. The solution to this quandary is to offer a different therapeutic contract. Unless you have discovered a formula for motivating underachievers, do not promise or even imply that you can do this. Instead, offer to help the adolescent discover what he or she wants—offer to help that adolescent reach his or her goals. Explain that you cannot do anything to raise a student's grades; only completing homework and studying can do that. Some parents will be unhappy with this, but they will recognize it as truth. If they still want your help, it will be with an understanding of what you can do and what you cannot do.

─────────── **CASE ILLUSTRATION** ───────────
Bob, Shirley, and Jack

Several years ago, Bob and Shirley called me full of concern for their 15-year-old son, Jack, a gifted artist and long-time underachiever. Jack had been diagnosed with attention-deficit/hyperactivity disorder by a local family doctor and was taking whichever medication was most popular at that time. Jack complained about various side effects; sometimes the medicine helped, and sometimes it did nothing for him. I could see little objective evidence that it was helping, but his parents were convinced that it was.

Bob and Shirley were two of the most genuinely nice people and the most concerned and supportive parents I have ever met. They were very aware of their son's artistic gifts and equally aware of how fierce the competition was for spots in the region's best art schools and how failing grades, even in nonart subjects, could undermine his chances of admission and of obtaining a scholarship. Their initial inclination, and mine, was to institute some sort of structure, a system of rewards and punishments, to ensure that Jack would do his schoolwork, prepare for tests, and achieve at a level at least close to what he was capable. So we tried many strategies in what I see now was a naïve hope that externally imposed consequences could make up for Jack's apparent lack of internal focus. This went on for some time. There were several 4- and 6-month periods when I did not see or hear from the family because things were going so well. There were also several month-long periods when we met weekly, trying first one strategy then another. Everything worked a little; nothing worked very well.

And then one day, a lightning bolt illuminated the sky. I asked Jack what he wanted and how he proposed to get it. What he wanted, it turned out, was to get good enough grades to gain entry to the most prestigious art school in his city and to have that accompanied by at least a partial scholarship. How he proposed to get it was to have his parents (and me) leave him alone to get his work done and his portfolio prepared as he saw fit.

He made a compelling argument. It was, after all, his future. I in turn made this argument to Bob and Shirley: If Jack is truly unable to handle scheduling his assignments and responsibilities, won't it be better for him to fail now, when he has the option of making up failures in summer school and reapplying to art school, than to fail out of art school or to be bounced from his first job for failing to get his work done? Failure now could be a truly valuable experience, not a tragedy. Let him try it on his own, I argued. Let him succeed or fail on his own. They agreed, though not without considerable anxiety. He did not fail. He got into that prestigious art school and will graduate this spring.

The reason this strategy was successful for Jack was because it focused not on his grades, but on his autonomy, his feelings, and his goals. The risk when seeing a case like this is that one will forget that the goal of therapy is to help patients integrate their feelings, thoughts, and actions. Sometimes that means taking the chance that they will get poor grades.

CASE ILLUSTRATION
Ricardo

Fifteen-year-old Ricardo was not doing well at his boarding school when Maria, his 25-year-old sister, called to ask if I could see him in therapy. Maria explained that their mother, Esmeralda, spoke English only haltingly, and Ricardo's father (the parents were divorced) spoke only Spanish, so she was arranging for his therapy. I agreed to see him and encouraged Maria and Esmeralda to drive the 2 hours to be present, if possible.

In that first meeting, I learned that Esmeralda's command of English was much better than her daughter's description had led me to believe. It was certainly far better than my knowledge of Spanish or any other non-English language, as I explained to her.

Ricardo's academic deficiencies were significant. He had missed many assignments, and his grades consisted of more Ds than otherwise. More significant, Ricardo had recently left campus without permission to go home because he was worried that his mother's paramour might be assaultive with her or his younger siblings. Ricardo had also accumulated more detention hours, mostly for cutting classes (more than 100), than he could possibly serve. He had developed a reputation as a fighter. As a result of this and his low grades, Ricardo was on probation.

In our first individual meeting, Ricardo told me that he was still worried about his mother's welfare, her drinking, and what he referred to as "her issues." He denied ever being depressed or anxious and said that he was trying to "lay off fighting." He said that he was uncertain about college and a career but had thought of being a Navy Seal or a lawyer. For the remainder of this appointment, Ricardo told me about the rules at his school, which were many and largely arbitrary. I took pains to explain that I was not working for his school, had no formal relationship with his teachers or anyone else there, and would not share information (with the usual caveats regarding imminent risk of harm to self or others). I was also intentionally very forthcoming about my reaction to what sounded like a very authoritarian environment at his school. When I heard something that would have annoyed me if I were a student there, I said so. If it would have angered me, I said so. And if it would have intimidated me, I said so. In this and subsequent sessions, we talked a lot about the unreasonableness of school rules and the apparent harshness of some of the teachers. I focused on helping Ricardo learn to separate wheat from chaff so that we might identify possible allies and supporters among the faculty. And I strongly, clearly, and repeatedly advised him to refrain from fighting. We were able to form an alliance: the middle-aged, middle-class White therapist and the Hispanic adolescent from the inner city. Admittedly, part of the alliance was based on the adage "My enemy's enemy is my friend," but I would like to think that there was more to it than that.

Ricardo stopped fighting and gradually worked off enough of his detention hours that the dean forgave the rest of them. He made up missing homework and after 3 months had a B average in most subjects. Things had settled down at home, and so Ricardo rarely voiced worry about his mother or siblings. The gap that still existed between our personal frames of reference became clear when Ricardo returned from a long weekend at home. He told me about spending time with a friend from the neighborhood, a boy of his age. He described his friend as always being in trouble and as being involved in selling drugs. "He carries a gun now. A *big* one." I commented that his friend was perhaps living on borrowed time. Ricardo replied, "Five or 6 years, that's all he has. Five or 6 years at the *most*." This provided a great opportunity for us to talk about whether it was truly a good idea to hang with this particular friend in the future.

Eating Disorders

Therapists who work with adolescents will inevitably encounter cases with eating disorder features.* This is more likely than it was in the past for two reasons, one positive and one not. The positive reason is that therapists, doctors, parents, teachers, and

---

* I wish to thank Rosalind Kaplan, MD, for her assistance in writing this section.

peers have become educated about eating disorders and are more likely to recognize them. The negative reason is that the increased incidence is not due only to greater awareness of the disorder, but to the greater frequency with which adolescents and young adults are actually developing eating disorders, and that these disorders, which used to be primarily seen in White, upper-middle-class girls, have crossed lines of race, sex, and socioeconomic status. Women of color and women in lower socioeconomic classes are now regularly diagnosed, and men account for about 10 percent of diagnosed eating disorders.

Eating disorders are classified as anorexia nervosa or bulimia nervosa, depending on whether bingeing and purging is present as a major feature. The third category, eating disorder not otherwise specified, is diagnosed when a patient meets some criteria for each of the two subtypes but not a sufficient number of criteria to make the diagnosis.

The most important point for therapists is that many patients with eating disorders hide them completely. For this reason, it is important for therapists who work with adolescents to routinely screen for eating disorders. Adolescents at particularly high risk include those who have family histories of eating disorders or of alcohol or drug abuse, those whose self-esteem is closely tied to body image, those who were obese as younger children, and those who participate in "body-conscious" sports such as gymnastics, dance, crew, and wrestling.

The etiology of anorexia, bulimia, and other eating disorders is mutlifactorial. Studies of identical twins raised separately and descriptive family studies strongly suggest a genetic component, but environmental and cultural factors also play a role. A number of psychological theories have been proposed, including a need for control when parents are intrusive, the wish to avoid sexual contact (there is a correlation between eating disorders and sexual abuse), and avoidance of other conflicts by focusing on food. Any or all of these may be valid in some cases, but each patient has his or her own set of personal circumstances. Our culture's fixation on appearance and particularly on thinness likely plays a significant role in the development of eating disorders. A study of young women in Fiji before and after the introduction of television showed that the incidence of eating disordered behaviors and body dissatisfaction increased dramatically 3 years after TV became available, and that those who watched more TV were more likely to feel "too big or too fat" (Becker et al., 2002).

Physical complications of eating disorders can affect every body system, and in very serious ways. Weight loss may induce amenorrhea (loss of menstrual periods), resulting in osteoporosis from lack of estrogen. Anorexia can temporarily slow the gastrointestinal tract. The frequent vomiting and laxative use associated with bulimia can cause permanent damage to the gastrointestinal tract. Dehydration may lead to kidney problems, and loss of electrolytes in purging may cause fatal cardiac arrhythmias, seizures, and muscle breakdown. Ipecac (used to induce vomiting) can cause other damage to the heart. Malnutrition may also cause liver inflammation, bone marrow suppression, and thyroid abnormalities.

If you find yourself treating an adolescent with an eating disorder, the first step should be to identify colleagues with whom you can form a multidisciplinary team, which should include, in addition to the therapist, an internist or pediatrician, a nutritionist, and possibly a psychopharmacologist if the therapist is not a psychiatrist. All members of the team should be well versed in the treatment of eating disorders, and there must be good communication among team members. Although some eating disorder patients may need inpatient care, outpatient treatment is preferable unless the patient is seriously compromised either medically or psychologically.

The internist or pediatrician will monitor the patient on a regular basis for signs of dehydration, electrolyte imbalance, and cardiac abnormalities. If any significant medical compromise is noted, the patient must be stabilized in a medical unit and then transferred to an eating disorder unit for ongoing treatment. Feeding in the inpatient setting is usually by mouth, but if necessary, nasogastric feedings can be instituted. Once the patient has completed an inpatient program, transitional day treatment or intensive outpatient treatment (several evenings per week) is typical before the patient returns to office-based outpatient therapy. Medication may play a role, particularly in the treatment of bulimia and binge eating disorders. Fluoxetine has been the drug most extensively studied, but topiramate may also have a role. Other medications are used as indicated for comorbid depression and anxiety.

More common in a typical outpatient practice than a patient with full-blown anorexia or bulimia is a patient with subclinical eating problems such as occasional vomiting or unnecessary dieting (but not health-endangering), as in the following clinical vignette.

——— CASE ILLUSTRATION ———
Janet

Sixteen-year-old Janet exhibited a number of eating problems. She often skipped meals, sometimes complaining that gastrointestinal pain made it impossible for her to eat. Once or twice a week, she complained of gastric discomfort and vomited intentionally. She had also induced vomiting several times when angry at her parents for refusing to give her access to the family car. On those occasions, she was completely aware of what she was doing, and why, and she openly shared this with her parents. As this pattern began to emerge, I asked an internist specializing in the treatment of eating disorders to see Janet. After evaluating her, the internist's opinion was that Janet had eating problems but not an eating disorder. Although she had lost 10 pounds during the previous 8 months, Janet's weight was still within the average range for her height.

I continued to see Janet for weekly therapy sessions focused on helping her to identify her feelings and find other ways to express her anger. The internist continued to monitor her weight and overall physical health.

Be Willing to Make Yourself Useful

Anna Freud's (1964) recommendation to therapists to be willing to be useful is not restricted to working with young children. Adolescents, too, need to know that we are willing to be helpful to them in concrete and meaningful ways. Sixteen-year-old Dean was a student at a local boarding school whom I had recently begun treating for mood issues. One of his ongoing concerns, shared with many boarding school students, was the prevalence and persistence of unnecessarily arbitrary rules. One of these was the requirement that students wishing to leave campus on Saturday afternoon for an overnight at home make a formal and written request to do so by the preceding Thursday at noon. Dean had missed this deadline by 20 minutes and so too the right to go home for a visit. This struck me as, if not Draconian, at least unfathomamable, and I made this clear. To point out what struck me as a silly rule, I asked if the school needed a count for a fancy catered dinner. Of course, they didn't.

Dean was disappointed and angry. He had anticipated a home cooked meal, a break from his roommate, a chance to catch up on his sleep, and most important, an opportunity to watch his younger brother play basketball. He told me that he had appealed to an administrator to no avail and that the school was rigid in this way, only permitting exceptions when a doctor's note was provided. I responded quickly that I would be happy to write a note if that would help. Dean said that it would, and so I gave him a very brief note saying that a visit home would facilitate Dean's progress in therapy. Having done this, Dean and I had a brief, but detailed discussion about how I would respond should the school administrator call asking for more information—I assured Dean that I would not provide anything beyond what the note said—and we moved on to other issues.

Therapist and Patient Goodness of Fit

When I first began to treat adolescents, the accepted wisdom was that all adolescent boys should have male therapists and all adolescent girls should have female therapists. Given the salience of adolescent identity issues, concerns about sexuality and body image that so frequently occur, this seemed only good sense. Some adolescents believe that they must have a same-sex therapist, and they are probably right. For many other adolescents, however, the gender of the therapist is far, far, less important than whether patient and therapist can connect. Discussions of sexual feelings and sexuality require trust and confidence, whether one's therapist is of the same or different gender. Discussions of romantic feelings require an equal measure of trust and confidence. I have probably treated as many adolescent girls as adolescent boys and have helped problem solve as many dating and sexuality dilemmas from a girls' side as from the boys'. Similarly, female therapists can be just as helpful to an adolescent boy as can a male therapist.

Depression and Mood Disorders

> O, that this too too solid flesh would melt,
> Thaw and resolve itself into a dew!
> Or that the Everlasting had not fix'd
> His canon 'gainst self-slaughter! O God! God!

> How weary, stale, flat, and unprofitable
> Seem to me all the uses of this world!
> —William Shakespeare, *Hamlet*, Act 1, Scene 2

Treating adolescents means treating depressed adolescents, sometimes severely and acutely depressed at that. The words of the most famous of all depressed adolescents could have been spoken last week by a depressed adolescent patient in your office or in mine. Unlike the Prince of Denmark, who correctly mistrusted his parents, most acutely depressed adolescents welcome the opportunity to fully unburden themselves to their parents. They accept and sometimes welcome parental involvement in their treatment in ways that are uncharacteristic of adolescents dealing with other issues. Therapists who take advantage of this openness to family involvement can make more rapid progress than is otherwise possible and can accomplish several specific goals. The first is to provide parents an opportunity to hear directly from their son or daughter, and from you as well, just how severe the depression is. It is remarkable how a parent's wish to avoid knowing that their child is in pain can combine with their adolescent's wish to spare their parents' worry. The result can easily be that parents suspect, but fear to confirm, that something is wrong, and adolescents believe, but fails to confirm, that their parents would do anything to help them overcome their depression. The second goal that can be met in this family meeting is to reeducate parents about adolescent depression. I refer to this as reeducation because any literate parent will have already read and heard before the information you are about to impart. Your reiteration will help them let the information in. And the most important bit of information you can give them is this: Asking their son or daughter how they are feeling will not lead to their becoming more depressed. Asking if they have thoughts of self-harm will not lead to their becoming suicidal. Do not stop yourself from explaining this because your patient's parents are psychologists or medical doctors. Just because they know things in their offices does not mean that they know them at home.

Some time ago, I was asked to see Max, a 16-year-old boy. While watching a television documentary about teen depression and suicide with his parents, Max said that he was sometimes worried about himself and his moods. At his request, Max and I met individually first. Max told me what he had been experiencing for the previous week: extreme sadness, no interest in friends or activities, little appetite, inability to concentrate, and frequent thoughts of suicide sometimes accompanied with the beginnings of a plan. Max assured me that he did not wish to commit suicide: "I could never do that to my family," but the thoughts were there nonetheless. I asked Max when he had first had these feelings. His response: "I can't remember, maybe five or six years ago. " And yet, over all this time, he had never told his parents or anyone else how badly he was feeling and how hard he had been struggling. Rather, he had tried to manage his depression by himself through exercise, nutrition, and "right thinking." I met with Max and his parents, who were as concerned and supportive as any parents could be. "Why," the three adults in the room asked, "had Max not asked for help before?" There were two reasons: He thought he could manage his problem by himself; he didn't want to upset or worry his parents. This concern about parents' emotional well-being is not unusual. Rather, it is so typical that I routinely ask about it in a first or second interview with depressed adolescents.

Unfortunately, acute adolescent depression with suicidal ideation is not unusual either, and it calls for rapid and aggressive treatment. There are times to let patients and families decide how intensive treatment should be—this is not one of those times. There are times when the possible advantages and disadvantages of medication as an adjunct to therapy can be discussed at leisure—this is not one of those times either. Sailors have a maxim that helps them decide when to reef, to reduce sail area, in windy or stormy conditions: "If you are wondering if it might be a good time to reef, it is." I use a similar maxim to help decide whether a psychopharmacology consult is indicated: "If I'm wondering if it might be a good time to ask for a psychopharmacology consult, it is."

In Max's case, my recommendation regarding medication involved a differential diagnostic issue that emerges only rarely in childhood but not uncommonly in adolescence. The diagnostic question is whether the patient's depression is varying in a relatively predictable way (e.g., more depressed in the mornings when serotonin is at a lower concentration in the bloodstream and relatively less depressed in the afternoons) or is cycling from depressed to not depressed or from depressed to manic. After Max had described his depression with a clarity that would reflect well on a psychiatry resident, I asked if the feelings were always there. Max said that he sometimes felt "really good," maybe "too good." Before I had a chance to ask what he meant by "too good," Max explained: "Do you know the little sparks you see sometimes when you plug something into the wall? That's how it feels in my brain."

It was beginning to appear that Max's moods were cycling. A quick phone call to Max's parents reinforced this impression. When they spoke to him the previous afternoon, he had seemed very low indeed. Several hours later and for no apparent reason, he was almost ecstatically happy. The final bit of evidence needed to feel reasonably confident that Max was indeed cycling arrived quickly in the form of this bit of family history: Max's paternal grandmother and uncle were both currently receiving treatment for bipolar disorder and had been since their late teens. Max was immediately started on the same medications that were helping his relatives. His mood swings began to decrease soon after that.

Diagnostic and medication issues having been addressed, therapy was able to focus on other issues, most importantly on exploring what had been keeping Max from letting others know what was going on inside him. Part of the reason for this was that Max had spent so much of his life trying to manage his feelings and to keep from being overwhelmed by them that he consciously avoided experiencing his own inner life whenever he could. This parallels the experience of most adults who seek therapy. They want to know themselves better and to be happier, but they would prefer to do it without dealing with a lot of complicated and sometimes unpleasant emotional experiences. One of the major differences between adolescents and adults in therapy is candor. When I suggested to Max that one of the things he and I might work toward, beyond mood stabilization, was a better understanding of his emotional life, this very bright and pleasant boy answered simply, "No, that's okay."

CHAPTER 11

Problems That May Be the Focus of Attention at Any Age

There are more things in heaven and earth, Horatio,
Than are dreamt of in your philosophy.

—William Shakespeare, *Hamlet*, Act 1, Scene 5

Disabilities

Children and adolescents with disabilities encounter the same emotional and interpersonal issues as their nondisabled peers. Some of the ways of working with nondisabled children and adolescents transfer directly; for example, the therapeutic relationship, learning to use your feelings and to trust your clinical intuition, and being ready to offer practical advice are all equally essential. But in working with children with disabilities you should have some familiarity with pediatric disabilities, those a child has from birth, such as cerebral palsy, as well as those that are acquired from disease (e.g., a spinal cord tumor or uncontrolled seizure disorder) or from trauma (e.g., spinal cord injury from a motor vehicle or diving accident). Just as in treating a child or adolescent with chronic illness, it is important to learn about the physical medicine aspects of the condition and the treatment. You have to know, for instance, that a spinal cord injury can result in loss of bladder control, even if it does not cause paralysis. If you do not ask your new adolescent patient about this, he may not tell you that worrying about loss of bladder control is the reason he is postponing returning to school after his accident.

There is a parallel between working with children and adolescents with disabilities and working with children and adolescents from different cultures, as discussed in Chapter 7. Learn what you can about disabilities in general, and your patient's disability in particular. Be humble about what you really know. And, most important, be willing to learn from your patients. There is also a deeper issue: the discomfort you may feel in being with a person who is disabled. This discomfort can take many forms: anxiety; a strong desire to not notice the walker, wheelchair, brace, limp, or speech impediment; an equally strong feeling of sadness or loss. It's important to be aware of what you are feeling so you can manage these feelings and use them to help your patient. As with other clinical situations, it's the feelings of which you are unaware that interfere with treatment. All of these feelings are normal for therapists to feel, and none need interfere with therapy as long as the therapist allows himself or herself to be fully aware of them and to be real with the patient.

You may be tempted to suggest to your patients with disabilities that they should "look on the bright side of life." Your patients have heard this before, from family and friends, from orthopedic surgeons, neurologists, and other medical specialists. Speech therapists, physical therapists, and occupational therapists have to be cheerleaders and coaches to do their jobs effectively. So by the time your patients with disabilities reach your office or you reach their hospital room, they have heard a thousand times how great they are doing and how much progress they have made. There is much ink spent on documenting the wonderful achievements of physically disabled people. But none of this changes the reality: Quadriplegics wish they were paraplegics; paraplegics wish they could walk with crutches, a cane, or a walker; those who use crutches, canes, and walkers wish they could walk without them.

The more real the therapist is about living with a disability, the better. And the reality for children who are physically disabled is that it stinks. I learned a lot about this from Maggie, a girl of 8 whom I saw at Children's Seashore House in Philadelphia. Maggie was born with cerebral palsy. She was able to walk only with a walker, her use of her hands was limited, and her speech was labored. That she was able to walk at all represented a huge triumph and was a testament to her family and her physical, occupational, and speech therapists and doctors. The developmental pediatrician who had seen her at 10 months had expected her to need a motorized wheelchair. The fact that she could walk, even though with a walker, was a near miracle. And yet, Maggie did not look at it that way. When I tentatively asked Maggie if she was ever angry that other children could do things she could not, her reply was "I'm so angry that I am the angriest girl in the whole world." Remarks like this have to be met completely honestly. And my honest response to this is that I would be angry, too. For me, any response implying that things could be worse or that other people have it worse would be phony. And yet, these are the things that young people with disabilities typically hear from well-meaning friends, relatives, and professionals.

They need their therapists to be different. They need us to be more real. And the truth is that to be physically disabled, having to use crutches, a walker, a cane, or a wheelchair, absolutely and simply sucks. Anybody who says differently is spray painting goat droppings and calling them nuggets of gold. This does not mean that we want to encourage disabled patients to spend every waking moment being angry. It does mean that we must validate the anger they feel and give them a place and time in which to feel it so that they can then move on to other feelings, and other goals as well.

Chronic Illness

Chronic Illness in children and adolescents can take many forms. Some chronic illnesses are with children for a lifetime. A diabetic child has to accept the change that has happened to his body and the adjustments he has to make in nutrition, in monitoring blood sugar, and in taking his medication. Such adjustments are huge for all children. The way children react to this new burden reflects their personality and temperament. Children who adjust well to changes, whether that change is parental divorce, the birth of a sibling, or moving to a new school district, also adjust well to pricking their fingers and injecting insulin multiple times each day. Children who are already having trouble adjusting to life circumstances will have greater difficulty adjusting to diabetes. And children who have been oppositional will be oppositional vis-à-vis their diabetes.

As should be obvious by now, I am in no way opposed to being directive when it is called for. Directly encouraging young patients to follow their physician's recommendations can be very helpful, as long as you have built a strong relationship first. If a 12-year-old decides to check his sugar five times a day and to follow his diabetic diet only to please you, that is just fine. The ultimate goal is for him to internalize the value of taking care of his body, but he may need to begin this process from a child's position.

Contextual ideas about unfairness and injustice have much to say about chronic illness. What could be more obviously unfair than for a child to develop a serious and incurable illness, such as diabetes? You will want to help the 12-year-old diabetic experience and express the full range of emotions associated with this life-altering diagnosis, including fear and anger at being betrayed by his own body. Acknowledging these feelings will do much more to help your patient than will reassuring him that he can still have a normal, active life.

Some chronic illnesses have cures that are almost as bad as the original illness. Children and adolescents with end-stage renal disease undergo hemodialysis three times a week. Dialysis patients typically feel ill the day before dialysis (toxins have built up in their body) and fatigued the day after (due to the dialysis itself and to losing fluid volume). While on dialysis, patients must stay on special diets and on very limited fluid-intake volumes. So dialysis patients look forward to the day when they may be able to receive a donated kidney and to undergo transplantation. The problem is that posttransplant, they are still renal patients on a regimen of multiple drugs (including steroids with nasty side effects). For many children, and especially for adolescents, this is a tremendous disappointment and a tremendous source of anger. As with diabetic patients, adolescents who tend to act out their frustrations in other areas of their life will act out their frustration with the lifestyle adjustments that their transplantation necessitates. The adolescents who are most aware of the extent to which they are frightened and angry are the ones who are most likely to be able to follow the required medical regimen and ultimately to do well on it.

Asperger's Syndrome

In the past 10 years, this previously little-known and poorly understood syndrome has become much better known, although not necessarily better understood. Asperger's syndrome is considered to be the high-functioning end of the pervasive developmental disorder continuum and is characterized by odd mannerisms, habits, and interests, a profound difficulty in establishing reciprocal interpersonal relationships, and the presence of at least normal language abilities. Children and adolescents with Asperger's syndrome often have significant difficulties with anxiety, depression, and obsessions and compulsions.

Neither psychological nor pharmacological treatment for Asperger's syndrome as a whole is currently available. However, medication and therapy are useful in addressing target symptoms, such as those noted earlier, and the combination of meds and therapy can result in great overall improvement in functioning, even though the patient still has Asperger's syndrome. Psychopharmacological treatment itself is complicated because children and adolescents with Asperger's syndrome, like those with other forms of pervasive developmental disorder, often have idiosyncratic reactions to medications. Frequent adjustments in medication type and dosage are the rule with Asperger's patients. Anxiety that is not adequately managed psychopharmacologically can easily lead to seriously disruptive behavior. The same is true for obsessive and compulsive symptoms. Adolescent boys with Asperger's syndrome are apt to become fixated on a particular girl they once sat next to in class or passed on the sidewalk. This kind of perseveration, when combined with the typical lack of social understanding and perspective-taking ability, can easily lead the adolescent to experience exhausting levels of anxiety and sometimes behavioral outbursts.

I once worked with Lou, a 16-year-old boy with Asperger's who had glanced at an attractive young woman in a parking lot while on a family vacation. Based on the passing glance (it was not at all clear that she glanced back), he became convinced that he and the young woman had a relationship, and he fixated on meeting her again. This chance meeting had occurred 2,000 miles from home, and my patient did not know the young woman's name and had not spoken to her. None of these impediments stopped him from perseverating about her and planning how he could see her again. The perseveration took a potentially dangerous turn when Lou began to be upset every time he saw a car with a license plate from the state where he saw the young woman. Upset and frustrated about not being able to find her, he became very angry that other people were driving cars registered in what he believed was her home state. He had fantasies of harming these people and their cars. This rage frightened him and his family. We talked about these feelings a great deal, and this, in combination with an increase in his mood-stabilizing medication, helped him gain a sense of control and something approaching calm. Rage and fantasies of hurting others are not diagnostic criteria of Asperger's syndrome. They can occur, however, and must be managed aggressively.

Attention-Deficit/Hyperactivity Disorder

Ten years ago, a publisher of professional books asked me to write a book about family treatment of attention-deficit/hyperactivity disorder (ADHD). I declined for two reasons.

First, there were so many books already available about ADHD that I could not imagine there being a market for another one. Second, I was not sure that ADHD was a genuine disorder in the sense that a seizure disorder is. I had seen many children whose attention wandered and who were very active and yet who experienced few, if any, impairments in functioning. I also knew many highly successful adults who were constantly on the go and who lost interest in activities and projects quickly, delegating the details to others.

In retrospect, I was obviously wrong about the market for books on ADHD. But I have not changed my mind about the apparent lack of veridicality of ADHD as a disorder. Its definition doesn't actually capture reality.

Despite my philosophical, or perhaps political, objections to thinking of children who have difficulties modulating attention and activity level as constituting a single disordered class, I recognize that such children and adolescents do exist and need help. I believe that the best way to help them is to identify their particular and specific problems and to address those, rather than focusing on the disorder issue. De-emphasizing diagnosis also makes room to consider a child's strengths.

Disorganization

Organizational difficulties are best addressed as directly as possible. If your patient is unable to find her homework papers, assignments, or handouts, have her bring in her backpack and dump it out on the desk or floor. Help her decide whether she will use folders or a three-ring binder. Help her schedule a time every day to sort and file. There are many, equally simple and quick techniques. In fact, some, such as the one I just described, may seem *too* simple and quick to spend precious therapy time on. But they do help. And if you don't teach your patient about them, who will? If your patient is receiving tutoring, it should be an easy matter for the tutor to monitor and assist with the organizational strategies you and your patient have put in place.

The kind of specificity that works for disorganization also works for inattention and activity-level problems. The activity level of young children is highly reactive to sleep deprivation. Before recommending medication for any preschool or school-age child, find out if he or she is getting enough sleep.

Medication for Attentional Issues

Medications used for ADHD appear to be safe, require minimal monitoring (i.e., no blood tests), and often have dramatic results. So they are prescribed freely by child and adolescent psychiatrists, pediatricians, family physicians, and others. This is not altogether a good thing, as it undoubtedly results in overdiagnosis and overprescribing.

The best way to avoid being part of the problem is to be sure that a child has received a very thorough evaluation before prescribing medication. At a minimum, such an evaluation should include direct observation, behavioral reports from parents and teachers, and an assessment that rules out other possible causes of inattention such as anxiety, visual impairment, hearing or auditory processing problems, intellectual limitations, sleep deprivation, traumatic stress, or mood disorder. Positive response to medication, especially to stimulant medication, should not be taken as confirmation of a diagnosis, because stimulants enhance concentration universally, not just in those with attentional problems. Although there are varying opinions about whether a computerized assessment procedure such as Conner's Continuous Performance Test should be routinely included in such an assessment, it has often been useful in my practice, so I continue to include it as part of my assessment battery.

Complicated and Uncomplicated Attention-Deficit/Hyperactivity Disorder

Discussions of ADHD sometimes treat it as a unitary initial disorder (even if one with subtypes) when it is not. There is variability in functioning, outcome, and response to intervention. Children who have problems with attention, concentration, and/or hyperactivity but who do not have other behavioral problems such as substance abuse or conduct disorder usually do well in treatment. For some of these children medication is a very useful component of treatment. For others, medication is unnecessary. And for still others, medication is essential.

On the other hand, children and adolescents I have seen who have the same kinds of problems with attention, concentration, and hyperactivity combined with substance abuse or conduct disorder generally do poorly in treatment with or without medication. Because medication can have such dramatically positive effects with uncomplicated ADHD, parents and doctors often try one medication after another in hopes of finding the magic bullet for children and adolescents with complicated ADHD.

Logic suggests that if children and adolescents diagnosed with A (ADHD) respond well to treatment (medication plus therapy) but children with A + B (ADHD plus conduct disorder/substance abuse) respond poorly or not at all to the same treatment, it is because problem B is not being adequately addressed. I do not offer this as a new insight, for I am very far from the first to say it. One problem is that the diagnostic criteria for ADHD are so broad that they can capture children who are merely temperamentally (as opposed to psychologically) hyperactive and inattentive. The second problem is that parents, and clinicians as well, may be seduced into believing that lying, screaming, punching walls, breaking doors, stealing from parents, cursing at teachers, threatening adults with physical harm, driving without a license, underage drinking, using drugs, and curfew violations are all part of "the ADHD picture." It is even possible to mislead oneself into believing that having strange ideas and engaging in bizarre activities are part of the ADHD picture. Of course, none of this is so. The idea of complicated ADHD itself is misleading. Those children and adolescents who have severe problems with mood, behavior, and cognition that have been attributed to ADHD have been misdiagnosed. The problems in the first list are characteristic of conduct disorder. Those in the second are suggestive of a psychotic process, including the manic phase of bipolar disorder. Conduct disorder will not respond to medications used in the treatment of ADHD, and some of these medications (i.e., psychostimulants) are regularly hoarded and may be abused or sold. Psychotic processes are often exacerbated by the use of stimulant medications but do respond to appropriate antipsychotic or mood-stabilizing medications; prescribing the right drug requires appropriate diagnosis, as does providing the right information to the psychopharmacologist.

Jack, the young art student I described in the section on underachievement in Chapter 10, had been diagnosed as having ADHD when he was 12. By 16, his age when I met him, every approved stimulant medication had been tried. Each had side effects that bothered him, and ultimately, he decided to not take any medication.

When you receive a referral of a youngster who has been previously diagnosed as having ADHD, do your own assessment to be sure that the diagnosis is accurate and that you are prepared to treat the problems you will be confronting and, most especially, so you can appropriately prescribe or provide information to the prescribing doctor. Just as you should not assume that the person referring the patient got the diagnosis right, do not assume that whoever is prescribing has sufficient information to make the decision.

About 6 years ago, I received a request to take over the psychological treatment of Frank, a 14-year-old boy with ADHD. At the time of the request, he was described as doing better than before but having a very rough time adjusting in school.

In the past, he had been disruptive, but this had not occurred for over a year. Because he was referred to me by a nationally known expert in the treatment of ADHD, I was inclined to accept this diagnosis without question. I met Frank with his family, reviewed the history, and met individually with Frank. He was seriously depressed, and something else I could not put my finger on. He talked to me, but he did not connect. He described distressing events and experiences, but his emotional expression did not fit what he was saying. I recommended a psychopharmacological consult to the family. I called my colleague in psychiatry and told her about Frank, his previous diagnosis, his depression, and my feeling that this was not a case of garden-variety ADHD. I explained the odd way he came across and told my colleague that I was concerned about how well grounded he was in reality. I think the way I put it was this: "I think he may be a little bit crazy." The psychopharmacologist agreed and started him on both antidepressant and antipsychotic medications. The combination of supportive therapy and these medications worked well. He was accepted into a special program in his high school combining learning support and emotional support features. He became part of the therapeutic community at the school, and he began to make friends for the first time since elementary school. Of course, it is impossible to go back and do the experiment the other way, but I do not believe the outcome would have been as positive if he had continued to receive treatment as a garden-variety ADHD patient.

——————— **CASE ILLUSTRATION** ———————
Joey

Doing part of one's professional training in a very large medical center can expose one to disorders and conditions that would not be seen in a smaller setting. When I was a fellow at Judge Baker Guidance Center in Boston from 1981 to 1983, I had such an experience. I was assigned to see Joey, an 8-year-old boy who was exhibiting marked distractibility, inattention, and problems focusing. Psychostimulant medication had been prescribed based on a diagnosis of ADD with hyperactivity. Joey's parents told the social worker (in those days, social workers saw parents; child psychologists and child psychiatrists treated children) that the medication didn't seem to be helping and that Joey disliked taking it. There was much discussion of how best to help them see that medication was indicated.

Meanwhile, I saw Joey every week. He was not getting any better and on occasion did things I was totally unable to explain. He was visibly upset by the fire extinguisher hanging in the hallway. He became distressed when the top of a small box of cereal tore unevenly. He stared out a window at nothing in particular. He asked to call his mother and in doing so pressed buttons with his thumb in a very awkward and peculiar way.

I enthusiastically accepted the offer of my very experienced supervisor, Pauline B. Hahn, to convene a case conference. Among the 10 participants in this case conference was the child psychiatrist and psychoanalyst Robert McCarter, who asked me only one question: "Has your relationship with the patient improved or grown in any significant way in the past 3 months?" When I responded that it had not, Bob McCarter reflected that many years earlier, when he was a resident, he had seen a child whose problems were similar to Joey's and who, it turned out, had a very rare degenerative neurological disease, adrenoleukodystrophy (ALD), since made famous by the movie *Lorenzo's Oil*. Dr. McCarter recommended getting Joey to a pediatric neurologist. I did, and unfortunately, Dr. McCarter's intuition was right: Joey had ALD.

I've not seen another child with ALD, but the lesson I learned in Boston has stayed with me. Slow progress is one thing, but when a case is making no forward movement at all, it is time to think about a consultation.

Sibling Rivalry

Some measure of competition for attention and affection among siblings is both normal and natural. When it becomes persistent and intense, it warrants attention. Issues related to all three of the components of the integrated model play a part in this problem. I have seen families in which parents engage in the most blatant form of favoritism, leading to intense experiences of unfairness and anger on the part of the less favored sibling.

Arguments among children are not at all unusual. Children of preschool and school age regularly argue about who sits where, who gets to take the first piece of cake, and who gets to talk about their school day first. Older children express disdain for younger children's interests. Younger children tease and annoy their older siblings. These issues hardly ever take families to the therapist. But sibling issues do come up in therapy quite regularly. Sometimes the sibling problems are potentially dangerous, as occurs when 5-year-olds are too aggressive with much younger brothers or sisters. Sometimes the sibling problems are not dangerous but are a source of continuing family tension, as occurs when a 16-year-old is constantly teasing his 12-year-old sister. One can sometimes handle sibling conflicts as just another instance of disruptive behavior, as it was in the case of Katherine in Chapter 8. Parents of younger children who are dealing with sibling issues find it reassuring to learn that they are not alone and for that reason may find bibliotherapy (e.g., Goldenthal, 1999) helpful. For other families, therapists have to rely on their connection with the patient and on their intuitions about the patient.

--------- CASE ILLUSTRATION ---------
Patrick

Several years ago I was seeing Patrick, a 16-year-old-boy who had been diagnosed as having ADHD. Much of his treatment focused on improving his interactions with his parents. An additional area of concern was his pattern of teasing his 12-year-old sister in ways that embarrassed her in front of her friends and hurt her feelings. My intuition about this boy was based on several factors: the way he talked about his sister, the way his parents described the relationship between their children, and the warmth of the family. My intuition was also based on Patrick's interaction with me; there was never anything mean or hostile in how he presented himself or how he talked about his sister.

With all of the data available to me, I decided to confront Patrick. Most of his visits had included his parents, but this time I invited them to step out for a cup of coffee. Then, when Patrick and I were alone, I said, "You know you love your sister. Why are you doing this?" I was not at all sure how he would respond. After all, he had been complaining about her habits; being too serious about schoolwork was the big one. Patrick's response was what I had hoped it would be: "I guess so."

Emboldened by my good fortune in striking the harmonious drum, I continued in a directive mode: "She's just a kid. She's your sister. You love her. Be nicer to her." With another adolescent or a different family, this would have been heavy-handed and a failure. With Patrick and his warm and tight family, it worked just fine.

Many sibling conflicts can be resolved if parents focus on understanding their children's emotional lives as much as they do on correcting their behavior. I wrote *Beyond Sibling Rivalry* (Goldenthal, 1999) to provide bibliotherapy for parents with those concerns. A partial list of headings and subheadings provides an outline for the kinds of recommendations you can make to help families in which sibling conflicts are a concern:

- Expect only the kind of sharing from your children that you would expect from yourself.

- Use family gifts to teach sharing.
- Be authoritative, not authoritarian.
- Do not threaten. Take action instead.
- Have some fun with them.
- Learn to read your child's emotional signals.
- Take your child's complaints seriously.
- Teach your children to stand up for their rights.
- Be alert for signs of unfairness.
- Look for each child's unique abilities.
- Acknowledge talents.
- Try not to be defensive.
- Celebrate differences.
- Be enthusiastic.
- Identify strengths.
- Acknowledge children's accomplishments without comparing them.
- Try out your child's point of view.
- Do not confuse criticism with encouragement.
- Remember that sarcasm is not a form of humor.
- Never compare your children to each other, to your neighbor's children, to your nieces and nephews, or to yourself as a child.
- See your children for who they are.
- Avoid putdowns.
- Listen to your children.
- Recognize efforts to achieve in school.
- Understand your child's scholastic strengths and weaknesses.
- Help your children resolve problems with their friends.
- Take your children's concerns seriously.

- Recognize efforts to be helpful at home.
- Be careful not to burden your children with your own issues.
- Remember that what they see and hear from you is what you get.
- Teach your children to take another child's perspective.

—————— **CASE ILLUSTRATION** ——————
Mitch

Much of sibling rivalry involves behavior that, from a parent's perspective, is annoying, frustrating, and tiring. Treatment for these behaviors is largely elective, but this is not always the case. Sibling rivalry can engender such intense feelings and equally intense behaviors as to be almost incredible.

Recently, Nancy and Fred called to make an appointment for themselves and their 5-year-old son, Mitch. They described Mitch as fighting and arguing constantly with his older brother, being mean to his younger brother, and being oppositional, for example, insisting that his demands be met immediately, lying, and being manipulative and having frequent and violent temper tantrums. He had also begun to smear feces.

Believing that he was hyperactive, they had him evaluated by a developmental pediatrician, who reported that Mitch "performed at age-appropriate levels in all areas, including orientation, gross motor skills, visual fine motor skills, temporal sequence organization, language skills, and preacademic learning. There were no concerns in his selective attention or activity, processing efficiency, or adaptation. Mitch's play skills were rich and well developed. He had good symbolic play, tolerated intrusion, and played cooperatively with the examiner."

In the office, Nancy told me that the problems had worsened since that evaluation. Mitch had become increasingly defiant and he smeared feces more often than before. Hearing this, I began to wonder if the developmental pediatrician had missed something major, or if Mitch had acutely begun to deteriorate due to a new and serious neurological condition or disease. I knew this developmental pediatrician very well and had complete confidence in her evaluation, so the first possibility seemed unlikely. I shared my thoughts with Nancy and Fred, adding that the only other thing I could think of was that perhaps Mitch was so angry about something that he just felt like urinating and defecating and was enjoying the effect it had on his parents. I then asked to spend a few minutes alone with Mitch to try to figure out what was going on.

The ensuing interview was not what I anticipated. Mitch made good eye contact and made several drawings in response to my requests. The drawings were somewhat immature but not bizarre in any way. In response to my questions about school, Mitch told me that he liked school and his teacher and that he had two best friends in his class. Interested in approaching the bathroom issue, I gradually asked first about lunch and the cafeteria. Mitch let me know that the food was not to his liking. Finally, I asked about the bathrooms: How were they? Mitch told me that he did not use the bathrooms in school. The interview continued as follows:

P.G.: Oh, what about at home?

Mitch: No, I don't use them.

P.G.: You know, I know some other boys who don't like to use the bathroom at home either. Would you like to know why?

Mitch: Uh huh.

P.G.: Well, some of them say the toilet seat is too cold. Some of them don't like the way the water in the toilet splashes. And some of them just like to pee and poop all over the place because they just want to.

Mitch: (giggles).

P.G.: And some of their parents usually say "Ew, doesn't it bother you to pee and poop in your pants? That's yucky!" And the boys are so mad that they just pretend they like it just because they are so mad.

Mitch: (giggles and laughs).

I never would have thought that old-fashioned anger would be sufficient for a child to manifest symptoms I had previously encountered only in children with very significant developmental delay. And yet here was little Mitch, well orientated, interpersonally appropriate, and developmentally on track in all assessed cognitive domains, and it was beginning to appear that he was using the two things over which he had complete control to express his anger and to get even.

Working on a hunch, I held up an open hand and invited Mitch to punch it, expecting a tap. His punch stung! I then reached for a cushion from my chair and held it in front of me, once again inviting him to punch it. While he enthusiastically attacked the cushion, I practiced appropriate sound effects. When he seemed to be tiring after several minutes, I assumed the guise of personal trainer: "Come on, you can do more! Just two more!" I was still not sure where this might lead, but two things were evident: He was enraged, and he was very happy to have something to hit. I invited Nancy into the office, sending Mitch to the waiting room. I then gave Nancy a summary of my 35 minutes with Mitch and gave her a prescription to buy a gym-quality punching bag with all the necessary hardware and gloves to protect Mitch's hands. I also instructed her to tell Mitch's brother that the bag was not his. I suggested that she get it set up immediately.

She called three days later to confirm Mitch's next appointment and to bring me up to date. She had bought the bag, a stand to hold it, and the gloves. Mitch loved it. And, most interesting, he had not soiled or relieved himself on the floor for 2 days. Therapy was not over, of course. It had just begun. But the change at home had been dramatic, and in addition. Nancy and Fred now saw how urgently they needed to address Mitch's emotional needs.

Synthesis

CHAPTER 12

Your Own Therapy Model

This above all, to thine own self be true,
And it must follow, as the night the day,
Thou canst not then be false to any man.

—William Shakespeare, *Hamlet*, Act 1, Scene 3

At the beginning of this book, I introduced the idea that readers would be encouraged to make their own contributions to the integrated model. I have made the case that clinical work with children and families benefits from being flexible and inclusive and from integrating multiple theoretical frameworks. I have argued that one may make a useful and practical model by combining behavioral, psychodynamic, and family systems perspectives. I have illustrated this contention by describing the model I use and showing how I combine social learning theory and contextual family therapy ideas with ways of working typically associated with the psychodynamic tradition. For this model to achieve its maximal utility for you, it needs to be tailored, and you must be the tailor.

Tailoring the Model to Fit Your Practice Pattern

My own practice is the psychological equivalent of an old-fashioned general medical practice. I regularly see preschool children, school-age children, adolescents, their parents, and sometimes their grandparents, and I see them for a very wide range of problems. The treatment model you have read about in the previous section reflects the nature of this practice. Although I have seen patients in inpatient, psychiatric, and tertiary care pediatric hospital settings in the past, I no longer have a hospital practice. Neither do I prescribe medications. Although I have treated children with disorders in the pervasive developmental disorder spectrum for many years, I am far more likely to be asked to see children with Asperger's syndrome than with more severe disorders, including autism. In the area where I live and work, these children and others with developmental disabilities are more likely to be followed by specialist child psychiatrists and/or developmental pediatricians working in one of two nearby pediatric medical centers.

Another factor that significantly affects my practice and treatment model is the issue of managed care. Because I am on no managed care panels, I do not have to justify my treatment approach or petition to obtain 10 more sessions. The issue of treatment length is decided in the office, not on the phone with the representative of a managed care organization. Sometimes treatment is extraordinarily brief. My standard toilet training intervention takes four sessions or fewer. But in other cases, such as when treating a depressed adolescent, therapy may be twice a week for several years.

This model is intended to be general enough to be of use to any clinician who works with children and families. It is intended also to be specific enough to be immediately applied to specific clinical problems. This book includes examples of many different kinds of clinical issues and problems, but it is limited to my experience. Your practice setting and the population you serve are unlikely to be identical to mine. And so the model may require adjustment, modification, or additions to suit your practice and your patients. The integrated model is designed to accommodate those adjustments, modifications, and additions without changing its essential character. It is designed to bend, and above all to stretch, without breaking. As you consider how you might want to make this model of working your own, it may be helpful to review its major points.

Intuition

Clinical intuition and its value has been hotly debated among psychotherapists for many years, often with reference to Meehl's (1954) book, *Clinical versus Statistical Prediction.* Although Meehl concluded that when data from paper-and-pencil measures are combined and evaluated statistically, they do a better job than clinicians at some kinds of predictions, he did not, as is widely assumed, denigrate the clinician's expertise or intuitive insights. During much of his very long and distinguished academic career, Meehl unapologetically practiced psychoanalysis and psychoanalytic psychotherapy. Intuition and intuitive understanding need not be mysterious processes. In a clinical situation, huge amounts of data are available to us at every moment. Explicitly taking note of every potential data point would require multiple video and audio recording devices and teams of graduate student coders. Each moment would require pages of transcription and more pages of interpretation.

An adolescent walks into your office for the first time in a week, and in the first seconds, you notice changes. She is dressed more casually than she was for her previous appointment. Her skin tone is different, and her hair is not pulled into its usual skin-stretching bun. She is not carrying her heavy book bag. Her posture is different. Her eyes crinkle when she smiles, and she laughs more genuinely. And this is only part of the information available to you in the first moments of this office visit. The list doesn't include how she sits, the words she chooses, when she pauses, or where she directs her gaze. Without stopping to record or quantify these observations, you rapidly integrate them into what I would call an intuitive understanding of her increased comfort at being in therapy and her willingness to use it and you to work through issues and make important decisions (e.g., whether to withdraw from AP history).

You may be treating an adolescent who has a history of self-mutilation. She tells you that she is upset because her best friend revealed to her that she had a fight with her boyfriend and that she (the friend) had cut herself. You ask your patient, "Did that make you feel like cutting, too?" You ask this question because you put together what you know about your patient (her sensitivity, emotional connection to her friends, history of cutting) with what she told you. You did not need to apply a regression equation to predict the probability of cutting.

Perhaps you have been seeing a 16-year-old boy with a history of very significant interpersonal difficulties. He tells you that he met a girl on a recent family vacation. For the first time, he accepts your oft-repeated suggestion that the two of you talk alone, without his mother present. Until now, he has always said that it didn't matter. You do not need to administer the Minnesota Multiphasic Personality Inventory to tell that he is beginning to develop a more mature sense of self.

Creating Your Own Therapy Model

A therapy model ought not to be cast in bronze to remain unchanged for centuries. Rather, it ought to evolve and change constantly. Every new patient provides an opportunity to learn and to incorporate what you have learned into your way of working. New knowledge about how to increase the effectiveness of treatment is also available in published research. Although many of these studies involve manualized treatments in ways that do not directly translate into clinical practice in the real world, you can easily abstract key procedures and incorporate them into your model. Another way that this model may be personalized is by adding techniques in which you have acquired expertise (e.g., hypnosis, dream interpretation, art therapy).

Listening to the Patient's Voice

Even patients who have serious impairment in some areas may still know more than we do in others. The following case illustrates how this may occur.

Some years ago, I was treating, Alan, a 16-year-old who had Asperger's syndrome. At one point in his treatment he told me that he believed he had obsessive-compulsive disorder (OCD) and that his medication needed adjustment. My first reaction to this was that Alan had found yet another way to feel bad about himself, this time by adding a diagnosis. I told him as much, fully believing that I was doing the right thing. Alan insisted that he had OCD. Thinking I would demonstrate that he was overdiagnosing himself, I picked up the third edition of the *Diagnostic and Statistical Manual of Mental Disorders* from my desk and began to read the diagnostic criteria aloud. There were few items that Alan did not endorse, providing specifics for each one. He was right: He did meet diagnostic criteria for OCD. And, after consultation with his psychopharmacologist, it turned out that he was right about the need to change his medication as well.

This experience reinforced my belief that patients can be very right about some things, even while desperately needing help in other areas of their lives. Alan could not begin to guess at another person's emotional state and had no way of telling if the pretty girl who smiled at him in science was interested, teasing him, or simply being polite. He could not bear to have anyone touch his map collection, and he never entered the room where they were stored without taking a shower first. (I learned all this in the context of his self-diagnosis.) But he could tell when his medication was not working as well as it had previously. It was well worth listening to him.

———————————————————————————

One can learn a lot about therapy from what patients say about previous therapies. One of my adult patients had a history of alcoholism. At one point in our meetings, I made reference to his having been a "drunk," a perfectly acceptable characterization among those who are in recovery and participating in an AA program. He agreed, and with the hindsight of many years of sobriety, recalled with dismay that none of his several previous therapists had called him on it, despite his being completely open about how much he was drinking. I realized how easy it is to miss signs of substance abuse when your patient seems to be doing well professionally and is as well-spoken and intelligent as this patient was. Ever since then, I have listened in a different way when the subject of alcohol arises, even when it is brought up by an adolescent.

This happened just this past fall. A relatively new adolescent patient made what seemed like a wise guy comment about his mother: "You tell her a secret, then she goes and gets drunk and tells the whole world your secret." If it had not been for the lesson I learned from that previous patient, I might have chalked this remark up to an adolescent's attempt to embarrass his mother in order take the heat off himself. That may well have been part of the story. But it was not the whole story, as I learned. I asked Marge, the boy's mother, "Do you drink?" The answer was candor itself: "I do drink, usually three or four glasses of wine, maybe a bottle." I asked a few more questions and learned that Marge sometimes drove after drinking ("usually not very far"), that she did tend to say things better left unsaid when she had been drinking, and that she had started drinking more after losing her job 3 years earlier.

She was an alcoholic, and she was depressed. Her depression would have become apparent after a while, but I do not believe that I would have identified her alcoholism. That patient's remark—that none of his therapists had followed up on what he said about his drinking—directly led to a modification of my standard initial interview. Now it includes questions about drug and alcohol use for everybody, not just adolescents who are acting out. Intake procedures and protocols for family histories should always be modified to reflect what we learn from patients.

Listening to Your Inner Voice

This book provides a blueprint and some tools. If therapy were a bridge or a building, those would be enough. A well-trained technician could read the blueprint, pick up the tools, and get the project in on time and under budget. Of course, therapy is not an engineering project, but a relationship between two people or among three or more people. Engineers do not have to contend with their feelings about a bridge, only with its structure. But therapy is guaranteed to bring up feelings, not just for patients, but for therapists as well. What Yogi Berra said about sight applies to hearing as well: You can hear a lot just by listening. It is important to listen as carefully to your own voice as you do to the voice of your patients. And it is important to know what that voice is saying about you, about your patient, and about what is happening in therapy at that moment.

At a recent appointment, Jackie, a 15-year-old, was uncharacteristically quiet. When she spoke, it was without much feeling. I waited for a while and began to realize that I was not sure where the session was headed, if anywhere. I was also beginning to feel bored and sleepy. I did a quick internal systems review: I had slept well the night before; I was not preoccupied by personal concerns. Then I realized that I was bored because nothing was happening. There was nothing going on at an emotional level, even though words were being spoken. Having done this reality check, I was ready to do something with what my inner voice had been telling me. I asked Jackie about it: "I can't tell what's going on with you today. I've been listening, but I just don't get a feeling for where you are. It's almost like there's something you don't want to talk about." After a brief pause, Jackie told me about a recent uncomfortable time with her boyfriend and her indecision about what to do about it. This sort of experience, repeated many times, has convinced me of the importance of listening to that inner voice.

Am I Having Fun?

It may not be true in all professional endeavors, but therapists who work with children and families ought to ask themselves this question once in a while. This does not mean that every moment of every day needs to be uproariously gleeful. It does mean that therapy with children, especially very young children, is not likely to be effective if the therapist can't laugh with his or her young patients once in a while. It also means that therapy ought not be "just a job," something one does between vacations.

Knowing Yourself

Much of what is important in therapy is extraverbal; it is not captureable on a printed page. There are many different ways to think and talk about this. Some of it is classic nonverbal communication: facial expressions of emotion, tone of voice, gesture, and posture. The concepts of transference and countertransference are useful in capturing how the histories of patient and therapist come into play. Another language I find useful is the language of perception and emotion. There are, I believe, three important overlapping interpersonal and extratheoretical ingredients in therapy: the therapist's use of clinical intuition, the therapist's self-understanding, and the therapist's capacity to tune into his or her internal experience, to listen to that inner voice. The rest, to borrow from Hillel, is commentary.

The Impossibility of Being Certain

Even all of this is not enough for therapists to know just what to do at each step in a therapeutic process. That is, in part, why a tolerance for ambiguity is such a strong characteristic of so many therapists, especially of those who train as therapists and choose to continue to practice rather than moving into administration. Meehl (1978) lists 20 characteristics of human beings that make it extraordinarily difficult to construct strong and falsifiable theories of personality and, by extension, of therapy. This list includes some items that require expertise in the philosophy of science to decipher as well as these more accessible items: unit of measurement, individual differences, unknown critical events (in a person's life), sheer number of variables, importance of cultural factors, and uniquely human events and powers.

I wrote this book with a certain kind of reader in mind, one who "prefers to have an intimate connection between theoretical understanding and the helping process" (Meehl, 1989, p. 383) but who is not satisfied with following a prescribed doctrine, whether that doctrine is psychoanalysis, behaviorism, or family systems therapy. For clinicians who continue to hope for that intimate connection, it is always worth trying to bring theory and practice closer together. It is my hope that this book will be helpful to you in doing this.

APPENDIX A

Checklist for First Sessions

Preliminaries

Begin by explaining that you will be taking many notes. If you are not a habitual note taker, inform patients that you will not routinely do this in subsequent sessions. This lets patients know that the interview aspect of this appointment differentiates it from therapy sessions that are to follow. In addition, those who experience your note taking as showing that you take their thoughts, feelings, and comments very seriously will not feel less important when you do not take notes during their regular therapy sessions.

Not every question on the list needs to be asked, but you should ask enough of them to tap each of the areas of concern. For example, if the child is evidently verbally gifted, I may ask only one question about language development. If the patient is an 8-year-old star on three soccer teams, you need less information about motor development, although you will want to make a mental note to follow up on how decisions are made about his or her extracurricular activities and how extensive they are.

Here is the list of questions to guide your history taking with parents:

1. Did you have any difficulties with pregnancy, labor, or delivery? (Follow-up questions as needed.)
2. Was your pregnancy full term? Did your child come home with you?
3. Has your child ever been in the hospital overnight since then?
4. Has your child ever been seen in an emergency room?
5. Has your child had any surgeries or medical procedures?
6. Does your child have allergies of any kind? What kind?

7. Has your child ever taken medicine on a regular basis? Does he or she take medicine now?

8. Who is your child's pediatrician (phone number, address, permission to contact)?

9. Do you have other children (names, ages, health status)?

10. If an only or oldest child: Was this your first pregnancy?

11. If not, have you had any difficult pregnancies? Miscarriages?

12. When did your child first sit up? Stand? Walk?

13. When did your child say his or her first word? First combine words in a phrase?

14. Were there any difficulties with feeding?

15. What was your child's temperament as a newborn? An open-ended question is generally sufficient here. If not, ask if the child was an "easy" or "difficult" baby. If the parent seems to need further prompts, you can ask if the child was easy or hard to soothe, especially sensitive to changes in environment or textures of clothing, fussy or irritable.

16. When did your child first sleep through the night?

APPENDIX B

The Psychology of Psychological Testing for Children

About a year ago, I received a call from Jerilyn and Jim. I had seen their daughter Katherine, now a high school senior, several years earlier, and they wanted my guidance in making educational plans for their son. They were sure that 13-year-old Jack was quite bright. He earned excellent grades throughout elementary school with little apparent effort. He was a genuinely upbeat kid, got along with everybody, and expressed a desire to do well in school. He talked about his interest in going to a top college and then into business. If his drive on the soccer field was any indication, he was far from lazy. But since 6th grade, his grades had slipped dramatically. When his parents quizzed him on history or math, he seemed to have every fact at his fingertips. When it came to tests in school, though, he was unable to get that knowledge on paper. Jim and Jerilyn were confused about how such a bright boy could be earning such mediocre grades.

This is the sort of confusion that often leads parents to request a psychological evaluation. Might I, they asked, have time to do some testing? This was a reasonable question, but the more important question was one they did not ask: Would I also take the time to get to know Jack well enough so that I could offer a sensible interpretation of the results? And, of course, there are the other questions: Would I have time to interpret the results, translate that interpretation into useful recommendations, and explain those recommendations to them, to teachers, and to their son?

I began by talking with Jim and Jerilyn for an hour about their son and their family. Then I met with Jack to get to know him, to try to see the world the way he did, and, above all, to forge a connection with him.

An earlier version of this article originally appeared in the *Hartford Courant, Northeast* magazine, September 12, 2004, p. 4.

Psychological testing does not provide an x-ray of a child's intellectual abilities, learning style, or potential for academic achievement. It does provide a good estimate of how readily a child acquires and uses new information, the way he or she approaches a learning situation, and the child's cognitive strengths and weaknesses. More important, a thorough psychological assessment will lead to recommendations for ways that parents, teachers, and other school personnel can help students use their strengths to maximal effectiveness.

In some ways, psychological tests are similar to the tests that pediatricians use. Both are used to answer diagnostic questions. A single test may be used to answer a specific question: What is Jack's blood pressure? or At what grade level is Jack reading? A single test, or combination of tests, may address more complex questions: Why is Jack's sore throat not improving? or Why is Jack not doing better in school? To answer the more complicated questions requires carefully selecting the appropriate tests and considering the results in the light of everything else one knows about the child. The process may also involve further testing.

The difference between testing in pediatrics and testing in child psychology occurs when we consider the extent to which the patient is involved in the testing procedure. In pediatrics, the child or adolescent has only to be cooperative with the measurement, whether it is via stethoscope, blood pressure cuff, or finger prick. In psychology, our success, and the accuracy of our conclusions, depends on achieving a spirit of collaboration with both the child and the child's parents. Without a complete history and a detailed clinical interview of the child, psychological testing all too often yields only enigmatic numbers. In the absence of an interpersonal context for interpreting the data, a psychologist is left to navigate in the fog with neither compass nor bell to guide him or her. With the help of a parent who provides information about early developmental history, about school or emotional issues that other family members may have experienced, the fog begins to lift. And when the psychologist can spend 40 or 50 minutes simply talking with and connecting with the child, the sun often breaks through.

This was what happened with Jack. The connection we formed in that single hour-long interview helped me make sense of the sheets of numbers that resulted from the testing and from the other information I gathered from his teachers.

His test results were a mix of highs and lows that could have reflected attention problems, motivational problems (as had been suggested by more than one teacher), or ability issues. A cookbook approach to their interpretation would have revealed little of value. Having had that hour with him, however, it became clear that he was as his mother described him: bright, engaging, and ambitious. His sincere insistence that nothing his teachers presented or asked of him was especially challenging was consistent with the top marks he had earned in elementary school. He said he was not especially fond of reading, but had no trouble with it. He was extraordinarily cooperative and polite. He cheerfully helped move the testing table to the center of the room.

The way he approached being tested also told me a lot about him. He worked hard and with great persistence. He never gave up, not even on the most difficult items. That some tests were easy for him was evident even before I scored them. He was apt to comment "That was fun" after completing nonverbal tests, the ones that involved applying his spatial skills. On the other hand, he just as spontaneously commented about the difficulty of some of the more challenging items on tests that were purely language-based.

After pondering the inconsistency for some time, I realized that Jack had done well in elementary school largely on the basis of his memory skills. His verbal memory was strong; his perceptual memory was remarkable. On verbal tasks that did not require memory, his abilities were significantly weaker. When he hit 6th and 7th grade, memory was no longer enough. He had not developed any study skills because he had never needed to study; information flew into his head and stayed there. He may have been a bit inattentive, but not to the point that it interfered with earning As and Bs in early grades. In 6th and 7th grades, teachers expected him to analyze and synthesize increasingly complex verbal materials. He had not learned to use his considerable strength in processing visual information to compensate for his relative difficulty in processing complex verbal information. In addition, as teachers in higher grades increasingly set strict time limits for tests, Jack's relative weakness in processing speed became a greater impediment.

As I went over the test results and my recommendations with Jack and his family, I asked Jack whether he learned more from the maps, figures, graphs, and illustrations in his science textbooks or from the purely verbal presentation in the text. Jack's answer was quick: the illustrations. Having formed a connection in the pretesting interview, it was a short path to talking with Jack about how he could learn to capitalize on his quick grasp of nonverbal information to achieve his academic and career goals. Together we took the first step to identifying the most comfortable and productive way for him to learn. If I had made the mistake of considering only the test scores, I might have concluded that Jack was bright but simply unmotivated, as a previous evaluator had suggested. If I had made the mistake of thinking of my interviews with Jack and his parents as activities I had to get out of the way before doing the "real assessment," I might have reached the same erroneous conclusion.

Only by using the nonverbal and verbal information from those interviews in combination with test data was I able to answer this clinical riddle and to formulate recommendations tailored to this child's needs. I aimed for recommendations that were most likely to help him quickly and that would not require huge changes in how he studied or how his teachers conducted their classes: that he take full advantage of all the information available in the graphs, illustrations, and charts in his textbooks, and that he be permitted to take his tests without a time limit.

APPENDIX C

Protocol for Relaxation Training

This protocol begins by orienting the child or adolescent to the idea of relaxation training or self-hypnosis. It continues with an explanation of diaphragmatic breathing, practice with diaphragmatic breathing, and the introduction of visual imagery to facilitate deeper relaxation. Biofeedback is also discussed. The language is intentionally informal, and intentionally ungrammatical at some points.

Depending on the child, you may want to introduce this session by saying that you will be teaching self-hypnosis. For some school-age children, this is a very exciting idea. For others, this idea may be anxiety-provoking, so talking in terms of relaxation training is preferable.

> Okay, now we're ready to start. First, make sure that you're really comfortable. Just let your hand flop on your lap. [Make sure that the child is not clenching his or her hands.] Everything okay? All right, we're going to start by just breathing, but we're going to breathe in a special way. We'll do it together. And if Mom or Dad wants to breath with us, that would be great.
>
> [To parents] It's great when parents do the breathing, too, because then you can help your child practice at home, and it can be something you do together.
>
> Now, the breathing we're going to do is called diaphragmatic breathing. Have you heard of that? [Some parents will be familiar with this from yoga or voice instruction.] There are two kinds of breathing. When you breathe in small, short breaths, you use mostly the smaller muscles in the upper part of your chest, the intercostal muscles. Today, what we're going to do is to use the larger muscle of the diaphragm to fully expand your lungs. The diaphragm is

kind of like a dinner plate that separates the upper part of your chest from your abdomen. It goes like this. [Illustrate with your hand.] So the idea is that when the diaphragm is pulled down and out, your lungs draw breath in, and when it relaxes and moves back up, your breath goes out. It's kind of the opposite of sucking in your gut. So when you breathe in, your tummy should go out. Like this. [Illustrate.]

[For younger children or children who seem to have difficulty getting the idea of diaphragmatic breathing.] If your Mom or Dad puts a hand on your tummy, they will be able to tell that when you breathe in, your tummy goes out, and when you breathe out, your tummy goes back in. You don't have to do a great big inhale like when the doctor says "Take a deep breath," just a regular-size breath will do fine. The idea is to draw the breath in, nice and easy, and then let it go out by itself. You want it to be a kind of circle, like a bicycle wheel going around and around. Okay, let's try it. Just relax, and close your eyes if you want to.

Do 10 cycles of breathing, counting each one.

Let's try 10 more.

Okay, now just relax and do your breathing for a few minutes. I'll be talking, but you don't need to answer or to open your eyes if you've closed them. All set?

[Wait for child to begin breathing, and then continue. Your voice should be as soothing as possible.] As you breathe, you can relax completely. The sofa [or chair] is doing all the work of holding you up. Your muscles can relax completely. Let yourself sink into the sofa [or chair]. Notice how all of your muscles are relaxing. You may begin to feel warmer as your muscles relax. Your breathing is so regular and easy. Completely relaxed.

As you continue to speak about how relaxed your patient is becoming, notice any changes you see in posture or skin tone and provide feedback on what you see. For example: "Your shoulders are so relaxed the muscles are stretching and warming. The muscles in your face are becoming completely relaxed."

Ten or at the most 15 minutes of this is enough for the first relaxation training session. It can be ended like this:

> Okay, in just a minute we'll stop the exercise and talk about what it was like. There's no rush, as soon as you are ready.

End by asking the child how he or she felt during the relaxation exercise and if he or she would like to work on it some more next time. Then add something like this: "Next time, we can add some relaxing and peaceful images if you want."

At the next appointment, remind the child and parents that you're going to be adding some images to help them relax even more deeply, and ask if there are any places that make them uncomfortable so you can be sure of avoiding those images. Begin by reviewing what you taught the child about diaphragmatic breathing and have him or her relax and begin, with the parents if both parents and child wish to.

After the child has done the breathing for 2 or 3 minutes (at a rate of about 6 or 7 breaths per minute), continue:

> Now I'm going to count backward from 10, and each time I say a new number, you will be a little more relaxed.

> Ten. Your breaths are very regular and relaxing.

> Nine. You're more relaxed, your muscles are relaxing everywhere; the muscles in your toes, your ankles, your legs, all relaxing.

> Eight. Now the big muscles in your legs are relaxing even more, and the muscles in the lower part of your back, more and more relaxed.

Seven. Breathing gently, nice round breaths, and the muscles in your back, and your shoulders are relaxing, they're getting soft and warm.

Six. Breathing and relaxing, the muscles of your neck are becoming more and more relaxed and the muscles that go up to the top of your head are relaxing, too.

Five. Now the muscles of your face are becoming warmer and softer, they are just so relaxed, breathing so gently and completely, the air going in and out all by itself, and the muscles of your upper arms are becoming so relaxed, as you continue to breathe.

Four. Breathing and relaxing, the muscles of your forearms and wrists are becoming more and more relaxed.

Three. As you continue to breathe your hands become so relaxed, just lying there so warm and peaceful.

Two. All the muscles in your whole body are so relaxed, just breathing and relaxing, just so relaxed and peaceful.

This is a choice point: You can stop here and resume at your next appointment, or you may choose to continue with imagery. If you choose to continue, begin this way:

Now that you are completely relaxed, we're going to add some visual images that will help you relax even more. If this is something you would like to do, just raise one finger of your right hand.

[Assuming that your patient does raise a finger, continue with the imagery.] As you continue to sit and relax and to enjoy being so relaxed, you can imagine a place you have been, or a place you might like to go, a beautiful and a relaxing place. It's a warm and quiet place. You feel totally comfortable, completely relaxed. There is beauty, perhaps water, too. You sit or lie in comfort, listening to the sound of your breathing and relaxing. Perhaps it is a beach, and you are lying on the beach. The sand is very soft and warm. The air is warm. You are lying on the sand, completely supported by the sand. Your muscles are completely relaxed. It is quiet. You might be alone, or perhaps you are with your family. You hear the wind rustling in some trees just a bit. Perhaps a few small birds fly by. You may hear tiny waves splashing up on the shore nearby. All the while, you continue to breathe and to relax.

[Pause, allow a minute or so to pass, and then continue.] In a minute, it will be time to come back to the office, and when you do, remember that you can always go to that beautiful and peaceful place whenever you want to, because it is your place. [Pause.] Now, as I count slowly backward from 5, you will gradually come back to the office.

Count backward very slowly, increasing volume gradually with each number. Most children will have closed their eyes, and some will have fallen asleep. When their eyes open, ask how they feel and if this exercise was helpful and something they would like to repeat. Explain that the idea is to do it a few more times in the office so that they can use it at home or anyplace else.

Some children, like my thunderstorm-phobic patient, like the idea of making a relaxation tape or CD. The best way to do this is in the office the second or third time you go through the breathing with imagery.

REFERENCES

Ackerman, N. W. (1966). *Treating the troubled family.* New York: Basic Books.

Becker, A. E., et al. (2002). Eating behaviours and attitudes following prolonged exposure among ethnic Fijian adolescent girls. *British Journal of Psychiatry, 180,* 509–514.

Boszormenyi-Nagy, I. (1987). *Foundations of contextual therapy: Collected papers of Ivan Boszormenyi-Nagy, M. D.* New York: Brunner/Mazel.

Boszormenyi-Nagy, I., Grunebaum, J., & Ulrich, D. (1991). Contextual therapy. In A. Gurman & D. P. Kniskern (Eds.), *Handbook of family therapy* (Vol. II). New York: Brunner/Mazel.

Boszormenyi-Nagy, I., & Krasner, B. (1986). *Between give and take: A clinical guide to contextual therapy.* New York: Brunner/Mazel.

Boszormenyi-Nagy, I., & Spark, G. M. (1973). *Invisible loyalties.* New York: Harper & Row.

Bowen, M. (1966). The use of family therapy in clinical practice. *Comprehensive Psychiatry, 7,* 345–374.

Bowen, M. (1978). *Family therapy in clinical practice.* New York: Aronson.

Dollard, J., & Miller, N. E. (1950). *Personality and psychotherapy.* New York: Mcgraw-Hill.

Erikson, E. H. (1950). *Childhood and society.* New York: Norton.

Erikson, E. H. (1968). *Identity: Youth and crisis.* New York: Norton.

Framo, J. L. (1982). *Explorations in family and marital therapy.* New York: Springer.

Frattaroli, E. (2002). *Healing the soul in the age of the brain: Why medication isn't enough.* New York: Penguin.

Freud, A. (1964). *The psychoanalytical treatment of children.* New York: Schocken. (Original work published 1946)

Freud, S. (1959). *Fragments of an analysis of a case of hysteria. Collected papers* (Vol. 3). New York: Basic Books. (Original work published 1905)

Garfield, S. (1994). Eclecticism and integration in psychotherapy: Developments and issues. *Clinical Psychology: Science and Practice, 1,* 123–137.

Goldenthal, P. (1993). *Contextual family therapy: Assessment and Intervention procedures.* Sarasota: Professional Resource Press.

Goldenthal, P. (1996). *Doing contextual therapy: An integrated model for working with individuals, couples, and families.* New York: Norton.

Goldenthal, P. (1999). *Beyond sibling rivalry: How to help your children become cooperative, caring, and compassionate.* New York: Holt.

Goldfried, M. R. (1980). Toward the delineation of therapeutic change principles. *American Psychologist, 35,* 991–999.

Goldfried, M. R. (1982). *Converging themes in psychotherapy.* New York: Springer.

Guntrip, H. (1971). *Psychoanalytic theory, therapy, and the self.* New York: Basic Books.

Klein, M. (1959). *The psychoanalysis of children* (A. Strickey, Trans.). London: Hogarth.

Levine, M. (1980). *The ANSER system.* Cambridge, MA: Educators Publishing Service.

Meehl, P. E. (1954). *Clinical versus statistical prediction: A theoretical analysis and review of the evidence.* Minneapolis: University of Minnesota Press.

Meehl, P. E. (1978). Theoretical risks and tabular asteristics: Sir Karl, Sir Ronald, and the slow progress of soft psychology. *Journal of Consulting and Clinical Psychology, 46,* 806–814.

Meehl, P. E. (1987). Theory and practice: Reflections of an academic clinician. In E. F. Bourg, R. J. Brent, J. E. Callan, N. F. Jones, J. McHolland, & G. Stricker (Eds.), *Standards and evaluation in the education and training of professional psychologists* (pp. 7–23). Norman, OK: Transcript Press.

Meehl, P. E. (1989). *Paul Meehl.* In G. Lindzey (Ed.), *A history of psychology in autobiography* (Vol. 8, pp. 337–389). Stanford, CA: Stanford University Press.

Minuchin, S. (1974). *Families and family therapy.* Cambridge, MA: Harvard University Press.

Norcross, J., & Goldfried, M. (1992). *Handbook of psychotherapy integration.* New York: Basic Books.

Paul, G. L. (1969). Behavior modification research: Design and tactics. In C. M. Franks (Ed.), *Behavior therapy: Appraisal and status* (p. 44). New York: McGraw-Hill.

Rotter, J. B. (1954). *Social learning and clinical psychology.* New York: Prentice-Hall.

Schaffer, R. (1983). *The analytic attitude.* New York: Basic Books.

Stricker, G. (1994). Reflections on psychotherapy integration. *Clinical Psychology: Science and Practice, 1,* 3–12.

Thorndike, E. L. (1911). *Animal intelligence.* New York: Macmillan.

AUTHOR INDEX

Ackerman, N. W., 33

Becker, A. E., 224
Boszormenyi-Nagy, I., 10, 29, 34, 39
Bowen, M., 33

Dollard, J., 15

Erikson, E. H., 15, 16, 17, 18, 35

Framo, J. L., 33
Frattaroli, E., 18
Freud, A., 10, 15, 18, 72, 136
Freud, S., 18, 107, 136

Garfield, S., 9, 34
Goldenthal, P., 29, 247, 248
Goldfried, M. R., 9, 34
Grunebaum, J., 23, 34, 39
Guntrip, H., 18

Klein, M., 135, 136, 179
Krasner, B., 29

Levine, M., 73, 79

Meehl, P. E., 139, 258, 265
Miller, N. E., 15
Minuchin, S., 45

Norcross, J., 9, 34

Paul, G. L., 52

Rotter, J. B., 10, 20

Schaffer, R., 287
Spark, G. M., 29
Stricker, G., 9, 34

Thorndike, E. L., 19

Ulrich, D., 23, 34, 39

SUBJECT INDEX